DONE DEAL

DONE DEAL

An Insider's Guide to Football Contracts, Multi-Million Pound Transfers and Premier League Big Business

DANIEL GEEY
Foreword by Gianluca Vialli

BLOOMSBURY SPORT
LONDON · OXFORD · NEW YORK · NEW DELHI · SYDNEY

BLOOMSBURY SPORT
Bloomsbury Publishing Plc
50 Bedford Square, London, WC1B 3DP, UK

BLOOMSBURY, BLOOMSBURY SPORT and the Diana logo
are trademarks of Bloomsbury Publishing Plc

First published in Great Britain 2019

A catalogue record for this book is available from the British Library.
Library of Congress Cataloguing-in-Publication data has been applied for.

ISBN: Hardback: 9781472947178; eBook: 9781472947185

2 4 6 8 10 9 7 5 3 1

Typeset in Scala by Deanta Global Publishing Services, Chennai, India
Printed and bound in the UK by CPI Trade

MIX
Paper from
responsible sources
FSC® C020471

To find out more about our authors and books visit www.bloomsbury.com
and sign up for our newsletters

To Issie and Livi:
*Keep your eyes on the stars
and your feet on the ground*

CONTENTS

FOREWORD BY GIANLUCA VIALLI

I signed my first professional football contract in 1980. I was 16, the club was Cremonese and the only advice I received was from the AIC, the Italian version of the Professional Footballers' Association. In those days, football was a self-sustaining ecosystem: the money stayed within the game, and there was no involvement from lawyers, banks or agencies – even agents were rare. Over a decade later, in 1992, I signed for Juventus from Sampdoria. Again, there was no agent and no lawyer: Paolo Mantovani, Sampdoria's president, asked what was important to me and then negotiated directly with Juventus on my behalf, securing the contract that would see me leave his club.

Around the mid-1990s, England's Premier League was breaking new ground: football was being packaged into a premium media product and sold globally. Money started flowing into the game. Many of my peers took on agents and lawyers to negotiate commercial deals and transfers on their behalf. For my final transfer as a player, to Chelsea in 1996, I took on my first agent. It was a huge learning curve for all of us as players, and we had to start thinking about ourselves in an entirely different way – as brands, media products, commodities to be bought and sold.

Over 20 years on, the football world is unrecognisable. The revenues from broadcasting rights have brought more money into the game than ever before, driving transfer prices, player salaries, sponsorship deals and commercial revenues to new levels. In this new world, it would be unimaginable for a young footballer to sign a contract – at a new club or their current one – without the help of their managers, agents, lawyers, and possibly a marketing/PR or image rights representative. Even more unthinkable would be a 28-year-old striker, with 59 caps for his country, trusting his club president to negotiate his terms with a buying club.

At the top levels of today's game, agents, lawyers, banks, marketing and PR agencies have all carved out considerable influence. The introduction of these industries and their ways of working have largely benefitted the sport and the players: standards have risen in terms of financial rigour, commercial best practice and legal protection for athletes with very short careers. That having been said, no transfer window goes by without a few sensational stories in the press about who really benefits from the mind-blowing sums of money involved – raising the question of what is going on behind closed doors and whether it's all above board.

I first met Daniel through a mutual friend, when he asked if I would be interested in getting involved in Football Aid, the charity he supports. Since then, I have got to know Daniel well, and always admired him as an authority on the legalities and business of sport. This book is a testament not only to Daniel's vast knowledge of his subject, but also to his ability to present even the most complex ideas in a clear and vivid way. I cannot think of a better person to reveal the inside story of this fascinating industry.

– *Luca Vialli*

THE CHANGING GAME

How we consume football has changed dramatically over the years. When I was growing up in the 1980s, watching live football was a novelty. Only the occasional game was broadcast on television and, in contrast to today, few column inches were devoted to football. This meant that the local newspapers such as the *Liverpool Echo* and *Daily Post* were my main source of information – two pages on a normal day and a few extra on match and post-match days – and I devoured every bit of football news I could.

Transfer gossip was very much in its infancy. Then came Ceefax, a television text information service, and suddenly there were up to 10 pages of football information per day on TV. The traditional rush home after school to grab the remote control, read Ceefax pages 302–312 and discover that Liverpool were linked to a particular player and how much he was going to cost was a revelation. Coming home to the news that Roy Keane had signed for Manchester United was a particularly dark day. This was my generation's internet, the first baby steps into the digital era.

By then, the World Cup was also very much front and centre. Discovering new players and their skills at major tournaments was an eye-opener and made me aware of a wider world of football, featuring exotic players and leagues.

By the time I was going to most Liverpool home games, the novel way of getting the best transfer gossip was through premium-rate phone numbers. No doubt prompted by the small fortune these lines were costing, my Dad became an early adopter and signed up to one of the first forms of the internet. Rather slow and making strange noises, the modem offered a constantly updated dose of football news and discussion forums.

Football became all-encompassing. During family dinners it was the glue of our conversation; Mum (and sometimes Dad!) spoke the most sense. We debated tactics, managers, personalities, games, rivals and history.

Then I attended university, and moved on to getting my daily fix from football news aggregator NewsNow. I even had the opportunity to write a dissertation on the changing FIFA transfer system and a journeyman footballer called Jean-Marc Bosman (more on him later; *see* page 42). This was the first indication that I could combine my two passions: football and law.

I soon found myself in an enviable position. Rather than just consuming football (which by now had become a major component of the global entertainment industry), I was able to offer my own perspective on football, blogging on issues and in turn amplifying my thoughts through a variety of retweets, internet searches, and Facebook and Instagram posts.

Since becoming a lawyer, I've been privileged to have worked on a number of high-profile football takeovers, transfers and disputes, meeting some fantastic people in the industry. The life of a football lawyer is, however, rarely glamorous. Deals may be finalised and photographed in the boardroom, but the nuts and bolts and the details are negotiated on WhatsApp, after mountains of emails, sometimes in the early hours of the morning and after 40 calls to your client each day. I've had moments when I've helped a client negotiate a transfer while picking my kids up from school, or I have been on holiday and ended up working because the deal has been agreed in principle and the player was flying in the next morning. I've helped with deals on the beach, in the snow, on boats, and (losing signal) up mountains. Seldom are negotiations straightforward, as some may presume. But with email and smartphones readily available, there are rarely barriers to finalising a deal.

Nonetheless, what continues to strike me is the somewhat fragile nature of the industry. Players are a bad knee twist or a tackle away from the end of their careers, or a tweet away from a ban; managers are sometimes just a few games away from the sack; agents are continually worried about losing their star players, sometimes having invested years of hard work for no reward; and owners, who may have saved their boyhood club from bankruptcy, are often castigated when results suffer.

Promotion, relegation, last-minute winners, missed play-off final and World Cup penalties, injuries, rehabilitation, contract renegotiations, player transfer requests and clubs forcing players out – these are the everyday actions that define the football industry. There is no black and white. What is important is context and nuance.

Why a story has been written is as important as what the story says. Everyone has an angle, from the player's agent wanting to negotiate a new and more valuable contract to the club wanting to manage the fans' expectations. The volume of content, articles, website reports, etc. can be bewildering, and is creating a broader content business that is changing the face of football, sport and entertainment.

The exponential growth in entertainment available from Netflix, YouTube or Sky Sports means there is more content vying for people's attention. No longer is sport as front and centre as it used to be. Binge on your favourite series, subscribe to your go-to YouTube vlogger and catch highlights of the live game if you've missed it. There is so much competition in the entertainment space that even when people are watching 90 minutes live, most are usually second-screening (using a second device to connect on WhatsApp or checking Twitter or Snapchat). Attention spans are reducing and consumption habits are fundamentally changing. Football isn't so scarce anymore and an almost infinite amount of entertainment content is readily available. Competition for viewers is stronger than ever.

The football spotlight remains incredibly strong. Some fans expect football players to be angels with perfect behaviour. Everyone is fallible, players included. Mistakes happen – and will continue to happen. When looking at the headlines, it's crucial to reflect that players, managers, owners and agents are a mistake, an injury and/or a press conference away from triumph and disaster. Football is particularly unforgiving, and a Twitter timeline after a team's defeat even more so. Any positive is usually drowned out by negativity. Context is important and is easily forgotten. Drama and controversy play out on a weekly basis.

Fans are no doubt the centrepiece for this beautiful game, but now more than ever it's vital to look behind the headlines and understand how the industry really works. This book aims to provide some context and nuance, as well as practical experience – from pitch to boardroom – of the off-field football matters that impact leagues, clubs, players and fans, and which shape the modern game.

CHAPTER 1

THE FOOTBALL ECOSYSTEM

The beautiful game is a complicated business. Luckily enough, it's set out in some detail in this book. To get started, it's vitally important to see how the different elements connect and interact; that's the reason for the ecosystem diagram set out on the following pages. Only by understanding how each football jigsaw piece fits together with all the rest is it possible to delve into the detail of the industry and uncover how things really work.

This book charts the interaction between the most important actors in the national and international football landscape. At the heart of the game are the clubs and teams. They employ the players, play in the various national and international leagues and competitions, pay agents for concluding transfer deals, receive money from broadcasters to broadcast matches to fans worldwide, enter into lucrative partnership deals with brands and receive money from fans for attending games and buying merchandise. The chart demonstrates the circulation of money flowing into and out of football.

Let's take Liverpool FC as an example. Based on the latest 2016/17 accounts published in 2018, the club received £73.5m from match-day activities; £136.4m from their commercial partnerships with brands, including Standard Chartered (£30m per season), New Balance and BetVictor; and £154.3m from broadcasting rights, mostly Premier League revenues. Those Premier League revenues are substantial: a significant proportion of the current broadcasting deal for the Premier League, valued at £8bn+, comes from UK broadcasters Sky and BT Sport paying more than

£5bn for exclusive UK rights. TV companies recoup such a large outlay through pay TV subscription services, which fans pay for in order to watch their team play on a weekly basis. Chelsea, the 2016/17 winners, earned £150.8m in one season as a result of the huge sums that broadcasters around the world will pay.

Similarly, a variety of TV companies also pay huge sums to UEFA to broadcast the Champions League competition. In the UK, BT Sport paid £1.18bn to UEFA for the privilege of exclusively screening live Champions League and Europa League matches until 2021. For details of how broadcasting rights are sold and paid for, and how the money is distributed, *see* Chapter 9, pages 196–227.

Back to Liverpool. Their turnover equalled £364.2m. By way of contrast, Manchester United's revenues were £581m, Real Madrid's totalled £580m and Barcelona's £557m. Liverpool's overall profit was £40m. Eighteen Premier League clubs made operating profit in the 2016/17 season. In that season, the previous winners, Leicester City, made a £92m profit. For details of how clubs maximise revenues, *see* Chapter 4, pages 71–132.

By way of outgoings, Liverpool spent £207.5m on wages and paid out £76m by way of transfers. (For details of how these transfers are structured, paid for and accounted for, *see* Chapter 2, pages 9–56). Similarly, clubs will pay agents a commission of 5–10% of the player's wages. Based on published figures for the 17/18 summer and winter window, Liverpool paid the most, £26.7m to agents. Collectively, Premier League clubs paid agents £211m.

When managers are sacked, compensation is often paid for terminating their contract (and usually the contracts of their backroom staff team). Ex-Liverpool manager Brendan Rodgers and his staff were reported to have been paid £16m. This can be a significant cost for clubs should they decide to change managers who are on long-term contracts.

The money flow is crucial. Due to the various financial control regulations (such as the UEFA Financial Fair Play Rules), clubs cannot usually spend more than they earn. For more details, *see* Chapter 4, pages 71–132. The main consequence of this approach is that clubs need to maximise revenues to ensure they can spend sustainably on player transfers, wages and bonuses.

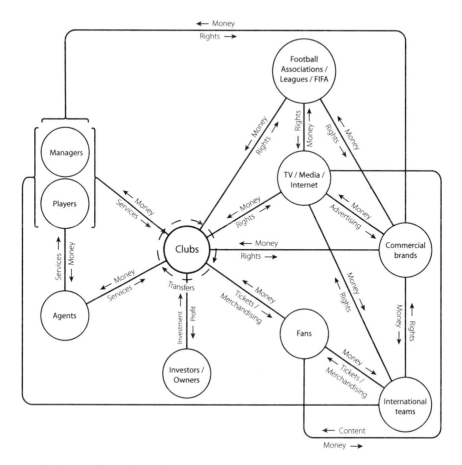

The increasingly complex football ecosystem, where clubs, players, agents and organisations interact and exchange services and rights in return for revenue. The amount of money circulating within the Premier League amounts to billions of pounds.

With this combination of record broadcasting and commercial revenues, millionaire and billionaire business people have taken significant interest in owning clubs. Over the last decade, iconic clubs like Inter Milan, Manchester City, Liverpool, AC Milan, Monaco and Paris Saint-Germain have all been bought in multi-million-pound deals. For details of how such deals are identified and completed, as well as the work that goes into taking over a club, *see* Chapter 4, pages 71–132.

The internationalisation of the game means that players are employed by their clubs but are released by their employers to play for their national teams. This has been fraught with issues in the past. Problems such as whether a player qualifies to play for a particular country, who should pay the player's salary if a player gets injured on international duty, and whether clubs should receive compensation for releasing their players have led to notable disputes in the past. (For more details, *see* Chapter 8, pages 181–195.) Nonetheless, international tournaments run by FIFA and UEFA can be the pinnacle of a player's career. A good World Cup or European Championship can put a player in the shop window for a lucrative transfer.

Brands like Coke, Budweiser, Hyundai, Visa and others have paid millions of pounds to be associated with such high-profile competitions. The money provided to the international federations as a result of the World Cup, Euros or African Nations Cup is passed on to national associations.

The money flow continues. Fans effectively fund the game through match-day attendance and buying pay TV subscriptions. Packed stadia, fanatical support and constant media attention mean that the global game goes from strength to strength.

Done Deal explains how the industry works, provides insight into some of the most topical areas of the beautiful game, and illuminates the multi-million-pound deal flow and the consequences for players, clubs and broadcasters alike.

CHAPTER 2

PLAYER TRANSFERS AND CONTRACTS

Turn back the clocks to August 2015, deadline day. As reported at the time, Manchester United are on the verge of finalising two high-profile, multi-million-pound transfers. The club are negotiating the sale of their first-choice goalkeeper, David de Gea, to Real Madrid for approximately £30m, including the part exchange of Madrid keeper Keylor Navas. Simultaneously, the club's negotiators are also trying to conclude a deal for Monaco wunderkind Anthony Martial for a staggering £50m+. While United manage to finalise the Martial transfer, de Gea and Navas are left without new clubs: the correct documentation was not uploaded to the FIFA Transfer Matching System in enough time, so the deal collapsed. A war of words breaks out, both clubs blaming each other. In the weeks that follow, de Gea signs a long-term contract extension and Martial scores on his debut against arch-rivals Liverpool.

This must have been a pressurised time for the lawyers, negotiators and commercial members of the United back-room staff. They were simultaneously negotiating playing contracts with a whole host of bonus provisions and performance clauses; securing image rights deals, to ensure club sponsorship agreements don't conflict with player sponsor arrangements; and negotiating with the various agents acting for the players and the clubs selling them.

In addition, they were finalising all the paperwork and documentation required for international transfers to take place. Navas will have required a work permit, complicating an already difficult set of negotiations and admin tasks.

It's taken you only moments to read the headlines, but what has just been described will almost certainly have taken weeks, if not months of organisation and negotiation. Some transfers make it over the line, like Martial's, and some don't, like de Gea's. This chapter will show the difficulty in making a transfer happen and the spider's web of jobs, tasks and complications that most fans never see or even contemplate.

Fast forward to the end of the 2017 Premier League summer transfer window, and records continued to tumble. A world record £1.4bn was spent by Premier League clubs; PSG bought out the contract of Barcelona's Neymar for £198m and paid a large loan fee to Monaco for Kylian Mbappé with the promise of a £167m transfer fee in the 2018 summer window. It was also the season for transfers that didn't (initially at least) materialise for a number of high-profile players. Philippe Coutinho submitted a transfer request to his club Liverpool, who refused three separate bids from Barcelona for his services. Diego Costa was left without a transfer out of the Premier League, and faced the prospect of being frozen out at Chelsea. He returned to Atlético Madrid in September but was not allowed to play until January 2018 because Atlético were banned from registering new players. Virgil van Dijk submitted a transfer request in order to push through a deal to Liverpool, who were willing to pay north of £70m to secure his services. It would not be until January 2018, however, that he joined Liverpool – for £75m, a world record fee for a defender.

Many of these issues – transfer fee negotiations, agents' commission, contract renegotiations, image rights deals, work permits, and international transfer clearances – are described below. This is the bread-and-butter work for clubs and agents alike. Take a glimpse into what actually goes on to get a deal done.

AGREEING TRANSFERS

Transfers have always been a vital component of the football industry. They allow teams to change the make-up of their squads, show ambition to their fans and increase the attractiveness of their team. They also enable the selling clubs to generate substantial sums, which can be reinvested into club infrastructure and the playing squad.

Read reports in the press, and transfers seem straightforward: a club targets a player and the deal is finalised. Easy. In practice, the process, from identifying the talent to signing the deal, can be complex. Back in the '80s and '90s, it was quite usual for players to discuss, negotiate and sign long-term contracts with their new manager, without the involvement of agents, chief executives, directors of football or chairmen. The opposite is now true. Today it is unusual that a player in the top four divisions is unrepresented.

In a transfer, there are usually at least two areas for agreement that need to be reached – between the buying and selling clubs, and between the buying club and the player. Although both sound straightforward processes, they are usually anything but. Agreeing multi-million-pound transfer fees is only part of the challenge faced by a buying club. Working with various agents is also required, in order to agree a weekly wage plus a fee for signing on, as well as loyalty and performance bonuses. The devil is in the detail.

It is important to remember transfers are far from straightforward. A football club registers players for its team. Clubs may want to buy a player who is under contract with another club and register him to play for its team. Clubs can do this by paying a transfer fee to effectively end a current contract and transfer the registration to the new club. The size of the fee depends on whether there is a buyout or release clause (*see* below, page 31) or an amount a selling club is willing to accept. Many players transfer to a new club without the buying club having to pay a transfer fee because the player is out of contract. This is commonly referred to as a Bosman transfer (*see* below, page 42). Transfers that involve fees are restricted to transfer windows. Typically, there is a winter and a summer window.

When buying a player, a club will usually identify a number of targets. A club may approach a selling club directly to ask permission to speak to a particular player or may engage an agent to liaise with the player's agent. Manchester United would have contacted Juventus to agree a transfer fee for Paul Pogba before Mino Raiola, his agent, could discuss his salary with the club.

THE TRANSFER FEE

The transfer fee depends on a number of factors, including age, current contract terms, international status of the player, length of remaining contract, nationality of the player and position (strikers being generally more expensive than goalkeepers). For example, Robin van Persie was 29 when he moved to Manchester United from Arsenal for £29m. His age meant he had limited resale value, but manager Sir Alex Ferguson believed that van Persie would contribute to the club's on-field value by scoring goals. Such logic meant that an internationally recognised player bought from a direct competitor was never going to come cheap. Manchester United paid a premium because they knew he would hit the ground running and be an instant, albeit short-term, guarantee of goals. As was so often the case, Ferguson was proved right: van Persie scored 26 league goals in the 2012/13 season for Manchester United, who were crowned Premier League champions after a win over Aston Villa – a match that featured a hat-trick from van Persie, then their leading goalscorer.

It can sometimes take several weeks or months to agree a transfer fee, which usually includes add-ons in relation to:

- the club achieving promotion;
- the club winning trophies;
- the club avoiding relegation;
- player achievements such as international team appearances and/or goals; *and/or*
- a sell-on clause to benefit the club when selling.

Sometimes it can take a matter of hours to negotiate a deal, especially when approaching transfer deadline day, but ultimately the fee depends on the relative strength of each party's position. For example, a player who has requested a transfer, but who is entering the last six months of his contract (and so can move for free six months' later), will be less valuable. As a result, his club may be in a weak position to maximise any transfer fee in comparison to a club with a star striker who has recently signed a five-year deal, and who is happy to remain at his current club.

It was reported, for example, that Naby Keïta's transfer from RB Leipzig to Liverpool in the summer 2018 window was dependent on where RB Leipzig finished in the Bundesliga. Both clubs had agreed to the transfer the previous summer. The transfer agreement included different transfer fees depending on Leipzig's league position. The fee was to be £48m if they finished in seventh position or below. They finished sixth, and the transfer fee was thus agreed at £52.7m.

What is FIFA TMS?

The FIFA Transfer Matching System (TMS) was set up in 2010 and is exactly what it says it is. Before an international transfer certificate (ITC) will be issued by FIFA, more than 20 pieces of information need to be inputted and 'matched' in the TMS by both the buying and selling club – including the name of the player, the clubs, the type of transfer, the agent and the transfer amount. If correctly provided, the ITC is issued, and the transfer can be finalised and the player registered with his new national association.

THE DETAILS OF THE TRANSFER AGREEMENT

A transfer contract is formed when the buying club and the selling club reach an agreement, which will likely involve:

- the transfer fee (likely to be paid in instalments);
- a sell-on clause if the player transfers again in the future; *and*
- any 'add-on' compensation – in the event, for example, that the buying club is promoted or qualifies for the Champions League, additional payments may be triggered.

A transfer fee is usually paid in instalments: for example 50% once the transfer has been completed, 25% on the first anniversary of the completed transfer, and 25% on the second anniversary. As detailed above, there may be add-on fees. For example, a buying club promoted to the Premier League may have included a clause in the transfer agreement whereby it would pay a one-off sum – perhaps £500,000.

Barcelona bid for Philippe Coutinho in the summer of 2017 for a headline transfer figure of £118m. Of this, only £82m was reportedly guaranteed, and that was payable in four annual instalments. The remaining £36m fee was contingent on, for example, Barcelona winning the Champions League and the player winning the Ballon d'Or. This meant that a transfer bid of £118m translated into an initial payment by Barcelona of only £20.5m. When the Coutinho transfer eventually happened, for a reported £146m transfer fee, it was unclear how much of this was guaranteed by Barcelona.

THE COST OF A TRANSFER

When newspaper headlines quote a transfer fee of £35m, many fans would be forgiven for thinking that a buying club transfers £35m to the selling club on the day the transfer happens, and that is that. In fact, the reports of a transfer are often different from the actual amounts paid to a club during the player's time at the club.

Let's suggest that Liverpool pay £35m for a Brazilian international player. The transfer agreement may state that Liverpool pay:

- £15m up front;
- £5m on both the first and second anniversaries of the player's transfer;
- £5m if the player makes 50 appearances for Liverpool; *and*
- £5m if the player wins the Champions League and the Premier League with Liverpool (£2.5m per win).

Therefore, on the first anniversary of the transfer, Liverpool will only have paid £20m. Obviously this could increase depending on the player and Liverpool's performance.

It is quite possible that a headline transfer figure is often never fully attained. Liverpool will never have to pay £5m if the player doesn't make 50 appearances or fails to win the Premier League and Champions League with them.

The £35m transfer fee is only one element of a much larger package. Usually a player's salary over the length of a contract will be a significant investment by the buying club. The average salary of a Premier League player in 2017 was £2.6m per year, or just over £50k a week. An elite international at a top Premier League club could be conservatively earning £5m per year, or around £100k per week. This means that a player earning £100k on a five-year deal will add an additional £26m in wages over the lifetime of the player's first contract (£100k × 52 weeks × 5 years = £26m).

It is important to be aware that the headline transfer fee quoted never usually refers to the investment that a club will have to make in paying significant wages over a long-term contract. A transfer fee of £35m, coupled with a salary of £26m, means very deep pockets are required.

Not only will a basic wage be negotiated but clubs will incentivise players to sign for them by paying additional amounts called signing-on fees and loyalty bonuses, usually paid in instalments over the length of a player's contract. Signing-on fees are usually paid on the anniversaries of signing the contract and loyalty bonuses at the end of one season or the beginning of the following season. These figures can be significant and may conservatively add £2–3m for an elite player over the length of their deal.

The extra expense of the signing-on and loyalty bonuses need to be factored into the calculations of a buying club to ensure they have wriggle room in their *overall* budget.

PERFORMANCE-RELATED BONUSES

Players will receive many different types of bonus, depending on their individual performance as well as the collective success of the team. Various success bonuses – including for an appearance, a win, a goal, and a clean sheet – will significantly top up a player's basic wage and can add as much as 20–30% extra on top of what a player is guaranteed to earn. That could mean an additional £1m that a club has to pay to particularly important players when the team is successful.

It is therefore important to note that a club with a number of significant performance-related bonuses will have a larger bonus liability if the team performs well on the pitch.

By contrast, top female players will earn only a fraction of the amounts on offer in the men's game. Top female players may earn £60,000–80,000 per season, which may include particular individual endorsement deals. In addition, England internationals are paid by the FA through central contracts. It is reported that up to 30 players per season are awarded central contracts (worth up to £30,000), which supplement a player's club income. The *annual* salary for a female player can equal the *weekly* wage of an elite male player. It was reported that US international player Alex Morgan was one of the top earning female players in 2015, earning £1.9m mostly by way of endorsement deals with Nike, McDonald's, Coke and EA Sports. Alex is the exception to the rule at present. Indeed, the average annual salary of players in the English Women's Super League in 2017 was reported by the SportingIntelligence website to be £26,000. Compare and contrast this to the average annual Premier League salary of £2.6m. Thankfully, the growing global popularity of the women's game means that this gap, though stark at present, may well start to narrow.

England players like Jill Scott and Steph Houghton are front and centre in a number of Manchester City's global marketing campaigns. In the #SameCity campaign, they are pictured alongside manager Pep Guardiola and senior male players. With commercial sponsorship and broadcasting revenues set to grow, this will filter down to the players as they become national and international superstars.

'The women's game is continuously growing. Young girls now have role models in the game and players are on full-time paid contracts. Manchester United finally have a women's team, which will certainly attract more attention. Players are now sponsored by some of the largest global brands. The FA Cup Final is played at Wembley Stadium, with record crowds and increasing prize money.'

Sam Miller, Broadcast Journalist

IMAGE RIGHTS CONTRACTS

It is common for top Premier League teams to enter into image rights contracts with their elite players who have a significant commercial value to their commercial partners. Sometimes those payments can be as much as 20% of the total basic salary of the player. A club will therefore have a potential image rights payment of £1m per year to make. Clubs may recoup significant amounts through higher sponsorship deals, using particular players in adverts and endorsement campaigns, but they will still pay the player for the privilege.

AGENTS' COMMISSION

A player's agent will be entitled to commission on a transfer. In large Premier League transfers, the buying club will usually pay the commission to the agent on behalf of the player. This may be 5% of the player's basic wages, and is usually paid in instalments, In the example of the £35m transfer fee to Liverpool described below and overleaf, the club will potentially pay the player's agent £1.3m in instalments over the length of the five-year deal.

From a headline £35m transfer fee, the total investment that Liverpool may need to pay could therefore reach as high as £71.3m over the length of the player's first contract: £35m (transfer fee) + £26m (wages) + £3m (signing on / loyalty bonus) + £1m (performance-related bonus) + £5m (image rights payment) + £1.3m (agent commission).

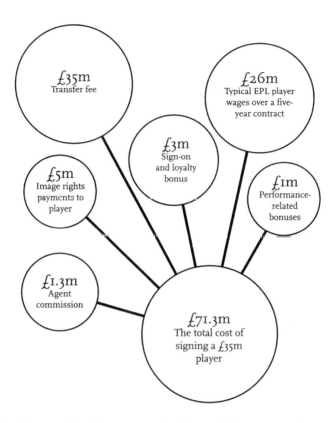

£35m
Transfer fee

£26m
Typical EPL player
wages over a five-
year contract

£3m
Sign-on
and loyalty
bonus

£5m
Image rights
payments to
player

£1m
Performance-
related
bonuses

£1.3m
Agent
commission

£71.3m
The total cost of
signing a £35m
player

The headline transfer fee is just one part of a club's overall investment. A player's salary when calculated over the full length of a contract can often match or top the initial transfer fee. There are also add-ons related to performance and off-field commercial activities.

TRANSFER COMPLEXITIES

Some phases of a transfer can make the process more complicated. There may be occasions when different agents claim to represent the same player. Finding the person with the authority to act for the player is sometimes not straightforward.

A buying club should not liaise with the particular targeted player until it has the permission of the selling club. This is usually granted once outline transfer terms have been agreed between seller and buyer, often indirectly through agents.

Then the work begins: fixing the transfer fee, structuring the various payments and the employment contract, and negotiating the image rights agreement (as discussed below). Such transfers may also have to address, where necessary, FIFA and national association administrative tasks. These will include international transfer certificates (when players move from different national associations), granted through FIFA's transfer matching system (FIFA TMS), medical examinations (to check they are healthy and able to play) and work permit applications (for non-European Union citizens).

It's fair to say that large transfers involving foreign players moving to the Premier League demand time-consuming scrutiny. For the larger deals in particular, agents as well as lawyers are having to become increasingly skilled at negotiating and concluding such transfers.

TAPPING UP

Under Premier League rules, clubs are not permitted to approach a player whose contract is due to expire until after the third Saturday in May of the same year (i.e. around six weeks prior to the contract's expiry). If a player is transferring internationally, a player can be approached in the last six months of his deal, with the view to signing a new contract starting after expiry of his old deal.

The Premier League and other leagues have rules in place to prevent 'tapping up' – an approach by a player, his agent or other representatives to negotiate a contract with a buying club without having first obtained the prior written consent of the club to whom the player is contracted. The wording of the Premier League rule states:

> Any Club which by itself, by any of its Officials, by any of its Players, by its Agent, by any other Person on its behalf or by any other means whatsoever makes an approach either directly or indirectly to a Contract Player . . . shall be in breach of these Rules.

In January 2005, Ashley Cole and his agent met Peter Kenyon (then Chelsea's chief executive), José Mourinho (then the Chelsea manager) and agent Pini Zahavi. The detail of what happened at the meeting was not clear, but the Premier League ultimately found breaches of the rules. The charges against all the individuals were proved – with the exception of Pini Zahavi, whom the Commission did not have the power to sanction. Chelsea, according to the investigation, were trying to convince Ashley Cole to sign for them while he was playing for Arsenal. The club were fined £300,000 and given a suspended three-point deduction. Cole and Mourinho were each handed fines of £75,000.

More recent examples have included Southampton complaining to the Premier League over Liverpool's reported approach to Virgil van Dijk. After Southampton had sold five players to Liverpool over the previous few seasons, Southampton were unhappy with reports that Liverpool had now tapped up van Dijk, and they asked the Premier League to investigate.

Within 24 hours, Liverpool had apologised to Southampton 'for any misunderstanding' and withdrawn their interest, and the Premier League's investigation ended. Ultimately, the transfer occurred in the winter 2017/18 window, but the issue no doubt caused problems for Liverpool and its relationship with Southampton. Before the transfer was concluded, Liverpool had to tread a very difficult line because Southampton's consistent message was that the player was not for sale – just as Liverpool had insisted to Barcelona (before his transfer was finalised) that Philippe Coutinho was not for sale either. Clubs can find themselves on both sides of the argument.

HOW PLAYERS CAN ENGINEER A TRANSFER

1. **Submit a transfer request.** The risk is that the request isn't accepted, and the player alienates the fans, causes a summer of instability for the club and sometimes finds himself training with the reserves. Recent examples have included John Stones's proposed but ultimately failed move to Chelsea in 2015 before transferring to Manchester City for a reported £47.5m, and Luis Suárez agitating for a move to Arsenal while at Liverpool before

ultimately moving to Barcelona the following summer for a reported £70m+.

2. **Go on strike.** Performance on the pitch is what ultimately matters. It's never as simple as playing badly, but managers, chairmen and teammates are acutely aware if players sit back, do the bare minimum or even go on strike. If the player is the star of the team and knows he is vital to the plans of the coach, such behaviour can destabilise the squad and ruin team dynamics. Robbie Savage recently explained that he 'downed tools' in order to push for a move from Birmingham to Blackburn. Carlos Tevez did not come off the bench for a Champions League match for Man City against Bayern Munich in September 2011. He denied that he had refused, but manager Roberto Mancini vowed never to play Tevez again . . . until a few months later when he was back on the pitch in advance of his Juventus transfer.

3. **Raise your game.** Play well and create demand for your services. Look at Leicester City, who surprised everyone by winning the Premier League in the 2015/16 season. They had a number of outstanding performers, players like Vardy, Mahrez, Kante, Drinkwater and Schmeichel, who have been or will be rewarded with lucrative playing contract extensions or transfers to world-renowned teams. Kante transferred to Chelsea for a reported £32m, and was followed to Stamford Bridge by Drinkwater for even more (£35m). Similarly, Gareth Bale couldn't get a game for Spurs in 2010, and even when he did, he played in 24 winless games for the club. Fast forward three years, to 2013, and his then record transfer to Real Madrid for €100m and his Champions League winner's medals have turned him into a global superstar.

4. **Contract, what contract?** FIFA rules can allow for a player to breach his contract and move to a new club. He will have to pay compensation to his old club, which will depend on his current ability and worth. Although not household names, players such as Matuzalém, Morgan De Sanctis and Lassana

Diarra have all been ordered to pay their previous clubs millions of euros after breaching their contracts. Needless to say, few players will go down this route: the risk of paying fortunes to a previous club is high, as is the prospect of years of distracting and expensive legal costs.

5. **Use the media.** Speaking to the press to say how unhappy you are with the team's ambitions is usually code for a player who wants more than what the club can deliver. It goes one of two ways. A player can be put on the mythical 'transfer list', thus burning his bridges with management and fans. However, if the player is the star of the team, he is in a strong negotiating position, and can use such leverage as a tactic to agree a lucrative new contract. Such was the case with Wayne Rooney when he questioned Manchester United's ambitions in October 2010.

6. **Wait it out.** A player allowing his contract to expire means his current club is not entitled to a transfer fee. This gives the player a large degree of bargaining power. In practice, a club is loath to let a valuable player leave 'on a free', so if the player/agent has indicated he will not renew his contract, they will usually decide to sell the player before his contract runs out, to maximise his transfer value. Examples include Raheem Sterling leaving Liverpool after explaining he was not going to sign a new deal, and İlkay Gündoğan moving to Man City for £20m from Dortmund despite having only a year left on his deal. The club decided to cash in on the value of the player who had also been injured for a number of months. Unfortunately, the player suffered a number of additional injuries in his debut season for Manchester City.

7. **Smart clauses.** Employ a clever lawyer and draft a transfer release clause. Savvy agents (with the help of lawyers like me) are inserting release clauses into players' contracts. The clause would work if, for example, a bid of £70m is received from a buying club. The selling club must contractually accept the bid and enable the transfer to occur. A number of players, including Demba Ba, Christian Benteke and Luis Suárez, have all activated such clauses in recent years. Jamie Vardy is reported to have a

£22m release clause. Similarly, reports suggested that former Liverpool player Emre Can would not sign a new deal without a release clause being inserted. He ultimately moved to Italian club Juventus on a free transfer.

8.   **Get relegated.** Being part of a relegated team is clearly negative, but it can offer a 'want away' player a means of escape. It is common for players to insert a relegation release clause, providing the opportunity for a move in a cut-price deal.

9.   **Cite personal reasons.** If the player's family haven't settled well because of the food, icy weather conditions for nine months in the year, language barriers, shopping or social life not being up to scratch, this puts a strain on the player's most important relationships and may force him to request a move to a more desirable city or country. When Dimitri Payet returned to Marseille after his protracted move from West Ham, one of the reasons cited was that his wife and children had never settled in England.

THE TRANSFER 'DEAL SHEET'

On deadline day, Premier League clubs can often be finalising transfer agreements until the very last minute. Indeed, Adrien Silva's transfer from Sporting Lisbon to Leicester in the summer 2017 transfer window was missed by 14 seconds – he had to wait to play until January 2018.

In order to give clubs some leeway for completing all administrative matters by the deadline, and providing documents to the Premier League and FA (and FIFA, where appropriate), the Premier League allows buying clubs to complete a deal sheet. This confirms a transfer deal has been agreed and allows for an extension in order to finalise the transfer. As explained on the Premier League website:

> For an 11pm deadline, the deal sheet cannot be used prior to 9pm and needs to arrive fully completed before the transfer window closes. Once the sheet arrives, clubs have got until 1am in which to submit the full paperwork. But if a club are looking to complete an international transfer, it still has to comply with the FIFA Transfer Matching System (TMS) deadline of midnight.

CR7 +JUVE = €?

The 2018 summer transfer window heralded the move of Cristiano Ronaldo from Real Madrid to Juventus. The transfer made headlines for a number of reasons. First was the eye-watering transfer fee, reported to be around €100m for the 33-year-old, plus his reported salary of €30m per season until 2022. Secondly, once the deal was announced by Juventus, its share price rose by 40%. It was also reported that Juventus had sold 520,000 Ronaldo shirts in the first 24 hours after the transfer was announced.

However, it was not all good news for Juventus. ESPN reported that Ronaldo's transfer caused a Fiat car-workers union to call a strike. The Agnelli family, who own 63% of Juventus, also own over 29% of Fiat. The union had complained of the economic sacrifices faced by Fiat employees while at the same time Juventus were spending such high sums on a single football player. Unfortunately for the union, only five workers turned up in protest.

FOOTBALL PLAYER CONTRACTS

Once a club enters into a contract with a player, there will be a variety of duties that the club and player must keep to until the end of the deal. The contract between a player and a club is important in order, for example, that a club can secure the future of its players who are highly valued – by way of both salary paid and transfer fee that could be received. Contracts protect the player (i.e. he will be paid) and the club (i.e. they can keep a player they don't want to sell or to demand a large transfer fee for). There are relatively few sectors where companies will pay huge transfer fees to release an employee from a contract. Lawyers (even this one!) are not in such a position as to have another law firm bid millions of pounds for their services.

All Premier League and Football League player employment contracts are based on a standard template contract and contain common clauses. The document is available online and sets out a wide variety of obligations. This obviously doesn't include the financial details for each individual player. Standard clauses include:

1. The player's salary and the amounts to be paid by the club.
2. The responsibilities of the player, including: attending matches; training; complying with club instructions (and not, for example, going skiing or riding a motorbike – Carlo Cudicini, the ex-Spurs and Chelsea goalkeeper, did the latter and broke his wrist and pelvis); not bringing the club into disrepute (by, for example, posting a tweet badmouthing the chairman or manager).
3. The responsibilities of the club – to release the player for national team matches, for example.
4. Disciplinary and dispute procedures where the club will investigate and decide upon breaches of contract, or failures to observe the contract (if, for example, a player fails to turn up for training, fights with other teammates or refuses to play for the team).
5. Termination of the contract by the club (e.g. for taking drugs) and/or by the player (e.g. for the club not paying his salary).
6. Community public relations and club marketing duties (such as meeting kids in hospital over Christmas).

The most important aspect for a player will be his salary. Sometimes this is based on a higher basic amount and a smaller variable amount. The variable figures usually relate to the number of bonuses a club may offer, and examples are set out below.

SIGNING-ON FEES

A signing-on fee in a player's contract will probably be worded as follows. The idea is that if the player is at the club for the times set out in his contract, he will receive a set amount:

> If the player remains at the club they shall receive a once-only signing-on fee of £100,000 in four equal instalments of £25,000 on 1 August in 2018, 2019, 2020 and 2021.

APPEARANCES

If the player is in the starting 11 for a Premier League match, he may receive an appearance fee.

Additional appearance bonuses can be inserted so that a player's weekly salary increases once a certain number of first team starts have been made. For example, a player's salary will increase by £1,500 per week after 25, 50, 75, 100, 125 and 150 Premier League starts.

The player may receive an additional one-off bonus after making a certain number of Premier League appearances. For example, the player receives £10,000 after each of 25, 50 and 100 Premier League starts.

Sometimes appearance and win bonus amounts vary for the various competitions in which the club is playing. For example, a Premier League win and/or appearance bonus may be greater than an FA Cup win and/or appearance bonus.

WINS

If the player is in the starting 11 for a Premier League match and the team win, he may receive, say, £2,000. Win bonuses can range from a few hundred pounds in the Football League lower divisions to £10,000+ in the Premier League.

Sometimes win and appearance bonuses are combined with a club position bonus in one clause so that: if the player is in the starting 11 for a Premier League match and the team's League position at, say, 11 p.m. on the Monday evening following the game is 1st to 4th, the player may receive £5,000 per win or £1,000 per draw.

The bonus amount changes depending on the position of the club after each Premier League match played. Usually, players aren't paid an additional bonus when the team loses.

SUBSTITUTE APPEARANCES

If the player is a substitute listed on the team sheet for a Premier League match, he may be paid 30% of the bonus (above) once he enters the pitch. Depending on the club, non-playing substitutes may receive no bonus.

GOALS

A number of clubs do not include individual achievement bonuses for goals and assists. The logic is that goal bonuses incentivise individual behaviour, which may conflict with team aims. In an extreme example, a striker who has a bigger goal bonus than win bonus may decide to shoot rather than pass to a teammate who has an open goal. There are still many clubs that provide a bonus if the player scores a goal in a Premier League match – £5,000 per goal, say. Some Premier League clubs are reported to pay £10–20k per goal, depending on how many have been scored in the season.

ASSISTS

Similarly, if the player directly assists by providing the final pass to the scorer of the goal for the team in a Premier League match, he may be paid £3,000 per goal assist. Assist bonuses can sometimes be as valuable as goal bonuses to particular players.

CLEAN SHEET BONUS

This clause is usually relevant for goalkeepers, defenders and defensive midfielders. So long as the relevant players usually start the Premier League match and the team does not concede a goal, a bonus of £5,000 could be paid.

CUP COMPETITION PROGRESSION/VICTORIES

As mentioned above, the club may vary the amounts they pay to their players in win, appearance, goal and clean sheet bonuses depending on the competition in which the team is playing. In addition, a bonus may be paid for reaching a final and/or winning the final.

LOYALTY PAYMENTS

A club will provide a bonus to incentivise its players to stay for the season ahead. For example, a player may receive loyalty payments during his contract totalling £120,000, payable in three equal instalments of £40,000 on 14 September, 2019, 2020 and 2021 (i.e. the payment is made after the end of each respective transfer window).

RELEGATION

As with positive bonuses, clubs will try to reduce costs – for example, in the case of relegation. If the club are now playing in the Football League Championship after being relegated from the Premier League, a player's basic salary could be reduced by up to 50%.

VARIABLE PAY AND INCENTIVES

Over the last few years, variable figures like those above have been used more often during contractual negotiations in order to reduce a player's basic guaranteed salary. Players may be offered lower basic amounts with the upside of higher variable figures. Whether this becomes more lucrative to a player will depend on whether the performance targets of the player and the club are met. There are many other variables that could also top up this amount.

An example: a striker wants £50k a week to sign for Arsenal, who are aiming to qualify for the Champions League. Instead of offering the player £50k, the club offers £35k plus £15k for each appearance made (so long as the player is on the pitch for more than 60 minutes of each game) with a bonus equal to £3k extra per win and £15k per week extra uplift, should the club qualify for the Champions League.

If the player doesn't play, he receives only £35k per week. If he plays and the team wins two games per month, and Arsenal qualify for the Champions League, his weekly salary will be over £70k.

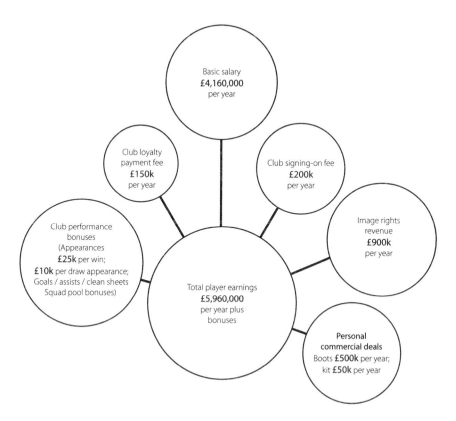

The earnings of an elite player are made up of various contractual components, including commercial deals, regular club loyalty and signing-on fee payments. Performance-related bonuses and a 30-goal season could boost a striker's earnings by as much as £1 million.

The decision for the player then is whether to accept a reduced/smaller basic amount or to gamble on a potentially higher variable salary. For players to take the gamble, the variable figure would have to be lucrative. Otherwise, a player who is injured for a long period of time will receive only the £35k per week.

Similarly, loyalty bonuses are typically paid after the end of each season as a reward for completing the season with the team. Savvy club owners will insist a loyalty bonus is paid to a player only in the September after the August window. This incentivises the player to stay with the club during the window. A player's decision to leave can sometimes be heavily influenced by the timing for particularly large bonuses. It was reported that Dimitri Payet was paid a £1m loyalty bonus by West Ham in September 2016, only for him to seek a transfer away from the club in the winter window a few months afterwards and sign for Marseille.

Loyalty bonuses can also be a major sticking point during a transfer negotiation. If we stay with the example of Payet, he will probably have had loyalty bonus payments due at each subsequent September over the length of his contract. When he moved to Marseille, there would have been a question mark over whether he was entitled to receive his future signing-on payment instalments (which are also usually spread over the length of a player's contract) and his loyalty bonuses. The basic logic is that a player asking to leave isn't being loyal and shouldn't be entitled to his remaining loyalty payment instalments. If the club wants to sell the player but the player is happy to stay, his agent will almost always demand the remaining signing-on and loyalty payments due because he is being loyal by not agitating for a move. Usually, for the transfer to happen when a player does not ask to leave, he will need to come to an agreement with his club to pay a percentage of his remaining outstanding payments. How much depends on the bargaining power and leverage of both sides.

'Things are beginning to change, as clubs are becoming increasingly savvy about the potential impact of bonuses on performance. Rather than simply rewarding good performance, well-designed performance-related play actually incentivises the player to do the best he can for the team. For some clubs, this means reducing the amount of fixed salary a player is offered but increasing the amount he can earn from making appearances and winning matches for his team. Clubs can also tap into a player's tendency for loss aversion, whereby they feel the pain of a loss more than enjoy the excitement of a gain.'

Omar Chaudhuri, 21 Club

SQUAD BONUS POOL

There are also end-of-season, squad bonus pool payments to players in addition to the individual bonuses specifically set out in each player's contract. This is usually at the club's discretion. It was reported that Cardiff City and Newcastle United players were unhappy at the size of the bonus pool distributed to the squad once they had achieved promotion to the Premier League.

The squad bonus pool is an additional amount of money to be shared between the players at the end of a particular season, depending on the success of the team. Let's say that a bonus pool amount of £2m is available to the players of a Premier League club if they are not relegated from the Premier League. (In practice, the amount can vary depending on the position in which the club finishes.) In order to reward the players who contribute the most on the pitch during the season, a points system is usually put in place. So 3 points are awarded for a player who starts each Premier League game, 2 points for any playing substitute and 1 point for a non-playing substitute. There will be 43 points available for each game (3 × 11, 2 × 3 and 1 × 4). Stay with me!

With 38 Premier League games, there will be 1,634 points available (38 games × 43 points). Therefore each point is worth just over £1,223 – i.e. the total bonus pool amount is divided by the number of points available (£2m/1634).

To give a practical example, a player in the same Premier League squad who starts 20 Premier League games is a playing substitute in 3, a non-playing substitute in 2, and is injured for the remaining 13 games will earn:

20 starts = 60 points
3 playing sub appearances = 6 points
2 non-playing sub appearance = 2 points
a total of 68 points × £1,223 = £83,164

RELEASE AND BUYOUT CLAUSES

Along with wages and performance bonuses, an increasingly key aspect of player contracts is the addition of release and buyout clauses.

A release clause is a clause in a player's contract that becomes effective if, for example, the minimum selling figure set out in the player's employment contract is triggered by a purchasing club. The player will then be entitled to speak to the buying club. The clause may also be triggered if another condition is met – for example, a particular transfer window or because a club does not qualify to participate in the Champions League. The result is that the clause automatically requires a club to accept a specific offer.

A growing number of Premier League transfers have been reported to have included release clauses. This was the case with the transfer of Demba Ba from Newcastle to Chelsea in 2013, and Joe Allen from Swansea to Liverpool in 2012. In the case of Allen, there were reports that the bid could trigger the release clause only if it came from one of five clubs, which included Liverpool. Liverpool also triggered Christian Benteke's £32m release clause to enable his transfer from Aston Villa.

What happened with Luis Suárez?

During the 2013 summer transfer window, when Suárez was still a Liverpool player, Arsenal bid their infamous £40m plus £1 to activate a clause that required Liverpool to accept any bid over £40m, or so they thought. This famously prompted Liverpool owner John W. Henry to tweet: 'What do you think they're smoking over there at Emirates?'

The Professional Footballers' Association (PFA) reported that the clause in Suárez's contract with Liverpool was a 'good faith' release clause rather than an automatic release clause. The two are very different. An automatic release clause means that the player must be allowed to speak to a buying club if the minimum release amount is offered. A 'good faith' clause means the parties are required to negotiate in good faith once a bid has been made. Importantly, a 'good faith' clause does not automatically mean the selling club have to accept the offer.

The problem with some buyout clauses is that they often remain confidential. This means that the player's agent potentially risks being sued for breach of confidentiality if the agent discloses the buyout figure to the buying club. As such, it is good practice for an agent to insert into a buyout clause that the amount and any other details can be disclosed as appropriate.

The PFA were reported to have arbitrated between Suárez and the club, explaining to the player the difficulty he faced by having the clause subjected to a robust legal examination.

Buyout clauses are widespread in Spain and are somewhat different to a release clause. They are usually set at a very high figure that is not necessarily the true market value of the player. The player must literally 'buy out' his contract at the stipulated amount – although in practice, it is the purchasing club who pays the amount via the player. In the past, this has been a complicated process because of the tax implications for the purchasing club, which transfers the buyout fee to the player, who in turn buys out his contract. This was highlighted by Manchester United's reported initial failed bid for Ander Herrera (in the window before he was subsequently bought) and Javi Martínez's successful transfer to Bayern Munich. The 2017 summer window, of course, saw the seismic buyout of Neymar's Barcelona contract by PSG.

When did Neymar become worth £198m?

How do buyout clauses such as Neymar's work?

In Spain, the buying club has to pay money to La Liga (the Spanish league) to activate the buyout clause, which is a contractual stipulation in a player's contract. Barcelona originally set Neymar's buyout amount at a figure that they did not believe anyone would bid. Nonetheless, PSG bid the correct figure and the clause was activated. When Lionel Messi signed a new contract with Barcelona in November 2017, the buyout clause was reported to have been set at £626m.

Could Barcelona or La Liga have asked UEFA to block the deal?
Barcelona and La Liga were unsure how any club would afford the buyout clause and comply with the UEFA Financial Fair Play rules (FFP) that stop clubs spending more than they earn (*see* page 110).

There was nothing stopping Barcelona from contacting UEFA, but once the buyout figure was met, there was little UEFA could do to stop the transfer.

How do PSG square such a big one-off fee with FFP?
From an accounting perspective, PSG paying in instalments or in a one-off payment doesn't make much difference. This is because PSG will account for the transfer in their FFP submissions by dividing the overall fee by the years of Neymar's contract. Even if it is paid in one lump sum, the accounting cost per season for a five-year deal, say, will be a fifth of the overall number.

It's likely that the club will have to push through a lot of pretty lucrative commercial deals or – even more likely – sell a number of players to recoup enough revenues to break even.

If PSG have made profit in previous years for FFP accounting purposes, that goes some way to subsidising any subsequent loss from the transfer of Neymar. Nonetheless, at the time of writing UEFA were investigating PSG's compliance with the FFP regulations.

In recent years the validity of release clauses has been brought in to question with some arguing they are increasingly meaningless. If an automatic release amount is triggered, a club will be contractually bound to accept the amount offered.

If the club who has the player's registration refuses to release him, it is likely an arbitration process would follow between the two clubs or the player and the club to assess the validity of the release clause.

In the case of a dispute between two Premier League clubs, the tribunal would have the power to rule that the clause is an automatic release clause, thus allowing the proposed buying club to speak to the player and proceed with the transfer. However, a significant issue could arise, in the UK, if the value in the release clause was so high that it went far beyond the market value of the player. A player may argue that he would be restricted from moving to another club because the release fee was extortionate.

Release clauses can play an important role and there will be instances when a player is willing to move down the football ladder, perhaps to achieve greater playing time in the short term or to sign a contract extension. He will do so on the condition that a release clause is inserted into his contract, which could be triggered if he plays well enough to attract a bigger club. Similarly, because the release clause is usually in the interests of the player and not the club, the player may usually have to accept lower wages, bonuses, etc. in order to insert the release clause.

Many have argued that Philippe Coutinho should have included a release clause in the deal he signed with Liverpool at the beginning of 2017. His subsequent move to Barcelona would have been easier, with the club obliged to meet his release clause. In practice, however, any such clause would have depended on the bargaining positions of the player and club at the time, and a release clause would probably have reduced his salary and bonuses. Since there was no release clause, Liverpool had the power – initially, at least – to refuse to sanction the move over the 2017 summer window. Coutinho eventually moved to Barcelona in January 2018 for £146m, making him the second most expensive player behind Neymar.

BUYBACK CLAUSES

Buyback clauses in transfer agreements give a selling club the security of being able to repurchase a promising player at a set fee, should the player excel in the future. Some high-profile examples of such clauses being activated include Álvaro Morata, from Juventus back to Madrid; Casemiro, from Porto back to Real Madrid; and Gerard Deulofeu, from Everton back to Barcelona. Liverpool also included a buyback clause in Jordon Ibe's transfer to Bournemouth.

In many cases, the benefit of the transfer extends to:

- the selling club, who receive a transfer fee for a player currently not getting regular playing time, but with the possibility of buying back the player if he plays well at a set fee;
- the buying club, who can purchase a player that they otherwise may not have been able to acquire (in addition, the buyback figure is usually significantly higher than the original transfer fee); *and*
- the player, who can play regular first team football, probably receive a pay rise and demonstrate their talent.

The buyback provision is usually based on a number of individual or cumulative triggers:

- the clause is usually activated within defined transfer windows (e.g. the selling club cannot buy back the player for a minimum of two seasons).
- The original selling club bids a set amount, which varies depending on the season that the buyback clause is triggered (e.g. £2m in the 18/19 windows and £2.5m in the 19/20 windows).

Should a buyback provision be triggered, there is usually a contractual obligation to enforce the contract and transfer the player accordingly.

Given that such provisions are commercial agreements between contracting parties, there is always the possibility of removing a buyback clause, should both parties agree – usually through payment made to the club that have the benefit of the buyback clause.

An interesting situation was reported for ex-Atlético Madrid defender Toby Alderweireld, who was on loan at Southampton for the 2014/15 season. Southampton entered in the loan deal with Atlético with the agreement that they had the option to purchase the defender for £6.8m.

Although not a buyback provision, the clause gave Southampton the ability to convert the loan into a permanent transfer unless Atlético paid Southampton £1.5m to remove the clause. In the 2015 summer window Tottenham bid around £11.5m, which Atlético accepted. Southampton, however, wanted to enforce the £6.8m purchase clause. It has not been publicly reported how the matter was finally resolved, but it is likely that Atlético provided compensation to Southampton in order for the player to transfer to Tottenham.

THE FIRST REFUSAL CLAUSE

A first refusal transfer clause gives the club who has the benefit of the clause the opportunity to be informed of any deal that the selling club is willing to accept for the transfer of the player.

This is different from a buyback clause because the selling club retains the power to decide whether to sell the player or not.

Typically, a buyback clause automatically triggers the transfer of the player, should specific conditions be met. In practice, the selling club will not have any way of refusing the buyback offer if the clause is intended to be an automatic trigger and is drafted correctly. The most common way for the original club to repurchase the player is through a set transfer fee that is inserted into the transfer agreement (e.g. if the club bids £15m in any of the second or third transfer windows).

In practice, these matters can become more complicated if there are different set fees depending on, for example:

1. the year that the clause is activated;
2. the player being called up for the national team; *or*
3. the player scoring a certain number of goals or making a number of appearances.

So, for example, a basic buyback clause could be structured as follows to ensure that the buyback fee will be set at:

- £5m should such a bid be received from the offer club in the Summer 2019 window; *or*
- £6.5m should such a bid be received from the offer club in the Summer 2020 window.

This brings into question what happens if a third club offers more? Does the original club have to match it? What if the third club then ups its offer in response?

This was a similar scenario to the example of Toby Alderweireld discussed above. In practice, a selling club can have the benefit of a stipulated transfer amount cancellation clause, just as Atlético did. This caters for a scenario where a third club bids more than the stipulated buyback amount.

Whether such a cancellation clause is inserted in the first place can depend on the negotiating position of the parties. If the original seller (who will have the benefit of the buyback) is in a strong position, there is less likelihood of such a cancellation figure being inserted.

If there is such a provision and the buyback cancellation sum is paid to the original club, the selling club is free to sell the player and accept a higher amount.

If the club refuses to pay the buyback cancellation sum or there is no clause in the contract, then the original selling club should be able to enforce the buyback clause – so long as it can agree personal terms with the player and that the player wishes to rejoin the club. (These factors may not be straightforward in practice!)

Some of the strangest clauses reported in footballer and manager contracts

1. **The great bake-off:** Rolf-Christel Guié-Mien reportedly asked Eintracht Frankfurt to pay for his wife's cooking classes.

2. **Astronomical:** Sunderland inserted a provision that stopped their Swedish international footballer Stefan Schwarz from travelling into space.

3. **All-out war:** In 2002, amid threats of military conflict in Iraq, manager Bernd Stange asked for a release clause from the Iraq Football Association in case war broke out. It subsequently did and he left.

4. **Ski school:** Stig Inge Bjørnebye was forbidden from emulating his father, an Olympic ski jumper. Liverpool refused to let him ski when back home in Norway.

5. **Who needs friends?** When Neymar played for Barcelona, his friends were flown to Spain every two months for an all-expenses paid holiday in Barcelona – a relatively common benefit among top players.

6. **The non-flying Dutchman:** It was reported that Arsenal legend Dennis Bergkamp, who has a fear of flying, insisted on a clause in his contract to ensure he was not forced to fly on away trips.

7. **Make mine a large:** Neil Ruddock, a defender playing for Crystal Palace, was reported to have had a weight restriction clause inserted into his playing contract in order to maintain his waistline. Erstwhile Palace chairman Simon Jordan told *FourFourTwo* magazine about the clause: 'When we were signing players like Neil Ruddock, Harry Redknapp had told me to get him on a weight clause in his contract otherwise he would turn up overweight.' Ruddock was reported to have missed his debut because the club didn't have shorts that fitted.

8. **No red boots:** When Rafael van der Vaart moved to Real Betis in 2015, it was reported that he could wear boots of any colour apart from red, the colour of Betis's local rivals, Sevilla.

LOAN DEALS

Loan deals are temporary transfers between football clubs. A club enters into an agreement that involves them taking a player on loan, and usually contributing to most, if not all, of the player's wages. The benefit to the player is the promise of first team action, and to the parent club a player who (hopefully) returns more experienced and ready to break into the first team.

In some cases, the club taking the player on loan will also pay a loan fee. When Falcao sealed a loan deal between Monaco and Manchester United, the loan fee was reported to be £10m for the season plus Manchester United paying all of his wages. In addition, there was a transfer fee agreed at the same time as the loan deal, by which the loan would become a permanent transfer if Manchester United agreed to pay the fee (reported to be around £40m).

There can be some difficult issues regarding loan deals:

- The Premier League regulations state that a Premier League player cannot play against his parent club.
- The Football League regulations state a Football League player cannot play against his parent club without the agreement of the parent club.

For this reason, loan deals in both leagues can be controversial. The rules are designed to prevent a potential conflict of interest, such as the player's parent club putting pressure on him to play badly ('If you want to have a future with us, we suggest you have a very average game'), or even the appearance of a conflict of interest, should a player give away a penalty or be sent off. Recently, Carl Jenkinson was not able to play for West Ham (where he was on loan) against his parent club, Arsenal. The manager at the time, Arsène Wenger, expressed his dissatisfaction with the current system in the Premier League:

> Once you are on loan, it should be a transfer – you play for the club. You cannot play for the club only in 19 games and not against another club. When I arrived, you could decide that when you loan the player

he could play against you or not. We had the case with [Jermaine] Pennant as well when he went to Leeds. I allowed him to play against us because at that time you could decide. Now, they have decided that you don't have the right, which is a little bit questioning the integrity of the players.

Wenger also offered the example of Romelu Lukaku, who could not face Chelsea when on loan originally to Everton. This gave Arsenal's rival an advantage because he could play against everyone apart from them. The rules protect top-performing loan players from playing (and harming) their parent club. There are some who view this as offering an advantage to leading teams with large squads.

This does cut both ways, though. Sometimes, in other leagues, it's the parent club that misses out. A prime example is Fernando Morientes, who was loaned to Monaco in 2004. Monaco played Real Madrid in the Champions League – and it was Morientes's goal that knocked Madrid out. Morientes gave his best in a game against his parent club, to prove the parent club was wrong in loaning him out.

Interestingly, this issue arose again in the Champions League before Atlético Madrid played Chelsea in April 2014. Atlético Madrid had Chelsea goalkeeper Thibaut Courtois on loan, under the terms of which Atlético would have to pay a fee to allow the Belgium international to face Chelsea. However, the club could not afford to pay the fee Chelsea wanted for the two games (reportedly £5m). Before the game, UEFA indicated that the payment clause influenced player selection and was therefore 'null, void and unenforceable'. By contrast to the Premier League and Football League, where loan players do not play against their parent club, the opposite approach in European competitions is very much the norm.

During the 2017/18 Premier League season, Chelsea had loaned five of their players to other Premier League clubs: Kurt Zouma to Stoke, Ruben Loftus-Cheek to Crystal Palace, Tammy Abraham to Swansea, Izzy Brown to Brighton and Kasey Palmer to Huddersfield. None of those players can play against their parent club, and while this avoids conflicts of interest, it has the impact of weakening opposing teams in 10 out of a potential 38 Chelsea Premier League matches.

HOW THE BOSMAN RULING CHANGED FOOTBALL

The Bosman ruling is regarded by many as the most significant case in European football to date. Jean-Marc Bosman was a footballer who played for the Belgium club Liège. His playing contract expired in 1990 but the club wanting to buy him (USL Dunkerque) did not offer a large enough transfer fee. As a result, Liège kept his registration and did not allow him to leave the club.

Bosman argued that such a situation was unfair and that he should be allowed to move to another club once his contract had ended. He took the case all the way to the highest European court – now called the Court of Justice of the EU (CJEU).

The outcome of the case was as follows:

1. **Free agents became the norm.** When a footballer came to the end of his contract, he was free to sign for any club based in the European Union (EU), and it was illegal for the club he played for to hold on to his playing registration.

2. **EU quotas became illegal.** At the time, quotas were in operation in European competitions. These set a limit of three 'foreign' players and two assimilated players in a team squad, and were also ruled illegal. Neither FIFA nor UEFA could impose on clubs any restrictions that discriminated against players on the basis of nationality. The subsequent UEFA Homegrown Player Rule, which is based on where a player trains rather than his place of birth (*see* pages 124–128), is a consequence of the Bosman decision.

3. **Players benefited from new horizons.** EU players had the right to move freely in the EU. The effect was that a large number of football players in the EU were able to leave on free transfers at the expiry of their contracts. Some of the highest-profile Bosman transfers in Europe over the years include Sol Campbell, from arch-rival Tottenham to Arsenal, and Steve McManaman from Liverpool to Real Madrid. The summer before McManaman moved to Madrid, Barcelona bid £12m for him, but the transfer fell through. Less than a year later,

in 1999, he was able to join Madrid on a free transfer. More recently, Michael Ballack, Robert Lewandowksi, Andrea Pirlo, Fernando Llorente and James Milner have been high-profile Bosman transfers. Players are now said to be in a stronger position to negotiate a more lucrative contract when their existing contracts begin to run down (usually when entering the final two years of the contract) because clubs do not want to lose the player on a free transfer. Conversely, buying clubs will pay higher wages and signing-on fees because there is no transfer fee to pay.

In some countries, further protection is given to clubs that have trained a player if he moves at the expiry of his contract before he is 24 years old. This is the exception to the Bosman rule, and compensation will be awarded by an independent tribunal if the clubs cannot come to an agreement. In the UK, Daniel Sturridge is one such example when he moved to Chelsea from Manchester City. Chelsea were required to pay £3.5m up front, rising to £6.5m once he played for England and started a certain number of games. Manchester City also received 15% of the £12m transfer fee paid for Sturridge by Liverpool in January 2013. More recently, Liverpool were ordered to pay an initial £6.5m to Burnley after Danny Ings joined the club in 2015. Burnley were also awarded 20% of any profit received by Liverpool if the player was subsequently sold.

'As a player approaches the final summer transfer window on his contract, his club needs to make a judgement on the likelihood of him signing a new contract. If the player doesn't seem likely to, the club will have to try selling him, or back themselves to persuade him to sign a new deal in the remaining 12 months. If the transfer window passes, and the player has only one season left and no intention of re-signing, he will be in a very strong position to optimise his contract with a new club. Consider that the buying club saves themselves 10, 20 or 30 million pounds on a transfer fee, and it is common for a player to make a large signing-on fee part of his conditions for signing. To avoid any of this, many clubs will try and re-sign their best players well before they have even 24 months left on their contracts.'

Nick Robinson, International Sports Consulting

SOLIDARITY PAYMENTS, TRAINING COMPENSATION AND THE TRANSFER LEVY

When a player transfer occurs, there are a number of associated payments that must be made.

TRAINING COMPENSATION

According to the FIFA rules, training compensation is paid by the player's new club to the training clubs that developed a player between the ages of 12 and 21:

1. when a player signs his first contract as a professional; *and*
2. each time the player is then transferred, until the season of his 23rd birthday.

FIFA provides a document on its website setting out the yearly training compensation costs for particular categorised clubs (1–4) in specific jurisdictions. For example, Real Madrid is a Category 1 club in UEFA's jurisdiction. Once the club category has been established for both the selling and buying clubs, the set training cost is multiplied by the number of years during which the selling club trained and improved the player.

Once the player is registered as a professional and then transfers, training compensation will be payable to every club with which the player registered since the season of their 12th birthday.

SOLIDARITY PAYMENTS

When a professional player is transferred to a club in another country for a fee before the expiry of his contract, any club that has contributed to his education and training is entitled to a proportion of the transfer fee paid to the selling club. In practice, the buying club usually keeps 5% of the transfer fee and distributes the money to the clubs where the player was registered between the seasons of his 12th and 23rd birthday.

So for a total transfer fee of £30m, 5% is £1.5m. This will be distributed to the clubs where the player was registered as follows:

- Season of 12th birthday: £75k – i.e. 0.25% of total compensation.
- Season of 13th birthday: £75k – i.e. 0.25% of total compensation.
- Season of 14th birthday: £75k – i.e. 0.25% of total compensation.
- Season of 15th birthday: £75k – i.e. 0.25% of total compensation.
- Season of 16th birthday: £150k – i.e. 0.5% of total compensation.
- Season of 17th birthday: £150k – i.e. 0.5% of total compensation.
- Season of 18th birthday: £150k – i.e. 0.5% of total compensation.
- Season of 19th birthday: £150k – i.e. 0.5% of total compensation.
- Season of 20th birthday: £150k – i.e. 0.5% of total compensation.
- Season of 21st birthday: £150k – i.e. 0.5% of total compensation.
- Season of 22nd birthday: £150k – i.e. 0.5% of total compensation.
- Season of 23rd birthday: £150k – i.e. 0.5% of total compensation.

If, for example, the player was registered with a non-league club between the ages of 12 and 18, that club will be entitled to £750k. This money is to be paid within 30 days of the player's registration with the new club. It often happens, however, that this money is not paid. Indeed, some clubs may not be aware that they are entitled to compensation for transfers – compensation that can be significant. It was reported that Neymar's original club, Santos, which trained and developed the player between 2003 and 2013, received €9m as a result of his record-breaking move to PSG.

PREMIER LEAGUE TRANSFER LEVY

A purchasing club must pay a transfer levy equal to 4% of the transfer fee paid to the Premier League in order for the player to register with the Premier League. The levy helps fund the premiums due under the Professional Footballers Pension Scheme.

Training compensation and solidarity payments relate only to international transfers and not to transfers between two Premier League clubs. Both training compensation and solidarity payments may need to be distributed among several training clubs. The obligation to ensure that the regulations are followed falls on the 'new' club (i.e. the purchasing club, or the club signing a player on his first professional contract).

The transfer window: the arguments for and against

The transfer window works just fine

1. Sport is special, and is not like any other business. Late transfers in a season could change the sporting strength of one team over another; this could distort the proper functioning of a full league season.
2. Clubs with only a few games left to play should not be able to buy players from a team that has nothing to play for – if, say, they are trying to win the league, qualify for the Champions League or avoid relegation.
3. The integrity of the game is one of the most important aspects of the league competition, and anything that allows teams to buy and sell players during crucial parts of the season may disrupt the playing field and ultimately the competition itself.
4. If transfers were available throughout the year, this would make it easier for other clubs to unsettle players. This longer-term instability might lead to greater player turnover, less connection between the fans and players, and less continuity throughout a season.

The transfer window doesn't work and needs to be abolished

1. The transfer window restricts the ability of a player under contract to move. Employees in any other industry may move to new organisations, so why is football any different? Is sport really that special? Why should there be periods when footballers can't move between clubs? Previously in the UK, players could move until the last Thursday in March. Such a system worked fine.
2. Why should players be allowed to move only during certain periods each year? This is surely too restrictive and unduly inflexible. Player rights should take priority over team stability.

3.   The window forces clubs to put in place contingency plans, because transfers have to be done during particular periods. Ending the transfer windows would mean clubs made fewer 'pressure' signings within a confined time.

4.   Currently, most people accept the status quo, and there hasn't been a judgement on the legality of the football transfer window – yet. FIFPro, the global players' union, have previously challenged the FIFA transfer system, and questioned whether the windows are legal. Nonetheless, FIFA and FIFPro signed a six-year cooperation agreement in the winter of 2017, which brought the case against the FIFA transfer system to an end.

TRANSFER WINDOW BACKGROUND

In early September 2017, Premier League clubs voted in favour of closing their transfer window in the days before the start of the season. Previously, the transfer window had remained open until the end of August. After 5 p.m. on 9 August, 2018, Premier League clubs were no longer able to register new players in the summer window. The duration of the window stayed the same (i.e. 12 weeks), so the window was opened on 17 May, four days after the end of the 2017/18 season. There is little doubt that this put Premier League clubs at a disadvantage because clubs in France, Italy, Portugal, Spain and Germany, for example, were still able to buy and register players up until 31 August.

This was a decision taken purely by the Premier League – one that required approval from 14 out of the 20 clubs to change the rules – but the chairman, Richard Scudamore, believes that other leagues may follow their example. So why did the Premier League clubs decide to restrict themselves?

In part, explained Mr Scudamore, to prevent the possibility of a player playing for one Premier League team before the window closes, then transferring to a team and playing against his original team soon after. Exactly that scenario did in fact occur with Alex Oxlade-Chamberlain moving from Arsenal to Liverpool for around £40m on summer transfer deadline day, 2017.

The problem for many (including Manchester United and Manchester City, who voted against the rule change) was that the decision does not stop other leagues buying and registering Premier League players. This means that a foreign club now has an additional number of weeks to plan and action their transfer acquisition strategy. It also means that foreign clubs have longer to destabilise Premier League players, encouraging them to leave – and leaving the Premier League club unable to replace that player.

Mr Scudamore was, however, right to suggest that other leagues may follow suit: UEFA has suggested the pan-European window should close on 31 July. Giuseppe Marotta, CEO of Juventus, confirmed that Italy's Serie A clubs agreed a transfer window cut-off of 17 August.

'CONTRACT, WHAT CONTRACT?'

As briefly described above, FIFA has a set of rules that allow a player to break a contract and move to a new club. A player will probably have to pay compensation to his old club, which will depend on his current ability and worth to his past and future club. The question is, does this mean that players can terminate their contract and move for limited compensation whenever they choose? The short answer is yes – ish! However, it may be very expensive for the player's new club and even the player himself.

If a player who has been bought for many millions of pounds decides to terminate or breach his employment contract with his current club, FIFA and/or the Court of Arbitration for Sport (CAS) will usually resolve the amount of compensation payable to the player's former club.

In some instances, a player may claim that he has not been paid and therefore he has just cause to terminate his contract. Similarly, if he has not played in more than 10% of matches, he could be entitled under the FIFA regulations to tear up his existing deal under 'sporting just cause'.

In any event, the question is usually about money and the amount that the player (and their new club) may have to pay to their former club. Article 17 of the FIFA Status and Transfer of Players Regulations sets out the factors to take into account, which include:

- the player's wages and other benefits from both the previous and current contract;
- the time remaining on the contract that had been breached;
- fees incurred by the former club when purchasing the player (e.g agents' fees); *and*
- whether the breach is within a protected period (i.e. whether it was within the first three years of a contract for a player whose contract was signed while he was under the age of 28, or within the first two years for a player over the age of 28).

There have been a number of cases in relation to this issue. Although perhaps not as widely known as Bosman, the cases of Andy Webster, Matuzalém and De Sanctis are examples where FIFA and CAS decided on the money paid to the player's former club (payable jointly by the new club and the player).

In the case of Webster, it was decided that only a small amount of compensation should be payable to the former club. This was calculated as £150,000, which was the remaining wages that Webster was owed by his old club. However, in the cases of Matuzalém and De Sanctis, CAS ruled that significantly more compensation should be paid to the former club.

Matuzalém, and the club to which he transferred, were ordered to pay almost €12m, a sum calculated in relation to his transfer value and wages. Similarly, De Sanctis and his new club were ordered by CAS to pay €2.2m, which included taking into account the cost of finding two replacement goalkeepers.

It's clear that CAS took the market value of the player into account when deciding on the compensation payable. To FIFPro and others within the game, it is unacceptable that a player be held responsible to pay at least part of a transfer fee that he had no part negotiating. What it means in effect is that the better the player and the bigger the transfer fee, the higher the cost and risk to the player to break his contract.

This was noticeably the case during the summer 2017 transfer window: even after requesting transfers, Virgil van Dijk, Philippe Coutinho and Diego Costa were all unable to move because their clubs did not want to sell. It's a gamble for a player to use FIFA Article 17 – unless the buying club provides a guarantee that they will effectively underwrite the compensation payable to the old club and not leave the player on the hook.

It's worth noting that if the breach of contract occurs within the protected period of the contract (as above), the player may receive a playing ban too. The effect of the protected period may be that more players run down their contracts and do not re-sign long-term deals in order to give themselves the option of prematurely ending their contracts while not being banned in the process.

PLAYER COMMERCIAL DEALS

Apart from players being paid for what they do on the pitch, a significant number will be paid by boot manufacturers and other brands to endorse particular products. At the most lucrative end, the *Forbes* Rich List of 2018 revealed that Ronaldo earned $47m from endorsements and Messi only $27m.

Most players even in the lower leagues will at least be given 'supply' deals, which means they won't have to buy their own boots. They're unlikely to have any brand deals outside of their boot agreement.

> *'In the pre-social media era, the majority of players were not exposed to many commercial deals; these were exclusively for those who were the best performers on the pitch, or the biggest characters off it through traditional media (newspapers, TV & radio). In today's social media age, many players are able to attract long-term and short-term commercial deals due to their large social-media followings and ability to engage particular fan markets. Forward-thinking agents are opting to hire external specialist agencies to deal with these matters, due to the complex nature of the crowded endorsement market.'*

> Ehsen Shah, founder of B-Engaged

PLAYER BOOT DEALS EXPLAINED

Clubs enter into lucrative sponsorship deals, while players and their image rights companies can also earn significant sums from brands wanting to partner with elite players. How does a contract with elite brands like Nike, Adidas, Puma, New Balance and Under Armour work in practice? A boot deal usually isn't just a boot deal. At the very least, the contract will usually require the player to wear and use the brand's products for training and in games.

For a number of elite players, wearing the particular branded football boot is only one part of an overall brand ambassadorial role that can include personal appearances and photo shoots, commercial and social media activity (Instagram live chats, or Twitter takeovers), corporate responsibilities and advertisements.

For all public activities – such as photo sessions and promotional appearances – a player will not only be wearing particular footwear and shin guards (plus gloves, if a goalkeeper) but will probably also be kitted out, depending on the circumstances, in the brand's clothes. As discussed below, some difficulties can arise depending on whether the player is appearing in a personal capacity, for his domestic club or for his national team.

The specific products/apparel that a player will be required to wear include athletic footwear, clothing and accessories like bags, gloves and hats. Such a product list may also cover sunglasses, golf clubs, sports equipment, headphones, personal care and hygiene products, watches and cases or sleeves for electronic accessories like tablets or mobiles.

As a result, the player will be provided with a variety of branded products to use. The flip side is that the boot deal may limit the opportunities for a player to sign additional deals with, say, the manufacturers of headphones or watches. The player may be limited to the use of only one set of branded products.

It can be important for the agent and lawyer finalising the deal to ensure that a player is rewarded adequately for giving away the opportunity to enter into additional deals with other manufacturers. If the boot deal is so wide as to cover a large number of products like sunglasses or phone accessories, the player should be aware that the scope to enter into additional commercial deals is limited.

The reality, however, is that most players will not have quite the same commercial appeal as Pogba, Neymar or Ronaldo, and thus will not have a large number of commercial sponsorship deals outside of their boot deal.

BRAND CONSISTENCY IS TRICKY

Issues can arise when a player has to juggle the obligations of his domestic club, his national team and his personal commercial partners. A player will have:

- Club obligations – training and playing in club kit, being pictured in a club shirt at a new kit launch or being part of an official club autograph signing afternoon. This is usually labelled 'club context'.
- National team responsibilities – wearing the training and playing kit and potentially endorsing commercial partners of the national team when away on international duty. This is usually labelled 'national team context'.
- Personal endorsement deals – a boot deal or individual ambassador deal not directly linked to the club.

So, for example, Gareth Bale plays for Real Madrid, sponsored by Adidas; plays for Wales, sponsored by Adidas; has a boot deal with Adidas; and has commercial partnership agreements with EA Sports and Sony. Importantly, Adidas has complete brand consistency across its apparel line, Bale playing in Adidas for both Madrid and Wales. Similarly, Neymar is endorsed by Nike while playing for both PSG and Brazil.

When appearing in a club context, the club will want to ensure the player is wearing club kit/apparel to satisfy their own kit sponsors and partners. There will be an obligation on the player to dress appropriately, though the club will normally allow him to wear the footwear of his boot supplier, even if it is a direct competitor of the team's kit manufacturer.

Indeed, when the player is on international duty, a club cannot stop its player wearing the international kit of a competitor. For example, Barcelona, sponsored by Nike, cannot prevent Messi from wearing the Adidas Argentinian kit and training wear. That is why having players like Bale and Neymar, who remain consistent in their endorsement messaging, can be of significant value.

Further, clubs in the UK who enter into image rights agreements with their players can potentially further control the range of additional commercial partners that a player can endorse – and will do so if they are in conflict with their own sponsors/partners. For example, it is unlikely that Chelsea would allow one of its players to personally endorse a rival tyre manufacturer to its main shirt sponsor, Yokahama.

Regardless of whether the player is playing club football, on international duty, undertaking off-field commercial activities or going out shopping, a boot deal can usually control more than what the player wears on his feet.

A DEAL CONTAINS LOTS OF PERFORMANCE CLAUSES

Clearly, elite players can earn significant sums from their boot deals. Boot brands will structure their deals in different ways. Some will call payment 'base compensation' or a 'retainer'. Usually, a standard type of clause whereby an annual payment is drafted as follows:

> In the first year of the contract (1 July, 2016 until 30 June, 2017), a fixed amount of £100,000 plus VAT will be paid in quarterly instalments if the player is named in the club's first team squad.

This would be subject to the club category requirements set out below.

The fixed amount paid will be determined by the calibre of the team for which the player plays. Most boot brands will classify particular clubs in different categories. For example, Manchester United, Barcelona, Real Madrid and Bayern Munich may be classed as Category 1 clubs, which means the brand will pay the player the full £100,000. Clubs like Chelsea, Arsenal, Atlético Madrid and PSG may be classified as Category 2 clubs, and the brand may pay the player only £75,000. If a player moves from Chelsea (Category 2) to Barcelona (Category 1), for example, the brand will pay the player an uplift because of the move – and vice versa.

There can also be specific reduction clauses in relation to the appearances made by the player for his club and international team. The basic amount is unlikely to be reduced if the player plays in at least 70% of competitive first team matches. However, if the player is injured and plays in, say, 40% of matches, the retainer amount can be reduced significantly.

Additional clauses can also be included for a player who is established internationally. For example, if the player doesn't play at least 80% of competitive club and national team games, the player's boot deal could be reduced by as much as 30%.

Similarly, there will be specific bonuses and reduction clauses depending on whether, for example, the club qualifies or fails to qualify for Champions League/Europa League competition. Additional bonus payments may be due if, for example, the player:

- is a member of the final 23-player squad of a European Championship or World Cup tournament;
- qualifies for the semi-final, final and/or wins the Champions League/Europa League; *or*
- wins the top national league competition.

The player will usually have been required to play in a designated percentage of the games. Such a number is usually calculated on the number of minutes the player is on the pitch rather than the number of matches the player plays.

BOOT DEALS CAN CONTAIN RELATIVELY RESTRICTIVE CLAUSES

There are matching opportunities and rights of first refusal, which give the player's existing boot brand the ability to re-sign the player or at least give the company an opportunity to match an offer made by any of its competitors.

Usually the brand will give three to six months' notice to the player if it wishes to extend a deal. If no agreement is reached, the brand may give the player its best offer in advance of allowing the player to negotiate with its competitors for a short period of time, usually one to two months. Should any better offers be put forward, the current boot manufacturer may have a period of time, usually up to 30 days, to match the competitor offer.

With the existing brand holding the right to match any new sponsorship offer the player receives, or even to automatically extend/renew a deal if the terms are matched, there have been examples of disputes between player and brand. It was reported that Mesut Özil wanted to switch to Adidas, though Nike (his boot manufacturer at the time) believed they had the power to renew their deal if they matched Adidas's terms. Ultimately, Özil signed a long-term deal with Adidas up to 2020.

BOOT DEALS ARE JUST ONE PART OF A PLAYER'S COMMERCIAL ACTIVITIES

A high-profile, elite Premier League footballer will probably have both an employment contract and an image rights agreement with their club. The player will usually be a shareholder in a company that has the benefit of the player's image rights to exploit. That company will enter into an agreement with the club to market the player's image rights as well as with other commercial brand partners. As such, apart from the player's employment contract, almost all other deals will be agreed between the player's image rights company and a variety of commercial partners, including the player's boot manufacturer.

Such an approach can offer significant tax efficiencies. Suppose that a player received £1m per year from his commercial deals. Without an image rights company in place, he would pay income tax (45%) and National Insurance (2%), totalling £470,000.

By contrast, paying the revenue into a UK image rights company means that only corporation tax is owed, currently at a rate of 19%, and due to reduce to 17% by 2020. Even at 19%, the tax owed is £190,000 – a saving of £280,000 per year for the player.

Even if a player does not have an image rights agreement with his club, he may wish to set up an image rights company if he is being paid a significant amount by a boot manufacturer.

THE TRUTH ABOUT TRANSFERS

Transfers are usually highly complex. Agents, players, club officials, lawyers and accountants are usually all needed to complete high-profile deals. Everyone will be making compromises to get the deal over the line, sometimes at the very last minute. The crux of a deal is contained in the transfer agreement between the clubs and the employment contract between player and buying club. The array of clauses, stipulations and conditions make for complex negotiations. It's fair to say that the transfer fee headlines only usually provide a small glimpse into the nuances that make up a successful transfer and player contract negotiation.

Alongside transfer and employment contracts are a growing variety of player commercial deals. These can be lucrative and restrictive in equal measure. Players are becoming more and more aware of their off-field commercial worth, with brands willing to pay significant sums for short- and long-term endorsement opportunities.

CHAPTER 3

AGENTS

From the public's perspective, being an agent – or, as FIFA now calls them, an intermediary – is a glamorous, high-profile and highly lucrative profession for what some think demands very little work or effort. They are often seen as the curse of the modern game, the people responsible for driving transfer prices and wages up or down, depending on their client's priorities. In light of such arguments, does the football industry really benefit from agents? Whisper it, but yes. Agents are essential and play an important role in delivering the spectacle that is modern football.

There are bad apples in any profession, but there are plenty of extremely hard-working agents, who are paid very well and do a fantastic job for their clients. One such 'super-agent' is Mino Raiola, who represents Paul Pogba and is reported to have made more than £40m from his client's transfer to Manchester United from Juventus. There was widespread condemnation, the former FA chairman David Bernstein being among the most vociferous critics: 'Even if they [the transfers] are being done within the existing regulations, figures of those sorts of size in agents' commissions are just immoral. It might not be illegal but it's immoral.' Those fees were in addition to the significant sums Raiola has made in brokering deals for Romelu Lukaku, Zlatan Ibrahimović and Henrikh Mkhitaryan. Such prominent agents inevitably colour the media's portrayal of the profession; not all deals are as high-profile or as lucrative.

There are thousands of agents working across the world's major football leagues. There are over 1,800 registered agents operating in the English Premier League and Football League alone. It's fair to say that the amounts made by Mino Raiola, Pini Zahavi (Robert Lewandowski's agent) and Jorge Mendes (Cristiano Ronaldo's agent) are very much the exception to the rule. Nonetheless, they make headlines – because elite clubs are willing to pay record transfer fees and wages for world-class, elite players.

Top agents are highly trained negotiators and impressive networkers, who provide connections to clubs that might otherwise struggle to make a deal happen. Granted, not all agents are as savvy as the next. But fans and the wider public usually have only a very distorted view of agents – believing that an agent only has to make a call, set up a meeting and then pocket significant commission. Such circumstances, in my experience, are rare. Indeed, Pogba's transfer to United – to offer just one example – will have taken many months to structure, will have included detailed and nuanced negotiations, and involved numerous clubs, executives, personalities and politics. Agents are masters at cutting through roadblocks and finding solutions.

'As an agent (also known as an intermediary), you must always have the best interests of your client at heart. Whether you are thinking about negotiating a new contract, moving to another club or working on sponsorship agreements, you should be informing your client about the important developments that are unfolding. This touches on a crucial part of an agent's repertoire. Loyalty and trust with the player you're representing is a fundamental requirement of the profession. Without these key skills, success is very hard to come by.'

Erkut Sögüt, agent for Mesut Özil

DOING THE DIRTY WORK FOR PLAYERS

Many agents do earn significant sums, but they are well rewarded partly because of the fragile and unpredictable nature of their job. The glamorous signing ceremony is only the tip of the player-management iceberg. The primary role of a player's agent may be to understand when, on the one hand, to aggressively push for a transfer or a new contract with the club, and when, on the other hand, to be the diplomat if a player is having trouble settling in, struggling with the management team or not performing on the pitch. An agent does his best work when managing and leveraging situations (both positive and negative) to the player's advantage.

Many agents take care of all their client's needs, from picking up their laundry to booking their holiday and organising a cleaner for their home. They are fixers, friends, confidants and truth-tellers all rolled into one.

Remember too that agents work hard in identifying and signing up young football talent and can often spend years representing players who never make the grade or generate any meaningful return. To add to this, agents will spend years building relationships with players while always facing the risk that the player, in whom they have invested serious amounts of time, has a change of heart and moves to a competitor.

If a player gets his head turned by another agent offering a more lucrative deal or a high-profile transfer, he may end the relationship with his current agent. That relationship may have involved many years of service by the agent without too much reward, and then end just as the player is on the cusp of a life-changing deal. It's true that the agent might sue, but the fact is, many agents are constantly looking over their shoulders worrying about another agent dangling a larger carrot. It's a difficult, insecure and high-risk industry.

To offset some of this risk, some individual agents find 'comfort in numbers' through formal or informal working relationships with larger football agencies, such as Gestifute, Base Soccer, Wasserman Media Group (WMG) and Stellar Football. The benefit is that there may be significant, additional resources to help a player with all of his on-field and off-field commercial needs. It may also be that some larger agencies have better relationships or networks with particular clubs, their chief executives, directors of football and scouts – which may assist with particular transfers or help when negotiating an uplift on an existing contract.

HELPING CLUBS

When buying a player, a club will identify a number of potential targets. They may approach a club directly to ask permission to speak to a particular player (which happens less than it used to) or may engage an agent to liaise with the agents of the players they have identified. In some cases, this could be deemed a type of tapping up (where a club will speak to another team's player without that club's consent), but it can also occur between two agents, each representing one side in the negotiation, who informally discuss whether a player may be interested in moving to that particular club. Should the outcome be positive, further discussions can take place between both clubs about a possible transfer. In practice, tapping up is difficult to police because formal complaints are rarely lodged. One exception is Virgil van Dijk: Southampton threatened to make a complaint to the Premier League after Liverpool manager Jürgen Klopp was reported to have met the player without Southampton's consent.

Liverpool were forced into making an official statement in June 2017:

> Liverpool Football Club would like to put on record our regret over recent media speculation regarding Southampton Football Club and player transfers between the two clubs. We apologise to the owner, board of directors and fans of Southampton for any misunderstanding regarding Virgil van Dijk. We respect Southampton's position and can confirm we have ended any interest in the player.

Southampton did not take matters any further and the Premier League did not conduct an investigation. Six months later, van Dijk joined Liverpool for £75m, a world record fee for a defender.

The benefit of operating via intermediaries is that the identity of the buying club can potentially be hidden (at least initially), avoiding a wasted approach. Major Premier League clubs are sometimes quoted inflated transfer fees (called an English premium, in part because of the massive £8.4bn TV deal agreed for 2016–19), so engaging an agent to agree a fee may reduce the transfer fee or keep it at a more reasonable level. For example, a Premier League team approaching an Italian team directly will almost certainly lead to the Italian club adding an English premium. This is where it can be common practice for the Italian club to quote one transfer fee for Premier League clubs and a lower transfer fee for all other clubs. Therefore, an agent acting for a Premier League team may be tasked to reduce the transfer fee or to try and get a better deal and take a cut of the cost saving.

Agents may also be willing to be used as scapegoats for a selling club that wants to drive a hard bargain for their star player or which wants a player to move on. Clubs need good agents for selling and buying players, and almost all clubs realise this. They build up relationships with trusted agents so that deals can be pushed through when they need to happen. This means that clubs cannot afford to burn bridges with some agents.

Agents understand who is in the market for a particular player and can match up a player who is no longer needed at one club with an opportunity somewhere else. A selling club's chairman or chief executive may not be aware of that opening. Agents have a fuller picture of the selling and buying market and can be of key value to selling as well as buying clubs.

Some may ask why clubs need agents to sell their players, but on occasion, agents can extract better transfer value for the clubs. They may have a more intricate network of clubs interested in signing the players, and the clubs benefit by outsourcing a process that might otherwise take up a significant amount of chief executive and management time.

Agents are also aware of the moving parts of various deals that can cause chain reactions. Individual club executives may not have this visibility. For example, an agent may know that one club is looking for a striker and will pay a transfer fee of £10m plus £50k per week in salary. He may also be aware that the same player is about to agree a deal with another club and therefore that club has to find an alternative striker. That agent will be able to offer alternative striker options – perhaps even before the club realises the player is going elsewhere.

The best agents are also fully aware of the market in which they operate and appreciate the club dynamics. For example, the chairman at one club may make the ultimate decisions while the owner at another club is 'hands-on' during transfer negotiations and any deal needs his approval. It has been reported that Roman Abramovich has at times asked the Chelsea manager to consider particular transfer targets, such as Shevchenko and Torres. In contrast, Liverpool owners Fenway have in place a transfer committee that recommends transfer targets to the current manager. Jürgen Klopp admitted that the committee persuaded him to buy Mo Salah from Roma. The forward went on to become the leading goalscorer in the Premier League in the 2017/18 season. Transfer decisions can thus be made by a 'committee of one' or by many, depending on the club in question. Agents need to be aware of all these nuances and personalities when trying to push or pull particular players to specific clubs.

GETTING THE DEALS DONE

Transfers can become a game of interlinked negotiations, in which each action has an implication and consequence for the various parties. One transfer can set off a chain reaction. Suppose Manchester City have a choice of two players and are negotiating hard to get the best deal. Such a negotiation and transfer may take until the last few days of the window. Once the club agrees the deal, the agent of the player that Man City have rejected may have been negotiating simultaneously with several other clubs, and one of those clubs may now try to complete the transfer. During the January 2018 transfer window, Man City expressed an interest in Arsenal's Alexis Sánchez, but as soon as their interest cooled City's neighbours United moved swiftly to secure the Chilean's services. Such negotiations will not just take place in the club's boardroom. They may include many months of WhatsApp messages, emails, calls and informal face-to-face meetings at games.

As the transfer is about to go through, another player in Man City's squad may now be unlikely to play as much and may be told to find a new club during the window. In fact, this is one of the reported reasons why Džeko left the club in 2016. Whether a club chooses to buy, waits to negotiate a particular deal or pulls out of a transfer will inevitably have knock-on consequences for other transfers that are directly or indirectly linked. An astute agent will be aware of all these types of situations at multiple clubs, throughout various leagues worldwide. An agent will be playing the equivalent of multiple games of chess at the same time, looking for opportunity and strategically planning a number of moves ahead.

ARE FOOTBALL AGENTS' FEES GROWING TOO LARGE?

From 2016, the FA has published details of every contract renegotiation and transfer from the previous season. It doesn't provide individual deal breakdowns but does give overall figures. This added transparency is to be welcomed and, interestingly, also sets out which agents actually get the deals done.

For example, between 2 February, 2017 and 31 January, 2018, Liverpool paid out almost £27m in fees to agents and intermediaries, according to figures provided by the English FA. In total, the 20 Premier League clubs spent over £211m during that same period.

Agents are unlikely to receive much sympathy from fans for the job they do, but in my experience they are very much a necessity for clubs and players alike, and many provide the skill set necessary to get a deal over the line.

Nonetheless, UEFA president Aleksander Čeferin was recently at pains to stress that agents' fees had reached astronomical levels. Čeferin reported that agents often try to dictate terms by telling buying clubs, 'Look, you will pay me 50% of the transfer or the player goes somewhere else.' UEFA calculated that more than €3bn has been paid to agents between 2013 and 2017, and has even suggested a cap on agents' fees. This was a recommendation previously floated by FIFA. It remains to be seen whether restricting what agents can earn is legal.

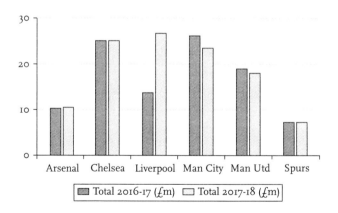

Agents' fees are often reflective of a club's transfer policy. Manchester City, after years of high investment, stabilised their spending in 2017–18, while Liverpool increased theirs. The relatively modest agent fees paid by Spurs are arguably indicative of the confidence they have in their current squad and in their youth development programme.

RULES FOR AGENTS

In 2015, FIFA changed its regulations, renaming agents as 'intermediaries' and introducing new rules for them to abide by. In practice, it put the responsibility on national associations like the FA to ensure agents keep to the rules. In response, the FA and a variety of national associations, including Spain's Real Federación Española de Fútbol (RFEF) and Brazil's Confederação Brasileira de Futebol (CBF), introduced their own regulations. The FA's regulations include the following areas:

Agents must be registered. To be used by a Premier League or Football League club or player, an agent must be recognised by the governing body. In addition, the agent must have a valid representation contract with a club or player, which usually involves the negotiation of a player contract and/or the transfer of a player's registration. These contracts must be lodged with the FA within 10 days of signing.

Reputation management. The FA's Declaration of Good Character and Reputation is very similar to its Owners and Directors Test (ODT; see pages 81–82) – also used by both the Premier League and Football League. The proposed agent must sign a declaration confirming among other things that he hasn't been convicted of certain specified crimes, banned from sport, disqualified from being a director or declared bankrupt.

Agents can be paid – just not too much. The FA recommends that the total an agent can be paid should not exceed 3% of the player's income or (in the case of an agent acting for the club) 3% of the actual transfer fee paid. The problem with such a recommendation is that agents usually receive 5–10% on particular deals. Since the recommendation has been in force, not much has actually changed – so far.

They're just kids. An agent can enter into a representation contract with a 16-year-old player so long as it is also signed by the player's parent or legal guardian and the agent has passed an advanced test. However, the agent cannot be paid for his services if the player is under 18, though players can sign professional Premier League or Football League contracts at 17. In practice, an agent's commission is usually backdated so that it is paid once the player turns 18.

Just the two years, thanks. The FA rules allow for a representation contract to be for a maximum of two years. This is seen as striking the right balance – a reasonable compromise between giving the agent long enough to build a relationship while also giving the player a straightforward way out if things don't go as planned. However, agents invest years of effort in a particular player and live with the risk that their player may have their head turned by a competing agent at the optimal time for a transfer or a lucrative contract renegotiation. Agents may be willing to put significant time into developing the relationship for minimal commission (because the player has perhaps not had the on field success as yet) in the hope that in a few years' time the player moves to a larger club and earns accordingly.

THE AGENT/FOOTBALLER REPRESENTATION RELATIONSHIP

For most agents, there are usually two distinct areas of focus: the first is recruiting players and the second is assisting those players in contract renegotiations and/or transfers. Getting the players to sign a representation contract is only half the job; keeping hold of the player and looking out for agents promising to do a better job for the player can take up serious amounts of time.

A football agent is rarely as glamorous a role as people imagine. It usually involves going to watch many, many football matches – though not all, if any, will be high-profile Premier League matches. For up-and-coming agents, the vast majority will be youth and academy matches as they try to build valuable connections with scouts, coaches, players and their families (where permitted under the rules).

Agents are constantly on the road, travelling across the country and often around the world in search of talented players. The need to recruit players must be balanced against the need to service the requirements of existing players. Sometimes big transfers need to be negotiated, but usually it is the more mundane tasks that require significant manpower. That is why larger agencies employ runners and/or plenty of administration staff, to help look after the players and their extended families. Football agency staff members could be tasked with anything: booking holidays, paying the utility bills, organising a taxi to pick up a family member from the airport, even taking the dog for a walk. Some players may require care 24/7 while others are self-sufficient. Therefore, when targeting particular players, agents will probably have done their homework, so that they understand which players will require significant care or call on their services only when absolutely necessary.

On any particular day, an agent may be renegotiating a boot deal for one player, driving to see an under-23s game in another part of the country, dealing with a second player who has posted something he shouldn't have done on Instagram (which is likely to involve speaking to lawyers and calming the club's annoyed chief executive) and liaising with a journalist about an interview for a third player.

At the time of writing, it is being reported that FIFA are recommending sweeping rule changes including the reintroduction of an agent's exam, an end to a player's agent representing multiple parties, fixed commission percentages and a transfer clearing-house for all monies to be paid into when a transfer occurs.

THE AGENT/FOOTBALLER REPRESENTATION CONTRACT

All agent/footballer contracts follow a basic template, available on the Football Association's website. In summary, an agent will want to ensure that a representation contract covers the following points:

- The player's details are right so that the information held by the FA or FIFA, for example, matches his representation contract when all the paperwork is being submitted.
- The contract is for the maximum two years possible under the rules, to ensure that players are not tied into a contract with an agent for too long.
- The contract is exclusive so that no other agent can represent the player. If another agent claims to represent the player, and the first agent is then cut out of the deal and loses out on commission, it is likely that the player will be sued for breach

of contract. The FA brought in additional rules in the summer of 2017 to try and avoid such situations in the future.

- The agent has the power to represent the player when negotiating transfers, employment contracts and all commercial deals. It is important for the agent that they can earn commission not just from on-field transfer and contract renegotiations but also from all commercial agreements (including boot deals, fashion brands, and brand ambassadorial roles). This ensures that the agent can provide a complete 360-degree service, enabling the player to maximise earnings on and off the pitch (*see* pages 50–55).

- The commission rate is set out. The rate for negotiating a player's new contract or transfer can be between 3% and 10% of the player's total salary. When negotiating commercial deals (a boot deal, say, or computer games endorsement deal), agents are usually entitled to receive up to 20% of the value of the deal. That can be a significant amount of money: a player like Paul Pogba can reportedly earn more than £3m p.a. from Adidas.

- Any disputes will be settled by the national association. For example, if the player leaves the agent during the term of the contract or uses another agent when negotiating a transfer and the original agent doesn't receive the commission, then the old agent will usually sue.

In many cases, an agent will also be acting for a club. Indeed, it has been reported that Daniel Levy, chairman of Tottenham, has asked agents to use some of the commission made in a deal to buy a corporate box at White Hart Lane. An innovative negotiation strategy!

BUT WHO ACTUALLY PAYS AGENTS?

Now, it may sound simple enough to suggest that an agent gets a commission of 5% – or, if they are lucky, 10%. The difficult part to explain is usually who pays the agent. You'd think it would be the player, right? Wrong.

The majority of Premier League and top-end Football League transfers involve the buying club paying the agent. Details can vary. A number of different structures are set out below. Brace yourself, it involves tax!

PLAYER PAYS

In very limited circumstances when dealing with Premier League players, a player may pay his agent for finalising a transfer. Under a player's representation contract with this agent, as set out above, the player may be obliged to pay his agent 5%, say, of his gross basic wage. This doesn't happen too often in practice.

Example 1: A player is paid £2m per year. The agent receives £100,000 (5%) from the player per year in one annual payment.

CLUB PAYS AS PART OF THE TRANSFER ARRANGEMENT

In practice, even if the player is required to pay his agent as set out in their representation contract, the player's agent can negotiate that the club pays the agent on the player's behalf. This benefit means the player doesn't need to pay his agent. However, paying an amount on a player's behalf is classed as a benefit in kind by the tax authorities and the player will pay tax on the payment by the club to the agent.

Example 2: A player is paid £2m per year. The agent receives £100,000 (5%) from the club paid on the player's behalf as a benefit to the player.

CLUB PAYS BECAUSE THE AGENT IS ACTING FOR THEM

Sometimes the buying club will pay the player's agent to act on its behalf during the transfer. You may think this is a conflict of interest – and you'd be right. In such a scenario, the player has to agree that his agent can work for both sides.

Example 3: A player is paid £2m per year. The agent will be paid for the work he does for the club and for the work he does for the player. The agent may then receive £50,000 (2.5%) from the club for the work done on their behalf and £50,000 (2.5%) from the club, as a benefit to the player, for the work done on the player's behalf.

Without getting too complicated, many deals are variations of Example 3. In Example 2, the player is required to pay tax on the £100,000 paid by the club on his behalf. In Example 3, the player will be paying tax only on £50,000 for the portion of the work done on his behalf – thus reducing his tax bill. To justify his £50,000 fee, the agent will have to demonstrate that he did work on behalf of the club, and this is usually set out in a separate representation contract between the player, the club and the agent.

At the time of writing, the Premier League is considering scrapping this approach and simplifying matters so that a player must pay his agent the commission due. This would be a radical change.

THE VARYING POWER OF AGENTS

There is rarely anything straightforward about being an agent. An agent's value is almost always in their network and their solutions-based approach.

An agent has to be a fantastic recruiter, to get the player in the first place; an excellent retainer of talent, to show the player that they are continually doing a good job; incredibly well networked, so that managers, directors of football, chairmen and owners will pick up the phone when there is a deal to be done; and must have an understanding of the wider market and which clubs are looking for particular types of player.

How powerful an agent is varies. For the agents who represent the elite footballers, their negotiating position can often be strong – but that always depends on whether they have been able to cultivate demand for the player at the right club, at the right time. Agents need clubs as much as clubs need agents. When the top players move clubs, agents are usually in a position of strength because there is no similar player in the market, meaning they are in a position to dictate (to some degree) salary and commission rates.

Since FIFA changed the way that agents are regulated, more agents have become registered. In the UK, there are more than 1,800 agents registered with the FA – there were only just over 500 at the time the regulations changed in April 2015 – but few agents end up actually doing deals. It's usually the same agents at the larger agencies doing the big deals. Rumoured changes, like the capping of commission fees, will be strongly resisted by agents. The issue is that wages have gone up, while the commission rate of 3–5% has stayed more or less constant. This means that agents at the top level are being paid more than ever before. Moves by UEFA, FIFA or national leagues to curb such remuneration would be highly controversial and most likely to end up in the courts.

CHAPTER 4

CLUBS

The revenues and rewards available for successful teams are substantial. Win the Premier League, and your club is guaranteed almost £150m. Enter into a lucrative shirt sponsorship deal, and you may receive tens of millions of pounds per season. The 2017/18 Premier League champions Manchester City signed the first ever sleeve sponsorship deal, with Nexen Tire, rumoured to be worth around £10 million a year. This income is *additional* to the main shirt sponsorship deal, which will itself be worth in the region of £50 million a year. Even so, the vast majority of European clubs have historically made losses. Some investor owners have injected billions of pounds in an attempt to win trophies and provide silverware for the club's fans.

With owners chasing their dreams, measures have been put in place to curb club spending. UEFA, the English Premier League and a range of other European leagues have implemented strict spending controls. And in the face of their own club's insolvency, many fans have welcomed such spending rules.

Throughout the years, many clubs have reinvested all their commercial revenues in order to maximise the chance of on-field success. The pressure to succeed can drive unsustainable transfer spending. This chapter charts how clubs make their money, the rules in place to ensure clubs do not spend their way to extinction, and why investors are as keen as ever to buy a club.

WHY BUY INTO FOOTBALL?

Before the Premier League was formed in 1992, wealthy owners, who were usually businessmen based in the local community, controlled a range of

English clubs. For example, Martin Edwards, whose father owned a regional meat business, was reported to have earned a total of £94m when he sold his remaining shares in Manchester United to the Glazer family, based in the United States. David Moores, whose father owned the Liverpool-based company Littlewoods, reportedly made £90m when he sold his Liverpool shares to USA-based duo Tom Hicks and George Gillett. More on them later (*see* pages 90–92).

A sea change was coming. As broadcasting rights became more valuable, the businessmen who had owned such clubs saw the value in selling – for significant profits. Until relatively recently in the Premier League, owning a club had been a loss-making exercise. Over the past four to five seasons, more clubs in the Premier League and across UEFA member countries have made profits. Historically, even when clubs were making significant losses prospective owners saw the potential of improving sporting and commercial revenues.

Now the likelihood of year-on-year profit has attracted new owners to the Premier League. In the 2013/14 season, 19 Premier League clubs made an operating profit. This is in contrast to the 2012/13 season, when 12 of the 20 Premier League clubs made losses equalling a combined overall loss of £291m. Such losses had been common for a significant period of time.

Many believe that the reason for such a dramatic turnaround has been the introduction of cost control rules similar to the UEFA Financial Fair Play regulations. These basically state that clubs cannot overspend and must live within their means. Interestingly, the rules introduced in time for the 2013/14 season helped Premier League clubs record collective profits of £198m in 2013/14 and £113m in 2014/15.

In the accounts for the 2016/17 season, published in 2018, 18 out of the 20 Premier League clubs made a profit. Manchester United recorded revenues of £581m, while Spurs made the highest profits of £58m. Only Chelsea and Sunderland made a loss.

FOOTBALL CLUBS AND FOREIGN OWNERSHIP

Even before Roman Abramovich became a household name in July 2003, Premier League clubs were attractive businesses. Constant speculation linked endless potential investors with one of the most popular leagues in the world. At the start of the 2016/17 season, 57% of clubs in the Premier League and Football League Championship were owned or controlled by foreign investors. By the 2018/19 season, only Burnley, Brighton, Huddersfield, Newcastle, Tottenham and West Ham bucked the trend, with newly promoted clubs Wolves, Cardiff and Fulham all foreign-owned.

In the period 2015–17 notable takeovers included:

- West Bromwich Albion, sold to a Chinese investment group led by entrepreneur Lai Guochuan;
- Wolverhampton Wanderers, bought by Chinese company Fosun;
- a majority stake in Swansea City, acquired by a consortium led by investors Steve Kaplan and Jason Levien;
- 49.9% of Everton, bought by Farhad Moshiri;
- 70% of Crystal Palace, bought by a group of US-based investors, including Josh Harris and David Blitzer;
- 80% of Southampton, sold to Gao Jisheng, founder and chairman of Lander Sports;
- Aston Villa, sold to Tony Xia, a Chinese businessman who subsequently sold on the club; *and*
- Leeds United, sold by controversial owner Massimo Cellino to Italian businessman Andrea Radrizzani.

Across Europe, many high-profile clubs have also been bought and sold, including Italy's Inter and AC Milan (to Chinese investors), and France's Marseille and Nice (to American and American/Chinese consortia respectively).

Indeed, according to the latest UEFA benchmarking report, 'More than 70% of all foreign takeovers in the top 15 leagues since 2016 have involved Chinese investors. In this period Chinese owners have taken over clubs in the Premier League, Championship, Serie A, Ligue 1, La Liga and Eredivisie.'

At the beginning of the 2016/17 season, there were 16 foreign owners in the Premier League compared with 10 in 2010/11 and three in the 2004/05 season. In the 2016/17 Football League season, 11 of the 24 Championship clubs had foreign owners/majority shareholders. The global appeal of the league is plain to see.

To date, the highest profile and most significant takeover involved the £790m purchase of Manchester United by the Glazer family in 2005. It remains controversial because the owners funded the purchase in part through loans secured against the club. Reports suggest that £500m+ has been spent on financing that debt to date.

2018/19 Premier League majority owners

Arsenal	Stan Kroenke (USA)
Bournemouth	Maxim Demin (Russia)
Brighton	Tony Bloom (England)
Burnley	Mike Garlick (England)
Cardiff	Vincent Tan (Malaysia)
Chelsea	Roman Abramovich (Russia)
Crystal Palace	Steve Parish (England), Joshua Harris and David S. Blitzer (USA)
Everton	Farhad Moshiri (Iran)
Fulham	Shahid Khan (USA)
Huddersfield	Dean Hoyle (England)
Leicester	Srivaddhanaprabha family (Thailand)
Liverpool	John W. Henry and Tom Werner (USA)
Manchester City	Sheikh Mansour (UAE)
Manchester United	The Glazer family (USA)
Newcastle	Mike Ashley (England)
Southampton	Gao Jisheng (China)
Tottenham	Joe Lewis (England)
Watford	The Pozzo family (Italy)
West Ham	David Gold and David Sullivan (England)
Wolverhampton Wanderers	Fosun International (China)

'From an international investor's standpoint, the Premier League offers a potentially tantalizing opportunity to own a team that is watched worldwide on a weekly basis. The value in live-sports media rights has grown so significantly that it attracts investors from all over the world. This will only continue to grow as parts of Asia and Africa get greater access to viewing these matches. The EPL has outperformed other leagues across Europe by being more balanced from top to bottom and putting the infrastructure in place for clubs to bring in the top talent and build the deepest squads. EPL club valuations should continue to grow and teams like Man U, City, Arsenal, Liverpool, Chelsea and Spurs will next trade for eye-popping amounts.'

Sam Porter, D.C. United and
Swansea City AFC

VALUING A FOOTBALL CLUB

Many elements come into play when valuing a football club, and these have to be carefully considered to ensure a price that is acceptable for both parties.

The main revenues and assets of a Premier League club are its players; central Premier League distributions; stadium match-day revenues; its facilities, such as the stadium and training ground; and its shirt, apparel and other commercial, merchandising and advertising deals.

There is no one-size-fits-all approach to calculate the true value of a club, but traditional factors such as income, profits, stadium capacity and usage, player spending and debt all form part of the financial consideration.

DOMESTIC COMPETITION PRIZE MONEY

In the modern era, a Premier League club's main source of revenue is through the competition or prize money it receives for participating in the league. In the 2018/19 season, each of the 20 Premier League clubs will receive a minimum of around £94m. This is distributed by the Premier League and generated through the centrally negotiated broadcasting and commercial deals. For each club, there is an equal share of £75m and then £1.9m per place and a minimum of £12m for appearing on TV. Even in the event of relegation, the club will receive parachute payments totalling at least £80m over two or three years (depending how long the club played in the Premier League). The FA Cup and League Cup competitions also generate revenue for participating, though the sums are much lower. For instance, the winner of the FA Cup secures only around £3.5m in prize money, plus gate receipts and around £150k for each time the club is on TV.

The significant Premier League revenues are, of course, attractive to investors or potential owners and are guaranteed as long as the club retains its status in the Premier League.

CHAMPIONS LEAGUE AND UEFA CUP COMPETITIONS

A team appearing in the UEFA Champions League can expect to receive participation and prize money, distributed by UEFA. Reaching the knockout rounds can bring in upwards of £40–50m. The revenue takes the form of television income and performance-related money, depending on the length of time a team remains in the competition.

STADIUM MATCH-DAY REVENUES

Historically, match-day ticket sales were a club's main source of regular revenue. In the days of standing terraces, as many as 100,000 people attended domestic club matches and, while those kinds of numbers are now the exception, stadium match-day revenues are still significant, especially since clubs cater for the highly profitable corporate supporter.

A new or expanded stadium can cater for additional levels of demand for each match day, from both corporate and non-corporate supporters. There was analysis before Liverpool's stadium expansion suggesting that Manchester United made up to £2m more per match day than Liverpool, thanks to their additional capacity and match-day merchandising revenues. Such revenue adds to a club's valuation, of course.

FACILITIES

A large-capacity stadium and a training ground, as well as other facilities already in place, will add significant value to a club and inevitably make it more attractive. Owners will otherwise need very deep pockets to invest in stadium and infrastructure projects, which can cost several hundred millions of pounds. Manchester City's new state-of-the-art stadium would have been viewed as a valuable asset prior to the club's takeover in 2008.

Other established Premier League teams like Tottenham have needed to raise over £500m to fund their stadium move. However, such investment will unlock significant long term growth via improved match-day revenues and a potential naming rights deal. On the move to the new stadium, Tottenham chairman Daniel Levy said, 'It is Tottenham's time to shine now. We have been competing against teams with match-day revenues that far outstrip ours and a restricted capacity that has meant our growing fan base has not been able to get to games. The new stadium will take us to another level globally.'

In their search for finance for the new Emirates Stadium in 2004, Arsenal borrowed more than £260m. This was offset by £100m, spread over 15 years, from Emirates Airlines for the stadium and shirt sponsorship, and by up-front payments from key sponsors like Nike. Keith Edelman, Arsenal's managing director at the time, stated that the projected turnover resulting from the new stadium was likely to increase revenues by around £55m per season.

Training grounds and any other owned properties are assets to be valued too, in part because of the land and infrastructure, but also for its commercial branding opportunities. For instance, Manchester United sold the naming rights to its Carrington facility for a reported £120m over eight years, naming it the Aon Training Complex.

PLAYING SQUAD

In determining how much a club may be worth, there is always debate around the value of the team's players. There is no exact science to valuing players. Ultimately it comes down to the market, and a willing buyer and seller after price compromises have been reached on both sides. Nonetheless, real insight and guidance can be found from a variety of sources. Internally, expertise can be sought from individuals who are responsible for the on-field part of the club. That might include chief scouts, directors of football, the manager and technical directors. All such individuals will have an excellent grasp of the talent and value of individual players as well as a good understanding of current market trends (i.e. whether there aren't many promising English right backs so a particularly high premium may be attached to such a player). By using such individuals as 'price barometers' a relatively accurate valuation picture can be garnered.

This approach can be complemented with a more nuanced, data-driven approach to player value. Such metrics can be used by data analysts to 'benchmark' and compare particular players in a squad against players with similar capabilities in other teams (locally and internationally). This allows a more objective measure when understanding the possible transfer value of particular players. In reality, combinations of the above approaches are relatively common and can assist in trying to assess a realistic market price for each player and the squad as a whole.

For example, in February 2016 billionaire Farhad Moshiri paid a reported £87.5m for 49.9% of Everton. At the time, the squad included John Stones (later sold to Manchester City for £47m), Romelu Lukaku (valued at £75m+, and later sold to Manchester United), Ross Barkley (£15m+, sold to Chelsea), Séamus Coleman (£25m), Gerard Deulofeu (£20m, bought by Barcelona), Kevin Mirallas (£15m) and James McCarthy (£15m) – all extremely valuable 'assets' that would have formed part of any valuation. The amount paid for almost half of the club was significantly less than the transfer value, at that time, of the most important members of the Everton first team squad.

'Prospective owners of football clubs usually value a playing squad based on past performance, rather than future potential. You might think that the two are closely related, but it's easy to fall into major (and very expensive) traps by mistaking that the former directly leads to the latter.

Firstly, because football is a low-scoring sport, it's not uncommon for the team that played better to lose, and vice versa. If a team goes on a streak of results that they didn't deserve, which happens all the time, then it's likely they'll be in a position in the league that doesn't accurately reflect their underlying quality. Teams that have been unlucky may be undervalued, and teams that have been lucky overvalued. Sophisticated statistical modelling can help investors get a better description of past performances, and accurately estimate where a team is likely to be in the short to medium term given their current underlying performance.

Statistical analysis can also help you evaluate the transfer market value of the squad. By using historical transfers as a benchmark, you can see what the market would pay for your players. Summing the squad value as a whole has no practical purpose though – you would never sell all your players at once. But we can help clubs work out the true value of their players; it may be that some are overvalued by the market because of recent, unsustainable performance, or systematic biases.'

Omar Chaudhuri, 21 Club

COMMERCIAL, MERCHANDISING AND ADVERTISING DEALS

Commercial deals and the revenues generated are significant elements to factor into a club's valuation. These will include shirt manufacture, front-of-shirt sponsor, sleeve sponsor and numerous commercial and advertising deals. Most Premier League clubs will have 8–10 such deals, but the larger, more global clubs will have agreements with partners ranging from car manufacturers to noodle suppliers.

LIABILITIES

As important – or arguably more important – when valuing a club is an understanding of its liabilities. A club loaded with significant loans or a crippling player wage bill will have a substantially lower valuation.

LOANS, DEBT AND INTEREST

It's relatively common for a club to have an overdraft and/or loans. For example, the club may have taken out a loan/mortgage to buy land to build a new training ground or may have exceeded their overdraft because money from another club for a player hasn't been paid. Such loans or short-term finance are usually sustainable so long as they form the basis of a business plan where such interest payments and overall repayments are taken into account.

Larger financial deals can occur when, for example, a club brings forward payments for particular events. This can happen in relation to transfers, broadcasting money or season ticket sales.

Finance on transfers can occur when a selling club wants all of its money up front. Usually, buying clubs pay transfer fees in instalments. For example, on a £15m transfer, £5m may be paid when the transfer happens, £5m on the first anniversary of the transfer and £5m on the second anniversary of the transfer. As such the selling club may have to wait two years to receive the additional £10m. Banks and financial organisations offer clubs the opportunity to access the value of those two further instalments sooner. The bank will offer to pay the club perhaps £9.7m straight away, retaining £300k as their 'fee'. They will then ask for the instalment transfer fees from the buying club when they fall due.

The reason why this is relevant is that a selling club may sell two or three players for many millions. If a potential buyer thinks that a club will be receiving additional instalments, the club is potentially more valuable. By contrast, a club that has received payments in advance will obviously receive nothing in the future because the instalments will go straight to the bank.

The same applies to ticket revenues. A potential owner may think he will be entitled to receive ticket money from the season that he owns the club. That may not be the case: the current owner may have agreed a loan from a bank in return for next season's ticket sales. This again makes the club less valuable, because those revenues have already been 'realised'.

Similarly, the valuation of a club may also depend on the repayments due on particular loans. For example, it is likely that the payments will be significant for a club that has recently built a new stadium and taken out a loan to do so. Only when looking through the individual documents will it become clear if the payments are affordable. Again, additional warning signs may include the club missing payments to players, staff, other clubs or the tax authorities. Court cases or tax investigations all point towards financial problems on the horizon.

This could have the effect of potential owners reducing the price they are willing to offer to reflect the fact that future payments may have to be made. In extreme cases, if club liabilities are especially high, a buyer may offer only a notional £1. Such was the case when former Chelsea owner Ken Bates bought the club in 1982. Certain conditions may be written into an agreement in case a club has to make future payments – for example, to the tax authorities for periods when the seller was running the club.

FOOTBALL CLUB OWNERSHIP

What with the glamour, prestige and revenues, who wouldn't want to own a football club? And can anyone?

The short answer is no. Any potential owner must pass a test. This test is called the Owners and Directors Test (ODT) in England, and used to be called the Fit and Proper Persons Test (FPPT). The FA, Premier League and Football League all have similar rules that govern who can own, control or be a director of a football club. This is to stop anyone who has been found guilty of certain offences or has been involved with insolvent/ bankrupt companies.

DISQUALIFYING EVENTS

It will be hard to buy a club if a potential owner is defined as being:

1. involved in the running or ownership (a stake of 10%+) of another Premier League or Football League club;
2. banned from being a company director;
3. previously sentenced to jail for a 12 month+ period, or for a crime that was dishonest;
4. declared bankrupt or previously involved in a club when insolvency events occurred;

5. banned or suspended by a sports or professional body;
6. guilty of breaching the betting regulations; *or*
7. named on the sex offenders' register.

The important part to mention here is that the potential owner will be required to sign a declaration confirming that none of the above applies. There are some additional considerations, too. It is common, however, for the Premier League and Football League to do background checks on potential buyers, and for a formal submission and meeting process to be undertaken so that League executives can ensure that new potential owners are suitable.

What does this mean in practice for a current owner? An owner who fails one of the above tests and then doesn't sell the club (as requested by the Premier League) puts the club at serious risk of being suspended. It would not be able to play matches and might even forfeit its games.

Richard Scudamore was the Premier League chief executive when Thaksin Shinawatra bought Manchester City in June 2007. In 2009, Scudamore insisted that the old FPPT did its job by forcing Shinawatra to sell his shareholding in Manchester City the following year to the current owners, Abu Dhabi United Group, because he realised that he would soon be in breach of the rules. Mr Scudamore explained that:

> Once his wife was convicted, our rules would define her as an associate of his and that would have caught him . . . the fact he sold the club so quickly was because of the application of our rule. He knew that his wife and him were not going to comply [with the FPPT]. So, in effect, the 'Fit and Proper Persons' test worked.

NOTIFYING THE PREMIER LEAGUE

A new rule was introduced before the start of the 2009/10 season, to ensure that any potential buyer would have to inform the Premier League in advance of any takeover, in order to obtain the necessary clearance. The declaration has to be provided 10 working days before the takeover is completed. In practice, in the build-up to the takeover, confidential talks will almost always take place between the potential new owner and the Premier League to ensure everything is in order. Mr Scudamore has stated that 'anyone looking to become an owner or director of a club would have to let us know in advance and we would give them an answer at the time of the proposed takeover as to whether they can or can't'.

An interesting example relates to south-coast club Portsmouth. In May 2009, owner Alexandre Gaydamak accepted a bid from businessman Sulaiman Al-Fahim to buy the club, which was an established Premier League club at the time. The Premier League had to be satisfied that Mr Al-Fahim passed the FPPT ownership rules.

On 21 July, 2009, the Premier League confirmed that 'Mr Al-Fahim has submitted all the documentation required to satisfy our fit and proper persons test.' On 26 August, 2009, the formal takeover, worth £60 million, was completed.

Then, on 2 October, 2009, it was reported that the Portsmouth players had not been paid their September salaries. Chief executive Peter Storrie hastily arranged a short-term loan in order to bridge any salary shortfall. It was announced on 6 October that Saudi businessman Ali al-Faraj, the source of the short-term loan, had bought 90% of Portsmouth, with Al-Fahim retaining a 10% stake. According to Mr Storrie, al-Faraj had already passed the FPPT when originally competing with Al-Fahim to purchase the club over the summer. There was therefore no delay in the subsequent acquisition of Portsmouth.

It is therefore a vital part of any takeover checklist to contact the Premier or Football league as necessary at the earliest opportunity to ensure any would-be owner and/or director passes the current requirements – now the ODT.

WHEN TAKEOVERS GO WRONG

An interesting example of how the Owners and Directors Test process can work out relates to Leeds United and its former owner, Massimo Cellino.

Very few fans in world football could have imagined that a yacht named *Nelie* would cause problems for Leeds United, the owners of the club and the Football League. That, however, is precisely what happened in 2014.

In March 2014, the Football League decided that Cellino, the ex-president and former owner of Leeds United, was disqualified from owning the club as a result of being found guilty of not paying import duties on a yacht named *Nelie*. He was fined €600k by the Italian courts.

In April 2014, Cellino successfully appealed against the decision because his lawyers explained that the guilty verdict by the Italian court was not 'based on dishonesty'. This was important because the Football League rules deem that the disqualifying event relates to having been found guilty of dishonesty. Cellino argued that the offence was not dishonest, so the Football League couldn't disqualify him. The appeal body accepted this argument because the written judgement of the Italian court had neither been published nor translated at this point and therefore the panel couldn't know whether the court considered the offence dishonest or not. If, however, the court subsequently ruled that the offence was dishonest, he would be disqualified.

In December 2014, that is precisely what happened. The Football League now had the benefit of the published, translated Italian court decision, making it clear that the offence was one of dishonesty.

Mr Cellino again appealed the decision to disqualify him, but he was unsuccessful. This meant that he was banned from owning or controlling the club until 3 May, 2015, at which time the offence became 'spent'.

In the end, many fans wondered why there had been an extremely long process to disqualify Cellino for only five months.

By way of recap:

1. In April 2014, an appeal reverses the disqualification because it is not clear the tax offence is a 'dishonest offence'. A 'dishonest offence' is a disqualification event under the Football League's ODT.

2. After Cellino's successful appeal, the Italian court decision is provided to the Football League. The Football League concludes the judgement does show dishonesty.

3. Cellino is therefore disqualified again by the Football League in December 2014. He cannot control or own Leeds and must resign as a director within 28 days of the decision. This didn't, however, mean he had to sell the club; it just meant he could not be involved at the club while the ban was in place. In practice, it meant he has no say at all in the day-to-day running or strategic planning of the club.

4. He was therefore disqualified until 3 May, 2015 – and continued owning Leeds after that date until he sold the club in 2017.

The following year, the FA and Cellino were at loggerheads again. This time, the disciplinary action related to a breach of the agent (intermediary) regulations, and Cellino was banned from running Leeds United for a year.

In December 2016, he was fined £250,000 for breaching the FA's Football Agent Intermediary Regulations in relation to the transfer of player Ross McCormack from Leeds to Fulham in July 2014.

Cellino appealed. The 18-month suspension was reduced to 12 months on appeal, and the fine was also reduced, to £100,000. However, the appeal itself was unsuccessful and meant that he was suspended from all football-related activity for one year until 18 February, 2018.

These two examples of disciplinary action taken against Cellino show the perils of club ownership. Once an owner is subject to the relevant FA, Premier League or Football League rules, significant sanctions can be imposed for various types of improper behaviour, including being banned from the very club where an owner has invested millions.

HOW A TAKEOVER HAPPENS

There are no hard and fast rules about how to start the process to buy a football club. Indeed, there are many avenues:

- a potential owner may be approached by an agent acting for a selling club, sounding out any interest;
- a potential owner may have undertaken a deep review of the landscape, identifying particular clubs of interest, and will then ask companies like 21st Club for a more forensic analysis of the club to understand their underlying performance, player infrastructure, squad depth and talent; *or*
- a potential owner will ask someone in their trusted circle – a lawyer, accountant or business associate – to get in touch with the club to ask whether the current owners are keen to sell.

An approximate valuation is usually established relatively early on in the process. This, however, is with the understanding that what the potential owner is prepared to pay may change after a careful look at the club's finances.

Nonetheless, once a potential owner has received positive signs about a potential deal, both parties will likely enter into a non-disclosure agreement (NDA). This is a confidentiality agreement so that information passed between both parties remains private, thus enabling the other side to sue if information is leaked. It gives the selling club comfort that detailed information they provide (i.e. finances, loans, contracts, disputes, etc.) cannot be disclosed without significant legal consequences. Similarly, a buyer will want to ensure that the seller doesn't disclose their identity so that the matter can be kept private and confidential for as long as possible. The NDA may also include a period of exclusive negotiation – say, 120 days – so that no other potential buyer can speak to the club. A buyer worried about competition may sometimes pay to secure a period of exclusivity.

Once the NDA is signed, the buyer will want to understand the true commercial position, and will ask for a lot of information. This phase is usually called the due diligence (DD) period. Information can include player and staff contracts; commercial contracts; bank loans, overdrafts and other debts; the company structure and ownership; property documents for the stadium, training ground and other land the club owns or leases; disputes with other companies; obligations to past players and staff; and current tax liabilities.

This may be just the tip of the iceberg. In many cases, it is efficient to set up a data room that allows the club to upload all the requested documents to a secure location for the lawyers and accountants to review. There can sometimes be thousands of pages of documents to review. Usually during this phase, particular questions and queries will be asked after reviewing documents, and further details will be requested.

Depending on the appetite of the buyer to investigate and understand every aspect of the club's business, the review can be finalised quickly, in a matter of weeks (or less), or it may take a number of months. A DD report is usually drafted by the buyer's lawyers and accountants to present and summarise the findings of the DD exercise. Again, the reports can be hundreds of pages or sometimes much shorter, depending on what the buyer wants to understand and the level of risk they are willing to accept.

During the beginning of the due diligence phase, it is also common to draw up a short, two- to three-page document setting out the important elements of the deal so that both parties understand what is on the table. This is called a deal sheet or a heads of terms. The document will usually contain the identified buyers and sellers, the purchase price, period of negotiation exclusivity, bonuses for the club remaining in the Premier League or being promoted, confidentiality clauses, and a timeline to complete the deal. This is usually signed by both seller and buyer, and gives confidence to both parties that the headline deal has been agreed.

Once the non-disclosure agreement and deal sheet have been signed by both parties, and the DD report has been finalised and reviewed by the buyer, both sides will start negotiating the actual agreement that transfers the shares of the seller to the buyer. This agreement is usually called a Sale and Purchase Agreement (SPA) and can be a mammoth document containing hundreds of pages of clauses, provisions, conditions, annexes, contingent payments – and more. It can take weeks, even months, to finalise.

What is the most important element?

The price

A purchase price is never straightforward. There will be guaranteed amounts paid, as well as contingent amounts if certain events either occur or don't (like relegation or promotion), and payment terms may be spread over a number of seasons.

The new owners will also need to ensure that they can fulfil the Premier League or Football League ownership rules – the Owners and Directors Test rules set out above (*see* page 81). Usually the selling club will liaise with the relevant league on a confidential basis to explain that a takeover may be occurring. As the process and negotiations between buyer and seller continue, the Premier League will ask for a meeting with any potential owners together with information about their investment, a business plan, and guarantees about the sources of their funds. The Premier League may also employ investigative teams to carry out research into the prospective owners to ensure they have 'no skeletons in their closets'.

After the SPA has been finalised, along with a number of additional documents (mainly in relation to share transfers and company board resolutions), a completion date is agreed. Sometimes the SPA is signed and an agreement is reached to complete the deal within a short period of time – say, within the following two months. This will usually involve the money being transferred to the sellers, share certificates being transferred to the buyers, and the buyer and seller agreeing to finalise the various remaining documents.

WHEN TAKEOVER DEALS COLLAPSE

There are a variety of reasons why a deal doesn't happen. The most common relates to price. Buyers will want to keep any figure as low as possible and sellers will want to maximise the club's value. Sometimes, that's as simple as it gets. However, usually the price and the deal will relate to numerous add-ons, including bonuses or reductions – for promotion or relegation – and how the payments are made (i.e. the percentage of the purchase price that is paid up front and the percentage paid in instalments).

In many cases, there is more than one seller, and the various selling shareholders may not all be willing to agree on the terms of the sale. Much will depend on whether a buyer wants total, majority or partial control over the club. For example, the initial deal for Farhad Moshiri to buy Premier League club Everton was for 49.9% of the club – and it was reported that there were particular clauses allowing him to buy additional shares in the club at a later date (which he did in September 2018). Buyers will usually want at least majority control if spending huge amounts to buy a club (usually over 50% of the shareholding of the club). Otherwise, they will not have the power to decide the direction of the club because they can simply be outvoted.

The due diligence report may pick up a major risk that a buyer cannot accept. For example, there may be a massive overdraft, or the club may not own its stadium, or it may have huge debts that will need to be paid off by any new owner. A potential owner may not be willing to accept these new conditions.

What follows are a few examples of club takeovers ending prematurely.

THE PRICE OF STEEL

Before George Gillett and Tom Hicks bought Liverpool from David Moores in 2007, it was reported that the consortium Dubai International Capital (DIC) were close to purchasing Liverpool. In the end, one of the reported reasons why Moores pulled out of the deal with DIC (according to former chief executive Rick Parry) was that the club had to put down a hefty payment to secure the steel needed to begin work on a new stadium. DIC didn't want to underwrite the order, which convinced Moores that they were not the right group to buy the club. Later, in 2010, Moores commented, 'With hindsight, we may have had a lucky escape there, as Dubai is not the buoyant market it was in 2007.'

THE SKY IS THE LIMIT

In 1999, football broadcaster BSkyB had its proposed £623m takeover of Manchester United blocked by the UK government, concerned about adverse effects on the UK football industry. Manchester United were then the Premier League's most prized asset, and owning the club would have given BSkyB a seat at both sides of the negotiating table. It would also have put Manchester United in a greater bargaining position when television contracts were renewed. Sensitive information that only United would be able to receive about competing bids could have been used to BSkyB's advantage. It was also argued that BSkyB might ultimately have exploited United's dominant position as a bargaining tool, which might not have been in the wider interests of the national game. For example, United might have chosen to resign from the Premier League or initiate the individual selling of rights. Stephen Byers, the trade and industry secretary at the time, was unequivocal in his opposition to the deal: 'Under almost all scenarios considered by the Monopolies and Mergers Commission, the merger would increase the market power which BSkyB already has as a provider of sports premium channels.'

THE OTHER SIDE OF CLUB OWNERSHIP

The financial opportunities presented by club ownership are significant. However, the millions involved make it a high-stakes game – as demonstrated by the examples that follow.

TWO COURT CASES AND A TEXAN SHOWDOWN

In October 2010, Liverpool FC became front- and back-page news. The owners at the time, George Gillett and Tom Hicks, had taken out a loan to buy the club in 2007 for £215m, and now needed to refinance the loan.

The loan came from the Royal Bank of Scotland (RBS) and others. In April 2010, RBS made it clear that they would extend their loan only until October 2010 – and only so that the sale of the club could be completed. A major condition was that Christian Purslow and Ian Ayre be added to the Liverpool board as non-owner directors. On the board already was Martin Broughton, and along with Purslow and Ayre he would now be able to outvote Hicks and Gillett by three to two. This was crucial because the owners would be outnumbered when the board made a decision on the sale of the club.

An initial court case arose after the board wished to discuss two companies willing to buy the club. Gillett and Hicks decided to remove Purslow and Ayre from the club board so they couldn't vote on which bid to accept. The owners didn't want to sell to either bidder, arguing that the values of the bids were too low.

The three non-owner directors took legal advice to understand their position:

- Was their removal from the club board by Gillett and Hicks illegal?
- Could they, as directors of the club, continue negotiating with the two preferred bidders?
- Did they have to go to court to make sure they had the power to sign off on the club sale?

The priority was to ensure that Purslow, Ayre and Broughton were able to outvote the two owners. The judge, Mr Justice Floyd, put the issue rather well in explaining that:

'The true position is that in order to secure additional loan facilities, the owners have released absolute control of the sale process which they are now seeking to regain. When it appeared that the sale was going forward on a basis which they considered unfavourable to them, they sought to renege on that agreement [the appointment of Purslow and Ayre].'

The court confirmed that Purslow and Ayre should be restored to the Liverpool board and that they had the power to sell the club.

Just to muddy the waters, RBS's lawyers received a letter from the owners after the court hearing, which enclosed a temporary restraining order (TRO) granted by a Dallas court. The gist of the TRO was to stall the sale of the club to Fenway Group (the preferred bidder after a decision taken on 6 October). Damages were also claimed, to the tune of $1bn.

The second court hearing was brought by RBS to stop the TRO taking effect. It's fair to say that Mr Justice Floyd, who had ruled on the first matter, was not best pleased. He went so far as to slate the owners' conduct as 'unconscionable', agreeing with RBS for the second time in two days. Tough stuff from the court. The next morning, the Texas proceedings were lifted, enabling Fenway to complete the sale.

This case is interesting because the owners were unable to lead the sale process and demand the biggest pay-off they could find. Instead, potential bidders at the time understood that if the non-owning directors consented to their bid because there were no higher finalised offers, and if they agreed to pay off the loan hanging over the club, there appeared little the owners could do about it.

GREEN AND GOLD: MANCHESTER UNITED

In 2005 the Glazer family purchased Manchester United for £790m. What was relatively uncommon at the time was that around £525m of the purchase price was borrowed against the value of the club. This essentially meant that the club had large interest payments to make on the loans used to purchase the club.

The club subsequently floated on the New York Stock Exchange in August 2012, with an opening valuation of $2.3bn. It has been reported that over £500m has been paid in interest payments and other fees to service the debt since then. Fans argue that such large sums should have been reinvested back into the team, facilities and community.

Indeed, in 2010, fan groups came together to investigate whether a large number of wealthy 'Red Knights' could band together and buy out the Glazers. For a time, protests continued, and green and gold scarfs (the colours of Newton Heath before the club changed its name to Manchester United in 1902) were visible around Old Trafford. Ultimately, it proved very difficult to raise the necessary money and the protests decreased. Nonetheless, the club was reported to have £464m worth of debt in 2017.

While the deal was no doubt an astute piece of business by the Glazer family, fans wonder what would have happened had the value of the finance costs (£500m+) been used to invest in the squad.

MARK GOLDBERG AND CRYSTAL PALACE

In 1998, Mark Goldberg had sold his successful IT recruitment company for over £40m. He decided to invest the money in his boyhood club, Crystal Palace. He initially paid £22.8m for the club (excluding the club's ground, Selhurst Park, which was then leased back to the club). Crucially, former owner Ron Noades retained ownership of the stadium, the club shops and the training ground. The deal was about to get even worse. Although the price was agreed while the club was in the Premier League, they were then relegated – which led to a huge drop in revenues even as the club's cost base remained astronomical. They had Premier League wages of £7–8m per year, while relegation meant that revenues had fallen from £14m to £4m. Ex-England coach Terry Venables had reportedly been paid a £135,000 fee just to open talks with the club and was subsequently paid an annual salary of £750,000 to become manager. A further report suggested that one agent had charged a commission of £448,000 to the club for introducing two unsuccessful trialists.

The club quickly spiralled into a near-fatal nosedive. Administration followed within nine months. Goldberg was declared bankrupt, lost his £40m and was banned from being a company director for 14 years. His example sits at the extreme end of what can happen when things go wrong post-takeover.

OWNING MORE THAN ONE CLUB

Over the last decade a number of companies and individuals have decided to buy shares in various clubs across the continent. For example, Sheikh Mansour owns City Football Group, which owns shares in Manchester City in the Premier League, New York City in the MLS (Major League

Soccer), Spanish team Girona, Melbourne City in the Australian League, Atlético Torque in Uruguay and Yokohama F Marinos in Japan. Similarly, drinks manufacturer Red Bull is involved in RasenBallsport Leipzig in the German Bundesliga, Red Bull Brazil, and the New York Red Bulls in the MLS. Red Bull is also the title sponsor of Red Bull Salzburg, in Austria. The Pozzo family own Premier League club Watford and Serie A team Udinese. This trend is likely to continue. Owners enjoy the benefits of joint collaboration across player exchange, technical support teams (analytics, medical knowledge), marketing, commercial and branding opportunities.

There is nothing to stop anyone owning more than one club, but the situation becomes complicated when the potential exists for two of those clubs to play against each other in the same competition. In the Premier League and Football League, an owner must pass the ODT (*see* page 81). These conditions include ensuring that they do not have the power to influence the management or administration of another Premier League or Football League club. This effectively means that the same owner cannot own a Premier League and Football League club at the same time.

Why is the owner of a club not allowed to buy a club in a higher or lower league? Specifically, because there is a risk that both teams could play each other in domestic cup competitions or if one was promoted or the other relegated. The owner of both teams could therefore be in a position to instruct one of the managers to lose, or to select certain players or to field stronger or weaker teams. The rationale is that off-field conflicts of interest should not impact on-field sporting success or failure. Anything that brings such issues into question should be avoided.

OWNING CLUBS IN DIFFERENT COUNTRIES

Ownership issues have also arisen when one company owns shares in more than one European football club competing in the same UEFA competition. In 2000, an investment company called ENIC had a 78.4% shareholding in AEK Athens FC and a 53.7% shareholding in Slavia Prague. Both clubs qualified for the UEFA Cup competition in the same season.

The Court of Arbitration for Sport ruled decisively: when two clubs qualify for UEFA club competitions and are owned or could be influenced by the same owner, one of the teams should not be allowed to play in the competition. The perception of a particular game could be damaged by the differing business aims of two clubs in the same competition.

Note that this also impacts the integrity of the competition itself. Suppose that in the group stages of the Champions League, Team A needs to win a match against Team B to qualify for the next round, while Team B is not in a position to qualify for the next stage. Both Team A and Team B are owned by the same company. Very difficult questions for UEFA will almost certainly follow if Team B fields a weakened team. The concerns of the company for one of its clubs to progress to the next highly lucrative round could lead to incentives to favour one of its teams, and this would not align with the integrity of the UEFA competition. The single aim of winning may be compromised.

A second potential problem is the prospect of a company favouring the more popular club if both teams are drawn against each other. Revenue-generating factors – such as which team will raise more prize money, and attract larger television audiences and advertising revenue streams – might take priority above the integrity of the game.

RED BULL AND THE CHAMPIONS LEAGUE

In June 2017, UEFA had to rule on this very issue. It appeared that Red Bull owned Red Bull Salzburg (RBS) and RasenBallsport Leipzig (RBL) – and both teams qualified for the 2017/18 Champions League competition. The concern was that Red Bull had decisive influence over both teams, which could impact the integrity of the Champions League. UEFA stated in its official report that Red Bull had:

- decisive influence over both clubs;
- high levels of income from Red Bull sponsorship deals;
- a formal cooperation agreement;
- unusually high levels of player loans and transfers;

- individuals who were/are connected to Red Bull in the operation of both clubs; *and*
- very similar visual kit and advertising branding.

In order to allow both clubs to compete in the Champions League, RBS agreed to remove certain individuals linked to Red Bull and to terminate a loan it had with Red Bull. In addition, the cooperation agreement between RBS and RBL was terminated, while the sponsorship agreement between RBS and Red Bull was amended to reduce the rights granted and the amounts paid by Red Bull. UEFA was now of the view that the RBS and Red Bull relationship was one of sponsorship, not ownership. Therefore, Red Bull did not have decisive influence over both clubs. Both teams were able to play in the 2017/18 Champions League.

CLUB REVENUES

Clubs receive significant performance- and commerce-related revenues. Many clubs earn the majority of their income from the broadcasting deals that are sold to a variety of pay TV channels. Premier League, La Liga, Bundesliga and Serie A clubs all earn monumental sums from selling their exclusive rights across the world and participating in league and cup competitions where sporting success can be worth tens of millions of euros.

Similarly, brands want to be associated with a variety of clubs in particular countries and territories, and will enter into shirt, apparel, stadium, training and betting partnerships for significant sums. In addition, fans and corporate sponsors attending matches and paying to watch games throughout the season generate further revenue.

PREMIER LEAGUE REVENUE

The Premier League distributes its UK broadcasting monies to its member clubs in the following way: 50% is split equally; 25% is based on the number of television appearances with a stipulated minimum amount – called facility fees; and 25% based on where that club finishes in the League – called merit payment. The overseas broadcasting monies received from broadcasters outside the UK is distributed equally among the clubs too. As of the 2017/18 season, the central commercial Premier League deals are with EA Sports (lead partner), Barclays (the official bank), Cadbury (the official snack), Carling (the official beer), Nike (the official ball) and TAG Heuer (the official timekeeper), who all pay sponsorship fees to the Premier League, which are equally distributed to the clubs (almost £4.8m each).

In the last year of the 2010–13 television deal, Manchester United received £60.8m for winning the League. Such was the increase in the amount paid by Sky and British Telecom for the next deal that in the following season, 2013/14, Cardiff City received more (£62.1m) for finishing bottom than United had for winning the League the year before. As champions in the 2016/17 season, Chelsea earned £150.8m while bottom-placed Sunderland earned £93.4m.

What Sunderland earned for finishing bottom was more than Juventus, Bayern Munich or Monaco earned for winning their respective Serie A, Bundesliga and Ligue 1 titles. The contrast is stark.

As can be seen from the table on pages 208–209, central distributions to the clubs continue to be lucrative. There are some interesting intricacies too. Although Manchester City won the League in the 2017/18 season, earning £149.4m in the process, their rivals Manchester United actually earned more money (£149.7m) because United were featured on UK television on two more occasions (28 as opposed to 26 times). Even more stark is the difference between sixth and seventh place. Arsenal finished sixth, earning £142m. Burnley finished seventh, receiving £119.7m. The difference was down to Arsenal being on TV 18 more times than Burnley over the season.

In addition, each place in the English Premier League is worth just over £1.9m. The 2017/18 champions earned £38.6m (20 × £1.9m) while West Brom, who finished bottom, earned £1.9m (1 × £1.9m). Even finishing bottom, however, West Brom earned £94.6m.

With every place in the Premier League now worth £1.9m, any clubs promoted to the Premier League will probably receive £180m+ based on their year in the League and a number of years' worth of parachute payments (see below).

PARACHUTE PAYMENTS

Parachute payments are funds provided by the Premier League to clubs relegated to the Football League Championship. These are primarily to provide a financial cushion for the relegated clubs to adjust to life outside the lucrative Premier League competition. Luton and Notts County were relegated along with West Ham in the 1991/92 season, just before the establishment of the Premier League, and go down in history for each receiving £1.5m in parachute payments without (to date) ever playing in the Premier League.

The Premier League has for a number of years distributed parachute payments over four years to relegated clubs. For the previous three-year broadcasting deal (from 2013 to 2016), the Premier League paid out around £65m over four seasons for clubs relegated during that period, including Burnley, QPR and Hull.

If a relegated club is promoted back to the Premier League, they lose any further parachute payments – because the club receives payments from being back in the Premier League.

THE £180M GAME

The Football League play-off game is now considered by many to be the most lucrative game in world football. The winner is rewarded with a place in the Premier League, where just one season will generate £180m as the bare minimum for the club. That is usually because of the following revenue uplifts:

1. **Central distributions.** This is by far the largest revenue boost for a promoted club, and there has been no better time to be in the Premier League. The amount of global broadcasting monies and central Premier League sponsorship deals is rocketing. Finishing bottom will typically earn a club around £90m+.

    Central Distributions for a club in the Premier League will mean a revenue uplift of £90m+ for a promoted club and significantly more if the club remains in the League.

2. **Parachute payments.** Depending on the length of time the club is in the Premier League, the parachute payments over two or three years could total £80m+.
   Parachute payments for a subsequently relegated club could reach £80m.

3. **Sponsorship.** The two largest club sponsorship deals are usually shirt brand and kit manufacturer agreements. For a promoted club with existing contracts, there will likely be uplifts for a team being promoted into the Premier League. If a team is out of contract, there will be a premium attached to a new shirt brand or kit deal. Nonetheless, the figures are unlikely to be too substantial. No promoted club is going to come close to Manchester United's £53m yearly Chevrolet deal. At present, the smaller Premier League clubs are reported to receive annually in the region of £2–5m in shirt brand deals and around £1–4m for a kit deal.
   Headline sponsorship revenues could provide up to £5m in additional revenues.

4. **Match day.** The majority of the lower Premier League clubs earn from £7m to £16m based on annual accounts lodged in the UK. By contrast, for the 2016/17 season, the average Football League Championship match-day revenue was around £6m. The marginal increase from being in the Premier League is likely to be relatively small in revenue terms – unless prices were hiked, which would probably be very unpopular.
   Additional match-day revenues may increase a club's bottom line by £1–3m.

5. The other slightly less tangible benefit of being in the Premier League is the value that attaches to the club. Clubs promoted will be guaranteed significant sums (as outlined above), which can make them attractive to investors. The effect of larger revenues combined with spending restrictions has made clubs more attractive to investors due to record profits in recent years.

All of the above should, of course, be balanced against the need for paying out promotion bonuses to players and staff, new contracts and salaries at Premier League level, team performance payments and greater investment in the playing squad – due to large transfer fees having to be paid and the subsequent increase in agents' payments, etc.

Nonetheless, even if a promoted club is immediately relegated back to the Football League Championship, it's worth remembering that the likely guaranteed amount for that one season will be in the region of £180m. Game on!

CLUB IMAGE RIGHTS DEALS

One of the ways that clubs can increase the value of their sponsorship deals is to promise personal appearances, advertisements and promotions with their top players. This can be achieved through image rights agreements with players (and managers), particularly at the top clubs.

Deals for image rights have been relatively commonplace in the UK and Europe over the last 20 years. Players and clubs will enter into agreements by which the club will pay the player an agreed amount in exchange for the ability to use the player's image in their general commercial, marketing and promotional materials. This deal sits alongside a player's playing contract.

An image rights deal can be tax efficient. For example, English club players will probably be paying 45% income tax on payments in relation to their playing contracts, but can transfer their image rights to a company that receives the payments on behalf of the player and pays corporation tax at 19% (currently), thus saving the player significant sums.

In fact, HM Revenue and Customs (HMRC, the UK's tax authority) has been concerned that some clubs have disguised a player's salary as image rights payments in order to reduce the overall tax burden for both the player and the club (*see* below).

IMAGE RIGHTS AND THEIR RELEVANCE

A player's image can include his name, nicknames, likeness, image, photograph, signature, autograph, initials, statements, endorsement, physical details, voice and other personal characteristics. The idea is that the above descriptions include everything that may form part of that player's image for the player and/or his club to then market accordingly.

A club and/or brand will be paying a player to endorse and promote a number of specific commercial deals. As commercial drivers push football into the entertainment and brand space, clubs are looking for a variety of ways to monetise and grow their revenue base. Clubs are entering into a multitude of commercial partnerships with brands that want to be associated with clubs and their high-profile players. In 2016, the *Financial Times* reported that in 2010 the Manchester United player Wayne Rooney earned £760,000 a year for his image rights.

HOW IMAGE RIGHTS DEALS WORK IN PRACTICE

Under the standard employment contract that each Premier League player enters into with his club, certain provisions allow for a club to use a number of its players to promote the club's sponsors. It is, however, limited in scope: the contract typically states 'the Club's use of the Player's Image must not be greater than the average for all first team players'.

For example, Mohamed Salah currently plays for Liverpool. If the club does not have a separate image rights agreement in place with one of its star players, it will be difficult to use his image with the majority of the club's commercial partners because that is not generally permitted under a player's standard employment contract. However, the club's commercial partners would probably want to use Salah's image more than that of a first team squad player who is less recognisable in other markets. So if Liverpool want to use Salah's image across a range of sponsorship opportunities, it becomes vital for the club to contract separately with him through a deal giving control of those rights to endorse particular products and services. If Salah owns his image through a company, the club will need to pay that company for the player's services.

WHY DO CLUBS AND PLAYERS ENTER INTO IMAGE RIGHTS DEALS?

In the UK, football players are taxed through the HMRC's pay-as-you-earn (PAYE) scheme. This means tax is deducted at the time of payment by the club. Premier League and Football League players will pay 45% tax on earnings over £150,000, as well as 2% National Insurance contributions. If a club is making a payment to an image rights company rather than a salary payment through the PAYE system, the player is not being taxed on that income at 45% but rather is paying corporation tax of 19% (falling to 17% by 2020). From a club's perspective, it does not have to pay employers National Insurance contributions at 13.8% on payments to the player's image rights companies either. The National Insurance savings for a Premier League club with 25 first team players with a strong commercial programme and a raft of commercial partners can be considerable.

As an example, if a player is paid £1.8m per year before tax is deducted, and the club puts in place an image rights structure with its players, the club could save up to £190,000 in tax payments per player per year.

In the past, HMRC had viewed this type of arrangement as a way for both the player and club to avoid tax, but more recently it has become more accepting of such arrangements within certain limits.

CONTROVERSY

During the early 2000s, many clubs entered into large image rights contracts – and came unstuck. This was primarily because teams agreed deals with players who sometimes did not really have an image to commercialise.

If a player had an image rights deal for £1m per year, HMRC were quite rightly interested to understand how that deal had been valued and how the club had exploited those rights as part of its wider commercial strategy. To offer an extreme example, imagine a *reserve* keeper at a Championship club being paid a large percentage of his overall package through an image rights deal. Questions would almost inevitably be asked about the commercial justification of such a deal. Indeed, HMRC investigated a large number of clubs during the early 2000s, and it is believed that almost all Premier League clubs for the period ending 2010 entered into settlement arrangements.

HMRC

HMRC recognise that image rights contracts are legitimate ways to structure payments to players in return for endorsing particular products and services. Clubs continue to understand that their star players are marketable assets off the field too. Given the popularity of Premier League matches in almost every country in the world, sponsors and commercial partners are keen to engage with high-profile clubs.

The questions HMRC will continue to ask may relate to the total percentage of the player's overall package paid to his image rights company, and how the club uses those rights. The days of more than 20% of a player's total package being provided by way of image rights payments by clubs to players are long gone in all but exceptional circumstances.

So long as clubs can reasonably justify image rights payments to their players through commercial opportunities, more deals will continue to be entered into, benefiting both clubs and players alike.

'HM Revenue & Customs in the UK recognise that under the standard Premier League contract, clubs only have minimal access to the players in a commercial capacity. Given the ever-increasing inventory of commercial partnerships, particularly at top clubs, there is a real need to secure increased access to the players to deliver to the commercial partners. If the player's rights are held by a company, the club has no choice but to contract with this company at an arms-length rate, for the ability to utilise those rights.'

Pete Hackleton, Partner at Saffery Champness

SPONSORSHIP DEALS

In the 2016/17 season, Manchester United were reported to have earned £268m from commercial, merchandising and sponsorship partnerships.

The two major sponsorship deals are for a shirt deal and the brand that appears on the shirt. For a player, a boot deal – usually with one of Nike, Adidas, Puma, Under Armour or New Balance – will be their most lucrative contract.

Brands are keen to be associated with clubs that have global reach, a broad fan base and a number of its players as international celebrities. Each of a club's major commercial partners will appear across the globe on various platforms, both physical and digital. Brands will be emblazoned on club shirts when the club plays in the relevant league and cup competitions, on advertising banners, post-match interview backdrops, dugouts, and various forms of advertising across the club's digital and online platforms.

Clubs seek out sponsors in a variety of ways. Many clubs have in-house commercial teams that go out into the market to source a wide variety of partners across many sectors. In addition, there are a range of commercial agencies that have excellent relationships with particular companies and brands. Such companies offer introductions to the clubs and then take a commission if a deal is done.

CLUB SPONSORSHIP VALUES

Premier League clubs generated around £226.5m in the 2016/17 season for their front-of-shirt sponsor.

It has been reported that the money paid by sponsors to be on the shirt of Premier League teams has almost tripled in value over the last seven seasons, from £100m in the 2010/11 season to £281.8m for the 2017/18 season. The 2018/19 shirt sponsorship league table, set out below, was reported by SportingIntelligence.com.

It is sometimes unclear whether the amount stated relates to any particular performance-related clauses such as finishing in a certain position or the minimum number of shirts sold. For clubs threatened with the possibility of relegation, there will usually be relegation reduction clauses in the event that the club has a deal for more than one season and the club is relegated.

For the beginning of the 2017/18 season, the Premier League for the first time allowed a secondary shirt sponsor to appear on the sleeve of its teams. This is predicted to bring in several millions of pounds for its elite clubs. For example, Manchester City's deal with Nexen Tire is reported to be worth £10m per season. Liverpool signed a deal with money transfer company Western Union, and Everton signed an agreement with mobile gaming and film company Angry Birds. Arsenal also tied up a £30m, three-year sleeve deal with Visit Rwanda.

A club like Manchester United will also have a training kit sponsor, which will be different from its first team kit shirt sponsor. In 2010, DHL paid £40m to sponsor its training kit, but in 2013 the club bought out the remaining part of the contract. In its place they signed an eight-year deal with Aon, worth £15m per year, to sponsor both its training kit and training ground. Their training facilities have been renamed the Aon Training Complex.

Chelsea have a playing kit sponsored by Yokahama Tyres, and training kit sponsored by drinks manufacturer Carabao. Liverpool have a new training kit deal with bookmaker BetVictor; airline Garuda Indonesia previously held the rights from 2014.

Club	Sponsor	Value	Sector
Manchester United	Chevrolet	£47m	Cars
Manchester City	Etihad	£45m	Airline
Arsenal	Emirates	£40m	Airline
Chelsea	Yokohama	£40m	Tyres
Liverpool	Standard Chartered	£40m	Banking
Tottenham	AIA	£35m	Insurance
West Ham	Betway	£10m	Gambling
Everton	SportPesa	£9.6m	Gambling
Crystal Palace	ManBetX	£6.5m	Gambling
Newcastle	Fun88	£6.5m	Gambling
Southampton	Virgin Media	£6m	Telecoms
Burnley	Laba360	£5m	Gambling
Wolves	W88	£5m	Gambling
Bournemouth	M88	£5m	Gambling
Leicester	King Power	£4m	Retail
Cardiff	Visit Malaysia	£3m	Tourism
Fulham	Dafabet	£3m	Gambling
Watford	FxPro	£3m	Forex Finance
Brighton	American Express	£1.5m	Finance
Huddersfield	Ope Sports	£1.5m	Gambling

Clubs will work hard at separating out various partnership assets to maximise the commercial inventory they can offer to potential partners. This can be taken to extremes: it was reported that the home strip for Swedish side Mjällby AIF contained 13 different sponsors and Puebla FC's home shirt for 2009 advertised nine.

In April 2017, Liverpool announced its first women's team kit sponsor after agreeing a three-year deal with cosmetic and beauty brand Avon. It meant that Standard Chartered were no longer the shirt sponsor for all first team playing kits. Across the city in July 2018, Premier League club Everton became the first professional English team to exclusively use their women's team to unveil the club's new 2018/19 season away kit.

SHIRT SALES

When David Beckham moved to Real Madrid, this seemed to herald the era of news stories about increases in shirt sales covering the transfer fee and wages for the new player. More than 1 million Real Madrid shirts were reportedly sold in the first year of Beckham's four-year stay at the Bernabéu. The same narrative is regurgitated whenever a big name moves – Pogba to Manchester United, Ronaldo or Bale to Real Madrid, Neymar to PSG.

The headline values that manufacturers attach to shirt deals for elite clubs can be very large. It was reported that the latest Manchester United deal with Adidas was worth £750m over a 10-year period. Adidas forecast at the outset that they believed United shirt sales would reach £1.5 billion over the length of the deal.

Indeed, Chelsea are said to have ended their current deal with Adidas early (after paying a hefty termination fee of around £40m) in order to secure a new deal with Nike, worth £60m per year. They did the same in 2005, agreeing an early end to their then agreement with Umbro by paying £25m to sign with Adidas.

Shirt manufacturers will pay such astronomical figures only if they believe they are going to profit from the deal. People suggesting that Manchester United would make an additional £40m in shirt sales revenues after signing Zlatan seem wide of the mark for the following reason. Kit manufacturers usually take 80–90% of all revenue from shirt sales. Clubs in return receive large, 'up-front' payments from their kit manufacturer. At best, the club earns 20% of all sales, though for many large deals, royalty payments to a club kick in only once a large number of sales have already been made – say, 2 million shirt sales.

Suppose Liverpool's home shirt retails for £50, and that the club is making £10 from each shirt it sells. To recoup the transfer fee spent on Sadio Mané (around £30m – and that doesn't include his wages), Liverpool would need to sell three million shirts. Bear in mind that Liverpool averaged 852,000 shirts sold per season from 2011/12 to 2015/16, and you see that it is usually impossible to recoup large signings from shirt sales alone.

To offer another example, it is reported that as Manchester United's deal with Adidas is so large, it may be that it receives no additional royalties on shirt sales until a certain sales milestone is reached. Let's say that after two million shirts are sold, the club receives a generous 20% of all shirt sales (again, for simplicity, £10 per £50 shirt). For the club to recoup Pogba's transfer fee of £89m, it will need to sell two million shirts to start earning the royalty, and a further 8.9m shirts to recoup the entire fee. The club sold an impressive number of shirts in the 2015/16 season: 2.9m, still nowhere near the amount needed to claw back their £89m transfer investment.

GLOBAL PARTNERS

The breadth of some clubs' commercial operations is now staggering. Take Manchester United in 2018: the club had 65 global and regional partners spanning airlines, wine, outdoor clothing, logistics, office equipment, video gaming, oil, paint, mattresses, headwear, noodles, watches, medical systems, drinks, pharma, financial services and media.

In their contract with Adidas, the club agreed that if it fails to qualify for the Champions League for two seasons running, the value of the apparel deal drops from £75m to £55m per year.

Through such strategic partnerships, the club is able to drive further revenues, which help the team succeed on the pitch. Noodle partners may not seem like an obvious fit, but the brand appeal of particular clubs provides lucrative revenue generating opportunities. Clubs like Manchester United have become global leaders at positively exploiting such partnerships.

FINANCIAL RESTRICTIONS

Within the last decade, football's authorities have taken important steps to clamp down on clubs 'chasing the dream' by spending big, and not having the revenues to service debt, wages and transfer fees. Clubs such as Leeds United and Portsmouth got into trouble because they were living beyond their means and their costs exceeded their revenues. In many cases, the wage bill was more than the club was earning. Clubs then made larger losses and could pay neither their footballers nor their local businesses, who had supplied goods and services to the club.

In the UK since 1986, there have been at least 81 clubs that have suffered an insolvency event. Fans have borne the brunt of overzealous spending. The authorities have been trying to find ways to avoid these financial failures.

Now clubs must spend only what they earn. Previously, there were no such penalties in place. This created an 'arms race', in terms of both transfer fees and wages. Some fans are annoyed that their club cannot spend as they wish, but in the long run the authorities believe that outlawing kamikaze spending makes it more difficult for a club to encounter major financial problems.

The football authorities have gone to significant lengths to ensure that clubs balance their books, do not spend more than they earn, and promote investment in youth development and in their stadia and training facilities. In the past, transfer fee and wage inflation spiralled upwards because each set of new and rich club owners injected more money into the European football club market. A 'keeping up with the Joneses' effect meant costs spiralled further because potential owners then had to outbid other high-spending clubs.

The beneficiaries were the players, earning ever more lucrative salaries, and the clubs eventually sought ways to help them limit their own spending. This may seem rather bizarre in the case of Chelsea or Manchester City, but it makes perfect sense; after spending £1bn+, Roman Abramovich realised that football clubs cannot endlessly outdo one another. Clubs have effectively asked the authorities to save them from themselves.

This process has happened at various national and international levels. Initially, UEFA was the body that looked into implementing cost control rules. UEFA and its then president, Michel Platini, had long been concerned that clubs making continual losses were not playing fair. The Premier League, and in particular its then chief executive Richard Scudamore, had been wary of curbing the ability of owners to subsidise their clubs, fearing that this would lessen the competition's attraction for global investors; that approach changed in 2010, after Portsmouth became the first Premier League club to go into administration. Rules regulating transfer and wage spending were implemented.

The cost of buying Neymar

There are some eye-watering numbers to consider. A world record transfer fee of £198m was required to buy out his contract at Barcelona; and a hugely lucrative long-term contract of perhaps £3–4m per month. All of this adds up to a possible total outlay for PSG of close to £500m.

Transfer fees for accounting purposes are spread over the length of a player's contract. £198m over a five-year contract is amortised by a club in its accounts to the value of £39.6m per season. This is regardless of whether the buyout amount was paid in one lump sum or not.

Practically, the yearly accounting cost would include his annual amortised transfer fee (£39.6m) plus his wages, bonuses and loyalty payments – perhaps another £50m. To fund such a purchase, a club would possibly have to find an extra £90m per season. There are only a few clubs that have such deep pockets.

For FFP purposes, such a deal must be financed through profits made, by selling existing players or by finding additional revenue streams.

FINANCIAL FAIR PLAY EXPLAINED

The Financial Fair Play (FFP) rules were put in place to ensure that clubs became more self-sustainable by breaking even in the medium to long term. UEFA, the Premier League and the Football League all have different regulations setting out spending restrictions that clubs must respect. These are called acceptable losses.

The result is that clubs can't generally spend beyond their means. It also encourages clubs to invest in sustainable and long-term revenue-generating assets like stadia or youth development – costs which are removed for break-even calculations.

Here at UEFA, Premier League and Football League level, the basics are set out:

- Clubs playing in UEFA competitions (Champions League and Europa League) can make losses of up to €30m over three seasons (€10m per season).
- Premier League clubs can make losses of up to £105m over three seasons (£35m per season) and can generally spend only £7m more on wages than they did in the previous season.
- Football League clubs can make losses of up to £39m over three seasons (£13m per season).

A club that moves between the Premier League and Football League Championship will be assessed in accordance with the average allowance that is permitted in the relevant division. For example, a club that had played two seasons in the Championship and one in the Premier League would have a maximum permitted loss of £61m (i.e. one season at £35m and two at £13m).

Sanctions vary depending on the regulations but include transfer embargos in the Football League, potential points deductions in the Premier League, and squad size restrictions and even expulsion in UEFA competitions.

So has anyone been banned? In short, yes; and many other clubs have had significant penalties imposed.

UEFA, the Premier League and the Football League all have the power to sanction clubs for breaches of their rules. For UEFA such sanctions include a warning, a fine, withholding of prize monies, points deductions, refusal to register players for UEFA competition, reducing a club's squad size, disqualification from competitions in progress and/or exclusion from future competitions. In 2015, UEFA took the ultimate sanction and banned Dynamo Moscow from future competition. This related to a significant overspend. The club's loss over the three-year period, as set out in the UEFA Club Financial Control Body (CFCB) judgement, was €257,268,000. This was over €200m more than was permitted under the FFP rules. As such, a ban was deemed appropriate by the CFCB and imposed on Dynamo for the 2015/16 Europa League season.

More recently, the CFCB has banned Galatasaray. The club had previously agreed to a 'settlement' deal whereby in exchange for agreeing to a range of penalties imposed by the CFCB (including strict spending requirements), they would not be banned from UEFA competition. Unfortunately, the club did not keep to those spending limits and were then banned from the Europa League for the 2016/17 season.

Other clubs, including Manchester City, PSG, Monaco and Inter Milan, have all entered into settlement deals (i.e. plea bargains) with the CFCB. As a result, they accepted a number of sanctions, including fines, squad size reductions and future spending restrictions. These sanctions have usually been handed down towards the end of each season.

As an example, what follows are the most important points from the settlement concluded by Manchester City with the CFCB:

1. A maximum loss of €20m for the 2013/14 season and a €10m loss for the 2014/15 season.
2. No more than €60m to be spent on transfers in the 2014/15 summer transfer window.
3. A freeze on players' wages for at least the next season.

4. A limit of 21 players to be registered for their 2014/15 Champions League season squad.

5. A €10m fine based on 2013/14 Champions League prize monies and an additional €10m fine based on their upcoming, 2014/15 Champions League prize monies. An extra €40m fine to be imposed in the event of the club failing to comply with the above conditions.

By 2017, UEFA had set out some revealing statistics demonstrating that their powers had started to move club spending behaviour in the right direction. In their benchmarking report, UEFA explained that combined club operating profits had risen to €600m in 2017, compared with combined losses of €1.7bn in 2011 prior to the introduction of FFP.

Similarly, in the final season before the Premier League cost control rules were introduced (2012/13), 12 of the 20 clubs made a loss, and the Premier League recorded a total overall loss of £291m. By the next season, and once the cost control rules were in place, that loss morphed into a £198 cumulative profit. Subsequently, in the 2014/15 season, Premier League clubs made an overall profit of £113m, and come the 2016/17 season, 18 of the Premier League clubs were making operating profits.

The biggest fine in footballing history

In 2012, the Football League put in place a set of regulations to limit the losses that its member clubs could make. These were called the Profitability and Sustainability regulations. The rules stated that clubs playing in the Football League Championship could not make losses of more than £8m in any one season. The sanctions were either a transfer ban if the club was still in the Football League Championship or a fine if the club had been promoted to the Premier League. The fining guidelines stipulated that, for losses over £10m, any fine would be on a pound-for-pound basis.

During that period, QPR went on a relative spending spree, paying significant transfer fees and wages for high-profile players. In the 2012/13 period alone, the club invested heavily in such players as Christopher Samba, Loïc Rémy, Ji-Sung Park, Júlio César, José Bosingwa and Stéphane Mbia.

In the 2013/14 season, it was reported that QPR posted a loss of almost £70m. Their reported wage bill was £75m – the eighth highest in English football, even though they were in the second tier. It appeared clear that this was more than the £8m permitted under the Football League rules. At the end of that season, they were promoted via the play-offs and under the rules, as they were no longer in the division, the Football League fined QPR.

QPR challenged the fine, raising arguments about the jurisdiction of the Football League and competition law arguments about the actual legality of the rules. In October 2017, three years after the Football League fined QPR, a panel came to the conclusion that the Football League was correct in imposing the fine. QPR stated that they planned to appeal the decision. It was announced in July 2018 that the club had settled its dispute with the Football League. QPR agreed to pay a £17m fine, and to a transfer embargo in the 2019 January transfer window.

Even though the Football League has subsequently changed its rules, the above rules remained in force for the period QPR were in breach. Former QPR chairman, Tony Fernandes, is surprisingly an advocate, despite the fine. In an interview with the *Daily Telegraph* in November 2017, he said: 'I support FFP. When we were in the Premier League mine was the casting vote to bring it in. I think the rules now are much more equitable. We've been spanked on the hand but we'd changed already. We are running now well within every rule, sticking to proper budgets.'

THE CRITICISMS OF FINANCIAL FAIR PLAY

The main argument raised by those opposed to FFP is that it restricts the amount of money owners can spend on player transfers and wages. This means that current, new and/or aspiring owners cannot challenge the established larger clubs with significantly bigger revenues and better players.

Successful clubs will earn more revenue, thus being able to buy better players and likely to be more successful on the pitch, which in turn drives commercial sponsorship as more partners wish to be associated with winning teams. Smaller clubs cannot usually generate short-term revenues in order to fund spending on transfers and player wages, which means, according to critics of FFP, that aspiring clubs are prevented from challenging the established clubs. Inadvertently, the regulations have caused greater inequality from the clubs. As a result, competitive balance (maintaining the uncertainty of results to maximise the attractiveness of the league or competition) is reduced.

UEFA are no doubt concerned about any potential gap between the high-spending clubs and the rest. The difference is that UEFA highlights that clubs spending more than they earn (and therefore risking financial difficulty) is an issue separate from finding longer-term solutions to competitive imbalance.

There have been plenty of legal challenges to the UEFA FFP rules, with a complaint from the European Commission, a reference to the Court of Justice for the EU, and court cases in France, Belgium and at the Court of Arbitration for Sport. All so far have been broadly decided in UEFA's favour.

THIRD-PARTY INVESTMENT

Third-party investment (TPI) in the football industry is now banned by FIFA. This involved the practice where a football club was not entitled to all of the future transfer value of their player.

It's important to understand why TPI was so widespread and the implications for the football industry. It played a large part in assisting some clubs, such as Porto and Atlético Madrid, to achieve on-field sporting success and profitable player trading off-field.

There were numerous models for TPI agreements, but the basic premise was that companies, businesses and individuals provided football clubs or players with money in return for owning a percentage of a player's future transfer value. This transfer value was also commonly referred to as a player's economic rights. Plenty of companies acted as speculators by purchasing a percentage share in a player directly from a club, in return for a lump sum that the club could use as it wished.

Companies also provided financial support for a young, up-and-coming player. This support took the form of meeting housing costs, making monthly payments to the player and his family, and paying training, travelling, equipment and school expenses. In return, the player agreed that the investor was entitled to a percentage of any future transfer fee when the player signed a professional contract with a football club.

These agreements have now been banned under FIFA regulations. The question to consider is how the practice became such a global phenomenon and caused so many issues to various leagues, including UEFA, FIFA, the Premier League and the Football League.

TEVEZGATE

Following the debacle of Tevezgate – or 'Who owned Carlos Tevez's economic rights at West Ham?' – the Premier League, Football League, the FA, various associations and most recently, FIFA put in place rules governing TPI. In a nutshell, it's a no-no. Only clubs can own a player's transfer rights.

But why have the authorities decided accordingly, and why is it so important that third parties do not own a player's economic rights? A brief summary of the case and its fallout follows.

On 31 August, 2006, both Carlos Tevez and Javier Mascherano shocked the football world by moving from Corinthians (a Brazilian team) to West Ham United, despite interest from larger Premier League clubs. The economic rights of Tevez were not owned by either club but instead retained by two companies: Media Sport Investment Ltd (MSI) and Just Sports Inc. The two companies also had the power to force West Ham to accept transfer bids from other clubs for both players.

West Ham submitted the player contract for Tevez to the Premier League, but not the TPI agreements giving transfer control to the companies. Wondering how West Ham had acquired such high-profile players, the Premier League contacted the club. West Ham assured the Premier League that they 'owned all the player rights' of both Tevez and Mascherano, and had registered them on that basis. Only later in the season, on 24 January, 2007, and after a freshly completed takeover of the club, did West Ham disclose the private TPI agreements to the Premier League. The Premier League then decided to refer this alleged breach of their rules to a Disciplinary Commission.

The Commission convened on 26 April, 2007 – two days before West Ham played Wigan in their third-to-last game of the season. It decided to fine West Ham £5.5m, and demanded that the club terminate the TPI agreement in order to retain Tevez for the remainder of the season.

On the basis of factors including West Ham's guilty plea, the closeness to the end of the season and the voluntary disclosure of the TPI agreements, the Commission decided – controversially – against a points deduction, which they stated would 'normally follow from such a breach'. West Ham subsequently contacted Kia Joorabchian, a director of MSI, and terminated their agreement.

This all became increasingly relevant – and even more controversial – as Tevez played a significant role in keeping West Ham from relegation in his last three games for the club. This feat – culminating in the 1–0 victory against Manchester United on the final day of the season, in which Tevez scored the only goal – came at the expense of Sheffield United, who were understandably not best pleased. Sheffield United appealed the Commission's decision, and the panel had sympathy for the club's plight, members even going so far as to say that they would have probably docked West Ham points had they sat on the original panel.

After prolonged legal wrangling, Sheffield United finally settled with West Ham. West Ham were reported to have agreed to pay Sheffield United £15–18m over five years. West Ham retained their Premier League status, though, while Sheffield United stayed in the second tier, albeit a bit richer.

To stop such things from happening again, the FA, the Premier League and the Football League all decided, around 2008, to fine-tune their rules and regulations. In short, they concluded a club must be the sole owner of these rights. The Premier League decided that, from the beginning of the 2008/09 season, an absolute ban on third-party ownership was required. A spokesman stated:

> The clubs decided that third-party ownership was something they did not want to see. It raises too many issues over the integrity of competition, the development of young players and the potential impact on the football pyramid. It was felt the Premier League was in a position to take a stand on this.

At that time, TPI was still common and widespread across much of South America and southern Europe, especially in Spain and Portugal.

THIRD-PARTY INVESTMENT CONCERNS

The FA, the Football League and the Premier League all argued that the transfer system primarily exists as a solidarity mechanism for football. Clubs are compensated for training and developing young players for the top leagues. Anything that undermines that process and diverts transfer market funds away from the grass-roots clubs (i.e. the lower-league clubs) was deemed bad for the game.

As the Premier League spokesman explained (see above), their major concerns related to integrity, young player development and money flowing out of the game. An internal FIFA report concluded that TPI trapped clubs in a 'vicious cycle of debt and dependence' and 'posed risks to players and to the integrity of the game'.

The main concerns about TPI included:

1. Conflicts of interest can occur between investors, club owners, agents and coaches. For example:
    a. The owner of a club also owns a transfer percentage in a player playing against his club. Are his loyalties to his club (to win a game) or to his player (to increase his transfer value)?

b. An agent owns a transfer percentage in a player, assists clubs in identifying players, and is also an advisor of a TPI fund. Does he recommend players he has an interest in?

The authorities were concerned about any possible conflict that might damage the image of, and public confidence in, the game, even leading to concerns about match-fixing or insider trading.

2. Clubs would become reliant on such investment, which in turn would lead to dependence on TPI companies to continue funding such transfers. TPI, so the argument went, encourages short-term profit making, with economic owners looking to the club to sell its players to realise their asset at the expense of on-field sporting concerns. The consequence would be the rapid turnover of TPI players at certain clubs, leading to fans having less connection with the players – and players having less loyalty to the club, knowing they might be transferred when the right offer is received. Clubs would be seen as short-term 'speculation tools', with the result that money left the 'football family'. The counter-argument is that clubs like Porto and Atlético Madrid have enjoyed sporting success during the last decade with the help of TPI companies funding their sporting transfer strategy.

THE ADVANTAGES OF THIRD-PARTY INVESTMENT DEALS

1. Before the Premier League and FIFA bans, such arrangements could supply world-class players worth upwards of £30m to teams that could not otherwise afford them. (Tevez was insured for £30m during his time at West Ham.) It meant that traditionally disadvantaged smaller teams could be galvanised by players who would not look out of place playing for Liverpool, Manchester United or

Barcelona. A growing number of clubs could not compete with the larger commercial and broadcasting deals of the bigger European leagues. Clubs in smaller European leagues, for example, needed to leverage their assets and seek innovative ways to obtain a competitive advantage enabling them to qualify for, say, the Champions League and Europa League.

2. Purchasing players is an inherently risky business. Clubs with less money to spend are usually more risk-averse when having to invest heavily in transfers. One way of reducing such risk is to share the financial burden. TPI contracts help a club with the transfer price for a talented individual or help to keep a player at the club (by paying part of his increased wages). In either event, the club benefits from external finance that cushions the club's position if the player is not a world-beater. Equally, both the club and the fund benefit, if the player is a success, by the receipt of a large transfer fee that is shared according to the contract. So, while the risks are high (the player might not fulfil his potential or might get injured), the potential gains can outweigh such risks.

Many have suggested that regulating TPI through transparency and disclosure obligations is a better alternative than an outright ban. One suggestion, before the ban was brought into force, was that no company should own more than 30% of a player, and that all the contractual details should be available for fans to see. So what's the current state of play with regard to TPI? The current FIFA Rule (Article 18bis) of FIFA's Rules on the Status and Transfer of Players states that:

No club shall enter into a contract which enables any other party to that contract or any third party to acquire the ability to influence in employment and transfer-related matters its independence, its policies or the performance of its teams.

This was not a specific ban on TPI but a ban on third parties from influencing a club's employment or transfer-related matters.

From 2014 onwards, UEFA and FIFA made a number of public statements concerning their aim to outlaw TPI. FIFA's then president Sepp Blatter explained: 'We took a firm decision that [TPI] should be banned but it cannot be banned immediately; there will be a transitional period.' FIFA then set up a working group to address the topic of TPI. So it came as a surprise to many that in late December 2014, while the working group was still debating several possibilities, FIFA announced that they were to ban TPI globally.

The ban came into force in May 2015, and agreements entered into from 1 January, 2015 could be only one year in length. This meant no new TPI contracts could be entered into.

Nonetheless, existing third-party contracts were allowed to continue until expiry, and in the following seasons some players have still been subject to TPI contracts. With each transfer window that passes, there are fewer and fewer TPI contracts as more expire or are bought out.

In 2007 the FA outlawed third-party ownership, since when any player registered to play in the Premier League or Football League cannot be owned by a TPI company. Both leagues banned such a practice after Tevezgate and then FIFA followed their lead. This meant that clubs had to show the Premier League and/or Football League that a player part-owned by a TPI company had been totally bought out by the club before they could be registered. This has occurred over various seasons with TPI players such as Marković, who transferred to Liverpool for over £20m, and Mangala, who transferred to Manchester City for over £31m.

Since the ban has come into force, a number of clubs have been sanctioned by FIFA:

- Belgian club Seraing United received a two-year player registration ban and a £120,000 fine.
- Club FC Twente of the Netherlands were fined 185,000 Swiss francs. The Royal Dutch Football Association had already banned

the club from European competition for three years after failing to reveal full details of a TPI contract with company Doyen Sports Investments.

• Santos of Brazil was sanctioned with a fine of 75,000 Swiss francs.

• Sevilla FC of Spain was sanctioned with a fine of 55,000 Swiss francs.

• Sint-Truidense VV of Belgium was sanctioned with a fine of 60,000 Swiss francs.

HOW PORTO USED THIRD-PARTY INVESTMENT TO ITS ADVANTAGE

In recent years, there have been exceptional managers at FC Porto, including José Mourinho and André Villas-Boas, but most football analysts point to its transfer policy as one of the key components for its continued league, cup and European success. Such a transfer formula is no secret. The club buys talented and relatively untested players (mostly from South America), bloods them in European competition, and after a number of good seasons shares the profit of a multi-million-euro transfer with its co-investors.

The old 'buy cheap, sell expensive' formula includes a twist. Porto usually bought only a share of a player's economic rights, leaving the rest to TPI owners. This made the acquisition cost even lower and minimised the risk of an expensive transfer mistake. Contracts with such third parties included clauses that allowed clubs such as Porto to increase their share in the player's rights at given times and for pre-agreed amounts. This enabled a club to raise its share in the player's economic rights after he had established his worth in Europe.

At the extreme end of the transfer spectrum, Real Zaragoza, a club in administration a few years ago, bought goalkeeper Roberto from Benfica, paying only a reported €86,000. The total transfer fee was €8.5m. In real financial difficulty, the club were almost totally subsidised by private third-party economic owners.

OVERSEAS PLAYERS AND WORK PERMITS

Just as in any other industry, players who come to play in the Premier League or Football League from around the world have to comply with immigration and employment law. At present, it is relatively straightforward for an EU player to join a Premier League/Football League club since the player can take advantage of the EU principle of freedom of movement. This, of course, may change depending on the outcome of the Brexit negotiations.

If a player from outside the European Economic Area (EEA) or EU wishes to play in the Premier League/Football League, a club must apply to the Football Association for an 'endorsement' for a work permit so that the Home Office can authorise the player to play for the club.

THE WORK PERMIT SYSTEM

Previously, in order to qualify to play in the UK, non-EU/EEA football players needed to have played in at least 75% of their country's senior international matches over the previous two years. There was an appeals process for players who didn't reach that target. Players must also have played for a country ranked by FIFA in the top 70 (averaged over two years).

Those rules no longer apply. The country must now rank in the top 50, and eligibility is determined according to a national team's ranking, as set out in the table below.

Official FIFA Ranking	Required percentage of international matches over previous 24 months
FIFA 1–10	30% and above
FIFA 11–20	45% and above
FIFA 21–30	60% and above
FIFA 31–50	75% and above

By way of example, let's compare a player from Brazil with a player from Turkey. Brazil is currently ranked within the FIFA top 10, so to qualify automatically for a work permit to play in the Premier League, a Brazilian player is only required to play a minimum of 30% of national team matches over the last two years. At the time of writing, Turkey is ranked 26, meaning a Turkish player would be required to play in 60% of matches over the last two years.

The two-year period is reduced to one year for players aged 21 or under at the time of application, making it potentially easier for young, outstanding talent to avoid being disadvantaged. A player can still appeal if initially rejected. If the above criteria are not met, the player can ask the Exceptions Panel to consider whether the player should be allowed to join the club, given his experience and value.

The appeals process is a points-based system under which the panel will award points depending on the circumstances of the transfer. If a player scores four points or more, the panel may recommend that the application is granted. However, the panel can still reject the application even if four or more points are scored. The most important criteria are set out below.

Criteria	Points
The value of the transfer fee being paid for the player is in the top 25% of all transfers to Premier League clubs in the previous two windows	3 points
The value of the transfer fee being paid for the player is between 50% and 75% of all transfers to Premier League clubs in the previous two windows	2 points
The wages being paid to the player by the applicant club are in the top 25% of the top 30 earners at the club	3 points
The wages being paid to the player by the applicant club are between 50% and 75% of all the top 30 earners at the club	2 points

If the player does not meet the above points-based system, there remains a second test that is more flexible. The panel can, for example, take into account the following circumstances:

- No transfer fee is payable – perhaps because the player has reached the end of his contract.

- Further arguments beyond the control of the player or national association – for example, a long-term injury or suspension that has prevented the player from appearing in the national team.

Clubs will not only be looking carefully at the type of player required to bolster their squad, but they may now find it more difficult to receive work permits for prospective targets. Under the old rules, when an initial work permit application was rejected, there was a high probability of success on appeal. Now, clubs need to consider the likelihood of targets satisfying the new automatic criteria.

The FA estimates that 33% of the players who gained entry under the old system would not have been granted a work permit under the new rules. Over the last five years, that means there would have been 42 fewer non-European players playing in the Premier League and Football League.

While this is true, it is worth remembering that the FA can do nothing to stop European players from playing in the Premier League or Football League because EU law means that the FA cannot discriminate on the basis of nationality. Brexit should make it easier to restrict the number of European footballers wanting to play in the Premier League and Football League.

THE HOMEGROWN PLAYER RULE

The UEFA Homegrown Player Rule (HGPR) was introduced for the 2006/07 season and requires each team entering European competitions to name eight homegrown players (HGPs) in their 25-man squad.

Similarly, Premier League clubs submit a squad of 25 players to the Premier League after the transfer window has closed. Those players will then be eligible to compete in that season's competition. Changes to the list can only be made in the January transfer window unless special permission is granted.

The Premier League introduced its own HGPR in time for the start of the 2010/11 season. The Football League has similar regulations. There is an important distinction between the rules, however. The UEFA HGPR states that four of the designated squad players have to be 'club-trained' and four must also be 'association-trained'. A club-trained player is a player who, regardless of where he was born, is registered between the ages of 15 and 21 with his current club for a period of three entire seasons or 36 months. An 'association-trained' player is similarly defined but trained with another club in the same association. The Premier League and Football League HGPRs do not distinguish between association- and club-trained, meaning 'homegrown' is defined as anyone registered with the English or Welsh Football Associations for three seasons or 36 months before a player's 21st birthday. All the rules permit an unlimited number of players under the age of 21 (regardless of nationality) to supplement each 25-man squad.

Importantly, there is no UEFA or Premier League restriction on how many HGPs must be selected in any starting team. Indeed, it would be possible for no HGPs to be in the match-day squad of 18 (i.e. 17 non-HGPs and one foreign-born under-21 player). On Boxing Day 1999, Chelsea became the first English club to field a starting 11 without a single British player. Now, almost 20 years later, this is commonplace.

The rules mean that players may be more attractive because they can qualify as a HGP for the relevant Premier League, Football League and UEFA squad lists, meaning that they may attract a transfer fee premium. When a club does not fill their HGP squad quota, this reduces the squad number that can be submitted. For example, Manchester City named only 20 senior players in their 2016/17 squad, and only four HGPs. (Players like Iheanacho, before he was sold, and Sané made the list in any event because an unlimited number of under-21 players can supplement the senior squad list.)

The HGPR and the Premier League squad list system made the headlines when Crystal Palace defender Florian Marange was unhappy not to be included in Crystal Palace's 25-man list because he was not a HGP. Marange left the club without making a single appearance. Individuals who do not 'make the cut' for the squad list and do not qualify as an under-21 player are significantly constrained in the number of appearances they can make until January, when clubs resubmit their squad lists after the transfer window shuts.

THE PRACTICAL EFFECTS OF THE HOMEGROWN PLAYER RULE

Cesc Fàbregas was born in Spain and plays for the national team. However, he qualified as an English HGP because he trained at Arsenal. Interestingly, when he moved to Barcelona, he was not classed as an HGP in the Barcelona squad submission to UEFA. Training with Arsenal during the relevant qualification period meant that under the UEFA HGPR he was English home-grown.

Similarly, when the Argentine player Érik Lamela was left out of the Spurs Champions League group stage squad in the 2017/18 season, it was reported that the quirks of the UEFA HGPR were at play:

- England international Eric Dier did not count as homegrown because he trained with Sporting Lisbon in Portugal and was effectively homegrown Portuguese. As a result, Dier took up one of the 17 places in the 25-man squad allocated to non-locally trained players.
- Left-back Ben Davies trained at Swansea City, who come under the jurisdiction of the FA of Wales, rather than the English FA. As Wales and England form part of two different associations, Davies could not claim that he had been 'registered with a club or with other clubs affiliated to the same association as that of his current club for a period, continuous or not, of three entire seasons or of 36 months' between the ages of 15 and 21. He was therefore classed as non-locally trained, and took up another of the 17 places in the team's 25-man squad. (Just to confuse matters, Davies *was* classed as homegrown under the Premier League squad rules.)
- Lastly, in the Premier League rules, a club can have an unlimited number of under-21 players to supplement the 25-man squad list. This is almost the same under the UEFA

rules, but those rules state that under-21 players must have been 'eligible to play for the club concerned for any uninterrupted period of two years since his 15th birthday by the time he is registered with Uefa'. It meant that Spurs' 2017 summer signings – Dávinson Sánchez, a £42m buy from Ajax, and Juan Foyth – did not count in Champions League competition for Spurs as under-21 players because they had not been training at the club for two years.

As a result, Spurs manager Mauricio Pochettino had to name all four players as non-homegrown, leaving the £30m Lamela to be omitted from the squad list. He was rather baffled: 'It's unbelievable that Eric Dier is not homegrown when he's playing for England. That is so strange, no?'

THE RATIONALE FOR THE HOMEGROWN PLAYER RULE

The HGPR was justified by UEFA as, among other things, a way of encouraging youth development and competitive balance. Creating a talented youth development structure could, it was argued, increase opportunities for domestic, young players to play in the first team and save clubs significant transfer fees or provide transfer fees when one of a club's star players is subsequently sold. Similarly, competitive balance (i.e. better competition between teams) is increased because the 25-man squad size allows only a certain number of established players to be registered for a particular competition. This has the additional effect of preventing the wealthiest clubs from hoarding the most talented players.

THE IMPACT OF THE HOMEGROWN PLAYER RULE

Some in the media embraced the HGPR, believing it offered the potential benefit of strengthening the chances of a country's national team. As the rule is not based on nationality, the logic for this argument is somewhat unclear. The basic idea is that players trained in a particular country are more likely to be able to represent that country internationally. However, the unintended side effect of the HGPR has been to encourage clubs to recruit even younger players from across the globe so that they subsequently qualify as a HGP. This may then mean there is less opportunity for domestically born youth players to play for their country. At present, however, this does not seem to be borne out. Statistics from the Premier League reveal that:

- 96% of boys registered at Premier League Academies (that is, aged 8–18) are British; *and*
- 90% of 16–18 year old boys at the Premier League Academies are British.

A question follows from this: why do so few domestic players look abroad for footballing opportunities? UK players may need to broaden their horizons and seek opportunity beyond the UK, which could in turn lead to a stronger, broader talent pool for the national team. Players like Jadon Sancho (Dortmund), Jonathan Panzo (Monaco) and Keanan Bennetts (Mönchengladbach) are showing that opportunities are available at elite European clubs for young British talent. Depending on the terms of any Brexit agreement, however, such opportunities across Europe may become more limited.

> 'UK-based players are faced with a tough choice. They can take a financial risk, and hope that moving to Europe translates to more minutes on the pitch (which is not guaranteed) or stay in the UK and fight for minutes, but with a higher and more stable salary. Another factor to consider is that often a player at a lower-end League 1 or top League 2 side can earn more than a player at a top Segunda or Ligue 2 side, so that players aren't as attractive to French or Spanish clubs, who could get a more experienced player, playing at a higher level of club, for less money. The financial imbalance makes it risky for both player and club when considering UK players moving abroad.'
>
> Nick Robinson, International Sports Consulting

BREXIT AND ITS IMPACT ON OVERSEAS PLAYERS

The UK's vote in the summer of 2016 to leave the EU has a number of consequences relating to work permits and free movement for football players.

The doomsday scenario suggested by some is that Brexit will result in a host of players failing to meet the current non-EU work permit criteria. Technically, this observation is true, but it sidesteps the point that the work permit principles currently applied to non-EU workers are unlikely to similarly apply to EU workers post-Brexit.

It's also highly unlikely that any EU players on existing Premier League contracts will suddenly be deported. Not only is it improbable that such working restrictions would be applied retrospectively, but practically it may take two years (and probably longer) to iron out the intricacies of Britain's new relationship with Europe.

The EU is certainly not incentivised to make the transition as smooth as possible. Quite the opposite; a rigorous, difficult and drawn-out negotiation would be a deterrent to other member states. However, even this is not a straight play-off between two of the biggest issues – tariffs versus free movement – though it does set the scene for the highly complex negotiations that will ensue. Believing that the current work permit rules which apply to non-EEA players wanting to play in the UK will similarly apply to European players is simply that – a belief. If the UK government's priority is to benefit from tariff-free trade within the EEA, free movement concessions from the UK government appear inevitable.

It may be that a tiered approach is likely. The strongest restrictions will continue for non-EU players. Perhaps a second, midway category will be applied, where EEA players will be in a more privileged position because of the concessions made by the UK government. The third category will be UK-born players, who will be in the most favoured category because of the ease with which they can be employed by clubs. However, in due course, a major overhaul of the work permit regulations for EEA players will be required.

An important additional point to consider is the FIFA Regulations on the Status and Transfer of Players. Specifically, Article 19, which limits the movements of players under 18 but permits transfers of minors between the ages of 16 and 18 if the transfer takes place within the territory of the European Union (EU) or European Economic Area (EEA). If Britain is no longer in the EU, it would be unlikely to benefit from this exception. Players like Fàbregas and Piqué, who came to the UK because Arsenal and Manchester United were able to take advantage of this rule, would not be in such a privileged position.

QUOTAS AND THE HOMEGROWN PLAYER RULE

If the UK leaves the EU (and is thus not bound by EU law involving nationality discrimination) nationality quotas may be reintroduced.

Currently, a fundamental EU principle is that discrimination on the grounds of nationality is not allowed. Some believe that discriminating against non-UK nationals – by quotas, for example – will help promote the national team by exposing more English players to top-level football. Premier League clubs will certainly not want to be restricted, because this will reduce the ease of recruiting top-class foreign players.

There was a proposal, driven by FIFA and first discussed in 1999, to impose a 6 + 5 rule. That would have required at least six domestic-born players to be in a match-day team, and a maximum of five foreign-born players. The proposal was shot down in 2010, in part after liaising with the EU, because of concerns that such regulations would have been illegal. Post-Brexit, however, it will remain politically difficult for the FA to impose nationality restrictions on the Premier League and Football League, but it could implement such regulations across its own FA Cup competition.

The previous political compromise between UEFA and the EU was the HGPR. The rule was drafted in such a way that it did not directly discriminate on the basis of nationality (i.e. where a player was born) but rather on where a player trained between the ages of 15 and 21. An unintended consequence was that it encouraged foreign players to play and be recruited into leagues and academies at a younger age. This had the side effect of displacing young, UK-born players so that 'foreigners' could meet the homegrown criteria. In theory, discrimination on the grounds of nationality could occur post-Brexit. Again, this seems unlikely given the political compromises needed to enable the UK to benefit from tariff-free or limited-tariff trade, which would otherwise harm UK exports.

THE IMPACT ON FREE TRANSFERS

The knock-on impact for the UK of no longer being bound by the judgements of the European Court is that some rulings may no longer apply. An obvious example is the Bosman ruling (*see* page 42), based on freedom of movement at the end of a player's contract. This will to some extent depend on the legal relationship that is established between the UK government and the EU post-Brexit.

Interestingly, EU law may still apply to a transfer if there is an appreciable impact within the EU (for example, a transfer involving a citizen of a member state in or out of the UK). In any event, the Bosman free transfer principles have already been applied to purely domestic situations, which do not involve issues of EU jurisdiction, including Campbell to Arsenal, Ings and McAllister to Liverpool, and Sturridge to Chelsea. It is therefore unlikely that the FA, Premier League or UK government will rush to impose additional restrictions on the free movement of its citizens or workers employed in the UK, with the effect of prohibiting a player's movement at the end of his contract.

FOCUSED ON FINANCE

The footballing landscape changed dramatically with the implementation of UEFA's FFP rules. It meant that clubs playing in UEFA competition had to adhere to relatively strict spending limits. After a number of high-profile cases where clubs were sanctioned, clubs across Europe realised that UEFA meant business. National leagues then set about introducing their own rules to regulate domestic spending. Since the implementation of the spending rules, club losses have decreased significantly. UEFA argues that the rules have improved the long-term health of the game, ensuring fewer clubs get into financial difficulty in the years to come.

Football clubs are at the very heart of the global game. They employ the players; compete in leagues and cup competitions; sell their lucrative broadcasting rights, either individually or collectively; enter into a vast array of brand, merchandising and commercial arrangements; and cater for the needs of their fans.

Business people will continue to buy and invest in clubs, and companies remain keen to align with clubs. While fans keep watching and broadcasters keep paying, clubs will continue to be attractive businesses for billionaires from across the globe.

CHAPTER 5

YOUTH DEVELOPMENT

Manchester United had just lost 3–1 to Aston Villa on the opening day of the 1995/96 season. Alan Hansen, the ex-Liverpool player and *Match of the Day* pundit, was stinging in his criticism: 'You can't win anything with kids.' There had been a major transition in the team that summer. Established stars like Paul Ince, Mark Hughes and Andrei Kanchelskis had been sold, and no replacements had been bought. The team on that opening day did depend on a handful of kids: David Beckham, Nicky Butt, Ryan Giggs, Paul Scholes, and brothers Gary and Phil Neville. Far from that being the end of an era, those academy players became the backbone of the team's success, going on to win the Premier League and FA Cup double that very season, and in 1999 the treble (Premier League, FA Cup and Champions League).

Kids have been essential for other clubs too. On the south coast, Southampton were put into administration, docked points and relegated to League One at the end of the 2008/09 season. A huge rebuilding job followed, putting major emphasis on youth development and the promotion of young players into the first team squad. This may have been in part because of the lack of money available to balance the books in the early years following administration. The Lieber family (then owners), along with Les Reed (vice-chairman and head of football development), were at the forefront of the turnaround. An incredibly impressive set of home-grown talent has trained and transferred from the club, including Gareth Bale, transferred to Real Madrid from Spurs for a then world record €100m; Alex Oxlade-Chamberlain, transferred to Liverpool from Arsenal for £35m after Arsenal paid Southampton £15m; Calum Chambers, bought by Arsenal from Southampton for £20m; Adam Lallana, bought by Liverpool from Southampton for £25m; and Luke Shaw, bought by Manchester United from Southampton for £27m.

Apart from the real benefit of having a raft of high-quality youngsters challenging at a young age for first team appearances, the financial upside is that Southampton received large transfer fees to compensate for the loss of the players they had trained. These sums were used to improve the training facilities and also reinvested into the first team squad. From the brink of bankruptcy in 2009, the club have implemented a youth development strategy and invested in an infrastructure overhaul that is the envy of many. Particularly famous is their 'black box', a live database that is fed by a range of analysts and which allows the club to monitor the progress of their own players and potential players and managers at other clubs.

In recent years, youth development has hit the headlines, partly after the introduction of the Elite Player Performance Plan (EPPP; *see* below). Brentford had their fingers burned when larger clubs signed two of their rising stars. Under-16 player Ian Carlo Poveda signed for Manchester City after two years with the club. Soon after, Joshua Bohui, an under-17 England international, was signed by Manchester United. By the terms of the EPPP, Brentford received set compensation rather than a transfer fee, and City and United were reported to have paid around £30,000 each.

Until a player signs a professional employment contract with a club when he turns 17, a club have limited financial protection (*see* below). Having been burned, Brentford came to the conclusion that an academy training and developing players from the ages of eight through to 16 was not financially viable – especially if the club could not protect their players from being signed by other larger clubs for a fraction of their market worth. They shut their academy, saving £1.5m in the process, and created a B team of players released from other elite clubs, happy to move to Brentford for a second chance.

THE ELITE PLAYER PERFORMANCE PLAN

The EPPP was introduced in 2012 and was a combined plan between the FA, Premier League and Football League to develop a stronger set of home-grown players. It works across three levels: Foundation, under-nine to under-11; Youth Development, under-12 to under-16; and Professional Development, under-17 to under-21. Clubs are categorised from 1 to 4, depending on a number of set criteria.

Previously, a club had not been able to sign youth players under the age of 18 from outside their local area – a catchment area defined as a 90-minute drive. That restriction ended when the new EPPP rules came in. Larger clubs can now target players from across the country. To ensure that clubs receive compensation for training, there are set compensation amounts that have to be paid by the new club when registered players move to another academy.

The compensation to be paid depends on the category of the club at which the player trained. For any child aged between nine and 11, there is a fixed fee of £3,000 to pay per year. This amount then rises considerably. Compensation for a player over 12 who plays for a Category 1 club is £40,000 for every year at the club. For Category 2 academies, that drops to £25,000 per year, and for Category 3, the fee is £12,500.

There have, however, been a number of reports about young kids who have been priced out of moving to another club, because the new academy either won't pay or can't pay the compensation required to register the player. Suppose that parents move to another city, and their 14-year-old child was at a Category 1 club. Any new club wanting to sign the player will have to pay a potentially huge sum of money. This leaves young players in limbo, and raises serious doubts about whether parents are fully aware of the terms of the contract they sign on behalf of their child.

In one reported situation, a boy who trained at a Category 1 club between the ages of nine and 10 decided to leave. When he wanted to join the youth academy of a Category 2 club some time later, his family found out that it would cost the new club £6,000 to 'sign' an 11-year-old. The new club couldn't afford the fee.

SCHOLARSHIP AGREEMENTS

A player can also be signed when he turns 16, by signing a scholarship agreement with their club. This is a two-year deal.

In practice, it is possible to sign a professional deal when a player turns 17. So, for a number of elite players, clubs will ensure that the player signs a professional deal at 17, which can be for a maximum of three years. This then removes that player from the EPPP system, and makes him subject to a transfer fee, should the player leave the club while under contract.

CLUB BANS OVER YOUTH RECRUITMENT

Over the last few years, a range of top clubs in the Premier League and La Liga – including Barcelona, Real Madrid, Atlético Madrid, Manchester City and Liverpool – have all fallen foul of the rules governing youth development transfers.

1. In April 2017, Liverpool were fined and banned from signing any academy players from English league clubs for two years after being found guilty of offering incentives to a Stoke City youth player to persuade him to join the club; they had paid for him and his family to attend a game and offered private education.
2. In May 2017, Manchester City were fined £300k and banned for two years from signing academy players registered with another Premier League or Football League club in the previous 18 months.
3. Barcelona were hit with a transfer embargo by FIFA for two transfer windows: the 2015 January and summer windows. Under the FIFA rules on under-18 players moving between countries, a player is allowed to move if, for example, their parents move to a new country for non-footballing reasons. FIFA concluded that Barcelona's recruitment of 10 youth players breached its rules.
4. FIFA imposed a one-year transfer ban in 2017 on Real Madrid for signing young players outside of Spain.

5. Atlético Madrid were also banned for buying any players in the two transfer windows in 2017. FIFA explained that the rules were in place to 'protect minors who move to other countries and prevent soccer clubs from exploiting them'.

Wait . . . what about a player who is out of contract? Can't he move on a free?

When an under-24 player in the Premier League or Football League is out of contract and moves to another Premier League or Football League club, the player's previous club will be entitled to compensation. Usually the Bosman rule means that any out-of-contract player can move without a transfer fee being paid, but in order to incentivise clubs to train players and invest in their development, a compensation fee is payable if the player moves 'domestically'. This fee is set by an independent tribunal called the Professional Football Compensation Committee (PFCC).

As explained in the player transfers chapter, when the out-of-contract Daniel Sturridge moved to Chelsea from Manchester City, Chelsea were ordered by the PFCC to pay £3.5m up front and a fee rising to £6.5m once he played for England and started a certain number of games. When Sturridge subsequently moved to Liverpool, Manchester City also received 15% of the £12m transfer fee in January 2013. More recently, Liverpool were ordered to pay an initial £6.5m to Burnley after Danny Ings joined the club in 2015. Burnley were also awarded 20% of any profit that Liverpool would receive if Ings were subsequently sold.

CALCULATING PROFESSIONAL FOOTBALL COMPENSATION

When deciding whether compensation is due, the PFCC will take into account a number of factors:

- the status of the buying and selling clubs;
- the age of the player;

- the length of time during which the selling club trained the player;
- the terms of any new contract offered to him by both the buying and selling clubs;
- his playing record, including any international appearances; *and*
- any interest shown by other clubs in acquiring the player.

So, for example, an 18-year-old transferring between two Premier League clubs, who has trained at the Premier League club for five years but has never played a Premier League game (despite starting a recent under-19 England game), is likely to be valued at a lower level on the PFCC compensation scale than a 23-year-old England international who has started 50 Premier League games, is on a weekly salary of £70,000 and for whom, a year earlier, a Premier League team bid £25m.

It is clear that the first player has great potential but the reality is that he is not currently at elite Premier League level. It would therefore be unlikely for the PFCC to award significant initial compensation. Rather, their sensible past practice has been to backload any potential compensation award with a small compensation award and higher performance-related payments (according to the number of Premier League and international appearances) alongside a sell-on fee in the event that the player is sold at a profit at any point in the future.

By contrast, the PFCC compensation for the out-of-contract 23-year-old England international earning £70,000 would probably be even higher than the amount Liverpool had to pay for Ings in the example above.

Ethan Ampadu joined Chelsea from League Two Exeter City in the summer of 2017. A tribunal settled the fee at a minimum of £1.3m, with the potential to rise to £2.5m depending upon appearances and a share of the sell-on fee. The potential fee would be a record for Exeter, but their chairman, Julian Tagg, expressed his disappointment: 'We feel this decision sends the wrong message in terms of financial rewards for those owners, chairmen, managers and coaches up and down the country who are also working as hard as us to improve their clubs by producing talented homegrown players for both club and country.'

A DIFFICULT BALANCING ACT

Clubs spend millions of pounds per year on youth development. The aim is to produce players for the first team, or otherwise to sell to larger clubs for significant sums. The question remains: are the regulations to the benefit of the players? If, by their early teens, they wish to move to another club, the financial compensation a new club may have to offer may be too large. Similarly, clubs need to know that the players they have invested in for years cannot move to another club without some compensation being payable. Transfer fees can now run into the tens of millions, so the most exciting teenagers (15- or 16-year-olds) may attract the attention of clubs throughout the world. There is a difficult balancing act for the relevant authorities to safeguard the interests of players and clubs alike.

CHAPTER 6

MANAGERS

The sight of one of the most high-profile football managers in the world climbing out of a laundry basket inside their dressing room was probably not what Chelsea players expected at half-time during a vital Champions League quarter-final match against Bayern Munich in 2005. José Mourinho had been banned by UEFA from entering the stadium after criticising the performance of Anders Frisk during the previous Champions League game against Barcelona. He was even branded by Volker Roth, head of UEFA's referee committee, 'an enemy of football'.

Mourinho's reported example shows the lengths that managers will go to, to get their instructions across. The pressure to deliver success at Europe's top clubs is monumental and any marginal improvements in tactical or motivational instructions can have a significant impact.

This pressure also manifests in a managerial merry-go-round, with club chairmen, owners and directors requiring on-field success for very different reasons. Some clubs like Chelsea will demand success at the highest level, with the team competing for the Premier League and Champions League titles on a regular basis. Since the Abramovich era, the club has frequently changed managers: Mourinho, Scolari, Hiddink, Ancelotti, Villas-Boas, Benítez, Di Matteo and Conte have all been recruited in their quest for silverware. Almost all of these managers did not last longer than two seasons, but the model has been hugely successful for Chelsea. Indeed, short-term managers have become the general rule.

Sir Alex Ferguson's 27 years in charge at Manchester United were hugely successful, but since his departure the club have since changed managers frequently, Moyes, van Gaal and Mourinho all arriving within the space of a few years. After Sir Alex, the Premier League's longest-serving manager was Arsenal's Arsène Wenger – by some distance. But at the end of the 2017/18 season, he too stepped down, which brought 22 years in charge to an end. With Wenger's departure, Eddie Howe became the longest-serving manager in the Premier League, having been in charge of Bournemouth for less than six years.

The pressure on a manager for success, from fans and owners alike, can be overwhelming, whether the requirement is for silverware and Champions League football (at a bare minimum), or for remaining in the Premier League. Teams that are underperforming (at the top or bottom of the league) may decide that another manager should take control and improve performance. This can lead clubs to sack their managers on a regular basis.

There have been various studies looking into whether a change of manager improves performance. Recent evidence suggests a positive benefit, or 'bounce', from changing a manager when things aren't going well. Whether this trend will continue into the future is another matter. A 2017 study by Sky Sports looked at managerial changes for a team in the bottom half of the Premier League, starting after Christmas 1992. Until February 2015, there were 38 changes made – and only 13 led to an improved league position. After February 2015, there were 10 changes, eight of which had led to an improved league position.

The churn rate is only increasing. The average lifespan for a manager in the professional game in England in 2017 was just over one year. In fact, when Warren Joyce was sacked by Wigan Athletic on 13 March, 2017, after just four months in charge, it was calculated that about one-quarter (26%) of clubs in England's top four divisions (24 of 92) had changed their manager in the last 100 days. Almost 60% of all managers only ever get one Premier League job, and out of 210 managers since 1992, only 85 got a second role. The insecurity of the role is considered a symptom of the short-term pressures facing clubs and managers alike.

The table below shows the managers who have managed the most Premier League clubs (the figures are correct up to the end of the 2017/18 season).

Manager	Number of Premier League teams managed	Teams
Sam Allardyce	Seven	Bolton Wanderers, West Ham United, Blackburn Rovers, Sunderland, Crystal Palace, Newcastle United and Everton
Alan Pardew	Seven	Reading, West Ham United, Charlton Athletic, Southampton, Newcastle United, Crystal Palace and West Bromwich Albion
Mark Hughes	Six	Stoke City, Blackburn Rovers, Manchester City, Fulham, Queens Park Rangers and Southampton
Harry Redknapp	Five	West Ham United, Portsmouth, Tottenham Hotspur, Queens Park Rangers and Southampton
Roy Hodgson	Five	Crystal Palace, Blackburn Rovers, Fulham, Liverpool and West Bromwich Albion

By the end of the 2017/18 season, David Moyes, Graeme Souness, Ron Atkinson and Steve Bruce had all managed four Premier League teams apiece.

UEFA's benchmarking report for 2015/16 highlighted the reality for managers employed in the top five European leagues (the Premier League, France, Spain, Germany and Italy). Across the five leagues, the percentage of clubs sacking their manager during the season was almost 50%. In the Premier League it was 40%, with Italy at 65%, France at 25%, Germany 56% and Spain at 50%.

The shortest Premier League managerial reigns

Terry Connor, Wolverhampton Wanderers – 13 games
René Meulensteen, Fulham – 13 games
Paolo Di Canio, Sunderland – 12 games
Iain Dowie, Charlton Athletic – 12 games
Chris Hutchings, Bradford City – 12 games
Chris Hutchings, Wigan Athletic – 12 games
Jacques Santini, Tottenham Hotspur – 11 games
Sammy Lee, Bolton Wanderers – 11 games
Bob Bradley, Swansea City – 11 games
Paul Sturrock, Southampton – 9 games
Les Reed, Charlton Athletic – 7 games
Steve Coppell, Manchester City – 6 games
Frank de Boer, Crystal Palace – 4 games

Source: The *Daily Telegraph*

Managers can be in a perilous and precarious position. Success is measured in on-field results. A bad run pulling a team into a relegation dogfight may mean a premature end to even a long-term contract. Similarly, a manager whose elite team is not challenging for Premier League and Champions League titles may not be living up to the owner's high expectations. In either case, the performance of a team has significant financial consequences. Under-perform and, for many clubs, relegation beckons. As a result, many club owners will quickly change manager and identify a particular manager with a track record of keeping clubs in the Premier League. Managers like Allardyce (Bolton, Sunderland, Crystal Palace and Everton), Tony Pulis (Stoke, Crystal Palace and West Brom) and Hodgson (Fulham, Crystal Palace and West Brom) have all developed stellar reputations for keeping clubs in the Premier League.

Given that there are no transfer windows for managers, sackings and appointments happen on a regular basis throughout the season. A team that has a bad start to the season may install a new manager by the autumn. Alternatively, towards the end of a season, when a club may be battling relegation with just a few games to go, an owner may gamble that a new manager can inspire a bounce from the players to avoid relegation. Some have suggested that a managerial transfer window be put in place, suggesting that this would slow down the managerial merry-go-round.

'Clubs have departments dedicated to player recruitment; the top teams employ dozens of scouts and analysts in order to try and identify the next big hit for their team. Despite this, close to 50% of transfers fail, if you measure success by the utilisation of new signings. Now consider how little time and resource clubs dedicate to head coach hire, and you realise why so few managers make it into their third year in the job.

Our models suggest that the most a key player in a team will add above a typical squad player is five points per season. This is pretty substantial – but the same analysis suggests that a leading manager can be worth double that. The trouble is, it can often be hard to identify who the good managers are; their influence is less visible than the players'. Proper surveillance – evaluating and comparing, across leagues, the relative change in performance of clubs under different managers, and assessing their suitability for your club – can mitigate this risk, but so few clubs do it.'

Omar Chaudhuri, 21 Club

THE MANAGER'S CONTRACT

When the inevitable managerial change comes, it can be at a significant cost, involving large payouts to sacked managers. This will usually be the remaining value of the contract. Ex-Chelsea and Tottenham manager Villas-Boas was reported to have been given a £12m payout when his contract was terminated by Chelsea. Previously, the club had paid £28m to his predecessor Carlo Ancelotti, and to Porto by way of compensation for luring Villas-Boas away. According to ESPN, another managerial casualty at Stamford Bridge, Roberto Di Matteo, was still being paid £130,000 a week a year after leaving the club. Similarly, Roberto Martínez was reported to have been paid around £10m when sacked by Everton.

In recent years, contracts have become more nuanced. The sacking by Manchester United of David Moyes in 2014, one year into his six-year deal, illustrates a more flexible approach. As reported at the time, his contract had been 'failure proofed', allowing the club to sack Moyes without paying him the remaining five years of his contract. There was a clause that defined the amount of compensation to be paid if Manchester United did not qualify for the Champions League. The club later confirmed that Moyes and his backroom staff were compensated to the tune of 'single-digit million pounds' – revealed to be £5.2m in the club's accounts published later in 2014. Therefore, even though the remaining value of his contract may have been £25m, the club ensured that the payout was nowhere near that amount if minimum performance levels were not met.

The trend towards performance-based termination provisions in a manager contract is likely to continue. Managers are likely to accept these if provisions are also made for exceeding expectations, which should trigger an automatic salary review. Typically, bonuses will be awarded for winning cup competitions, qualifying for the Champions League or avoiding relegation. Managers and their wider backroom staff can be awarded millions of pounds for keeping a team in the Premier League. One example that is set out in more detail below (*see* page 151) relates to Tony Pulis. For keeping Crystal Palace in the Premier League, he was awarded a bonus of £2m.

When replacing managers, some clubs will want to approach another club to recruit its current manager. It is now becoming more common for managers, like players, to have release clauses that allow them to speak to any club that matches the specific amount in the release clause. This was reported to be the case with Spurs and Chelsea, who paid Southampton and Porto respectively for their managers Pochettino and Villas-Boas.

There are also a number of restrictions that clubs will almost certainly wish to include in any contract to offer as much protection as possible. In the event that relationships between the owner/club and manager become strained, there are 'gardening leave' provisions – which can sometimes be up to 12 months in length but are normally around six months. Gardening leave provides the option to the club of removing the manager but stopping him from joining another team. Every managerial contract is different, and though such provisions are common, there are wide disparities between different clubs and their manager.

The intention of gardening leave is to delay the manager's move, thereby preventing a rival gaining an immediate competitive advantage. Ultimately, these clauses provide leverage. If the club losing the manager is not adequately compensated, it can enforce gardening leave provisions, meaning that the manager is contractually unable to move to his new club. To avoid this, the new club will usually have to stump up significant money. In cases where managers wish to leave their current job and the club wishes to retain their manager, the level of compensation rises. This occurred during the 2017/18 Premier League season, when Everton pursued the then Watford manager Marco Silva. Watford refused to accept Everton's approach in November 2017 after reportedly rejecting compensation of £10m. By January, Silva had been sacked by Watford after a poor run of results. In the meantime, Everton had appointed Sam Allardyce. Silva eventually joined Everton in June 2018.

A managerial contract will ultimately depend on the role envisaged for the manager and the organisational parameters within which the manager must work. Some clubs, especially outside the Premier League, have well-established directors of football who will deal with a variety of issues, including transfers, player recruitment and youth development. This leaves the managers to prioritise first-team coaching duties. Historically, Premier League clubs have had a more traditional structure, whereby the manager had total control over all on-field matters, including scouting, transfer negotiations and existing player contract renegotiations. Such an approach gave managers complete responsibility, which would lead to praise and blame in equal measure.

Ultimately, a manager's contract will set out their roles, responsibilities, powers and reporting obligations. This could be as detailed as who has final say over player recruitment and the appointment of key staff. For a neat example of what happens when the roles and responsibilities of a manager conflict with the powers of a director of football, consider the example of Kevin Keegan below (*see* page 147).

A number of other provisions that are increasingly being used in managers' contracts include:

- Clauses stipulating that the sacking of the manager automatically terminates the employment contracts of their coaching/backroom staff.
- Restrictions on taking club employees (coaching staff and/or players) to the new club. The intention is to minimise disruption to the club by losing its elite player coaching team.
- Restrictions after termination of the contract, to stop a manager from working for a direct competitor for the period of, say, one transfer window.

Some high-profile managers may also be handed image rights contracts. Image rights as a more general concept are described in Chapter 4 (*see* pages 100–103). In such contracts, the club and the manager agree to exploit and commercialise the manager's image and endorsement value when working in a club context. This can sometimes cause complications, however.

In May 2016, it was reported that one of the matters holding up the appointment of José Mourinho as manager of Manchester United was a conflict over his image rights. The suggestion was that his former club Chelsea owned Mourinho's image rights. In addition, it was believed that Mourinho's individual commercial deals, entered into before he joined Manchester United, may have been with competitors of the club's own sponsors. Negotiations apparently centred around his deals with Jaguar and the watch company Hublot – and presumably United's arrangements with their own sponsors, Chevrolet and Bulova. These types of commercial conflicts are becoming more frequent: players and managers have their own individual commercial deals, but clubs don't want to devalue their own sponsors/partner brands. As Manchester United have more than 60 commercial partnerships/sponsorship deals in place, the potential for conflict is huge.

HOW YOUTUBE EARNED KEVIN KEEGAN £2M

At the end of the summer transfer window in August 2008, Dennis Wise, then the director of football for Newcastle United, phoned manager Kevin Keegan to recommend a new signing. The player in question was Uruguay midfielder Ignacio González. Wise wanted to sign the player in part to court favour with two prominent South American agents – presumably so that the club would be in a stronger position to buy other talented players in the future. Wise suggested that Keegan watch the player on YouTube to see how good he was. Keegan did, and refused to agree to the transfer, who was signed nonetheless (and even though no club scout had ever seen the player play).

Keegan then resigned, believing that, as manager, he had the ultimate say over transfers. According to English employment law, a breach of a fundamental term of an employment contract can be classed as a 'repudiation of the contract', which gives the harmed party the ability to resign. This is classed as constructive dismissal. The decision had been made against his wishes, undermining his own position at the club. Keegan sued the club for £25m, which included compensation for the remaining value of his employment contract.

A Premier League Managers Arbitration Panel agreed that Newcastle had breached Keegan's agreement by signing González. The verdict found that 'the [YouTube] clips were of poor quality and provided no proper basis for signing a player to a Premier League club'. This did amount to a fundamental breach of his employment contract, and he was awarded £2m. Interestingly, Keegan in his press release explained that:

> I resigned because I was being asked to sanction the signing of a player in order to do a favour for two South American agents. No one at the club had seen the player play and I was asked to sign him on the basis of some clip on YouTube. This is something I was not prepared to be associated with in any way.

Ultimately, a YouTube clip led to an expensive payout for Newcastle United.

> *'Football disputes are on the rise due to the sums involved, short-termism in the industry, and the uniqueness of the legal framework in which the industry operates. In that context, average football managers' tenures are shorter than ever. With that reality comes the need to secure a pay-off for the manager or the conjuring up of arguments in order to reduce those payments. Similarly, players' rights are heavily regulated, with potentially millions at stake for them,*

their agents and commercial partners. All of this leads to a record number of disputes in a variety of different forums; both domestically and abroad, and in public or in private.'

John Merzhad, Sports Barrister

Why Sam Allardyce left England after 67 days and one game

Sam Allardyce left his job in July 2016 as Sunderland manager to take over as England manager after the team's below-par Euro 2016 results. As part of an undercover sting by the *Daily Telegraph*, in which journalists pretended to be football agents and investors, he was caught on camera explaining that he knew ways round the FA rules in relation to transfers. He also made fun of his predecessor, Roy Hodgson, and criticised Hodgson's assistant manager Gary Neville, and even Prince Harry.

It was reported that the FA hierarchy at the time (Martin Glenn and Greg Clarke) explained to Allardyce that his position as England manager was untenable. The FA argued that his behaviour fell short of the standards that an England manager should uphold. It may also have been the case that the FA believed Allardyce had committed a fundamental breach of his employment contract.

Both parties agreed that Allardyce would leave 'by mutual consent'. This type of wording is usually a result of both parties agreeing a financial settlement so that the matter doesn't end up in the public courts. Such a settlement almost always includes confidentiality clauses stopping either party from talking about the matter in public. The day after his enforced exit, a visibly upset Allardyce was quoted saying: '. . . entrapment has won on this occasion and I have to accept that.' Presumably the FA paid him a certain percentage of the rest of his contract. The actual sum was not reported.

Sixty-seven days in the job became the shortest reign of a permanent England manager.

MANAGERIAL CONTROVERSIES

Over the years there have been a number of high-profile incidents involving managers. These have included accusations concerning the acceptance of bungs and bribes, reports of sexism and racism, as well as bonus entitlements.

BUNGS AND BRIBES

Back in 1995, an FA panel found George Graham, then manager of Arsenal, guilty of misconduct for receiving £425,000 from agent Rune Hauge as a result of the transfers of Pål Lydersen and John Jensen. Graham was sacked by Arsenal and banned from football for a year. He subsequently managed Leeds and Arsenal's arch-rivals, Spurs.

By way of wider comment on bribes/bungs, it's worth noting that there have been a number of investigations alleging that payments were made to managers and/or members of clubs involved in transfer deals to ensure that the deal gets done. The FA's intermediary regulations make it very clear that all payments made in relation to a transfer or contract renegotiation have to be documented in the correct forms and that payments cannot be made to club officials.

In various investigative documentaries, managers and club officials have been accused of receiving money from a 'favoured' agent in return for using that agent on particular deals – so that both the manager and agent benefit from the deal happening. The controversy with such payments is that they are likely to be illegal under the UK Bribery Act (among other pieces of legislation), and possibly subject to criminal sanctions and a breach of various FA and league regulations. In addition, HMRC will probably be very interested in such payments: by their very nature, these payments are secretive, and it is thus unlikely that tax will have been paid on the payments. HMRC has the power to investigate and, if breaches are proven, to impose large fines.

BE CAREFUL WHAT YOU TEXT

Scottish manager Malky Mackay got into serious trouble for sending text messages that were subsequently leaked to the press.

Mackay was sacked by Cardiff City in December 2013 after a string of poor results. He had previously led the club to promotion to the Premier League. He had then interviewed for the manager's job at Crystal Palace in August 2014, and was close to signing for them before information was provided to a UK national newspaper that disclosed a number of text messages. Allegedly sexist and racist, they had been sent between Mackay and an ex-Cardiff City colleague, Ian Moody.

Mackay apologised for sending the text messages and rejected accusations that he was anti-Semitic or racist. Subsequently, the FA began an investigation. In July 2015, and somewhat controversially, the FA confirmed that Mackay was not to be charged with any breach of the FA disciplinary rules. This was because: 'The FA's policy in cases such as this has been to not bring charges in respect of private communications sent with a legitimate expectation of privacy.'

The FA did stress that they were undertaking a full review of how messages sent in private should be treated in the future. Nonetheless, many within the game and wider society viewed this as an example of the regulator not taking a tough enough line on such a serious matter.

THE RECEIPT THAT SAVED CRYSTAL PALACE ALMOST £4M

The chairman of Crystal Palace could never have guessed that a hairdressing receipt proving where he was on a particular day in 2014 would be worth almost £4m to the club – but that's exactly what happened in 2017.

Ex-Crystal Palace manager Tony Pulis was ordered to pay back more than £3.7m to his former club after leaving them days before their first league game of the 2014/15 season. Pulis had been entitled to a bonus of £2m for keeping the club in the Premier League for the previous season – so long as he was still at the club on 31 August, 2014.

The bonus was due to be paid on 31 August, 2014, but Pulis requested the money two weeks early. He promised the Crystal Palace chairman that he would stay with the club and that the money was urgently needed to help his family buy a property.

Those two promises formed the basis for the case against Pulis. Crystal Palace argued that both promises had been fraudulent misrepresentations, thus deceiving the club into paying the bonus early.

Crystal Palace paid Pulis the bonus £2m on 12 August, 2014. The following evening (13 August), he informed the club for the first time that he wanted to leave – and did so the following day. The club claimed Pulis wanted the bonus early so that he could leave the club with his bonus, to join another club.

The court decision, made public only after Pulis lost his first case and appealed, was unequivocal. After reviewing the evidence, the judge believed that Pulis had not been truthful when he stated:

- that he was committed to the club (the reason he got his money early); *and*
- that he needed to buy land for his family (despite little evidence to show that this was the case).

The main argument between the club and Pulis was the date of a 'heated players meeting'. Pulis claimed that he was committed to the club until the time when his bonus was paid, and changed his mind only because of the 'heated players meeting' – which, he said took place on the very same day as the payment of the bonus (i.e. 12 August).

By contrast, Crystal Palace argued that the heated players meeting took place on 8 August, and so couldn't be used to explain Pulis's change of mind on 12 August. The club argued he was looking for any excuse to leave after the bonus had been paid and the 'heated players meeting' gave him the perfect opportunity.

Ultimately, the court refused to believe that the players meeting took place on 12 August, as Pulis claimed. This was partly because Crystal Palace's chairman, Steve Parrish, had a hairdressing appointment (and receipt) on 12 August – the same time that the 'heated players meeting', which he also attended, was meant to have taken place!

The court decided that the meeting happened on 8 August, meaning that Pulis's explanation for his sudden desire to leave the club was unlikely. In his ruling the judge criticised Pulis's behaviour, stating that his 'conduct has been shown to be disgraceful'. Palace were repaid the £2m plus interest and legal fees, which added up to almost £4m. Pulis is reported to have paid the money to the club in early 2017.

WHEN MANAGERS ARE BANNED

Just as players can be banned and fined, so can managers. This is the same FA process as for players. When managers bring the game into disrepute, the FA will charge them accordingly. The specific charges can relate to using abusive or insulting wording, violent conduct and/or threatening behaviour to a match official or other participant. Usually the charge is based on FA regulation E3:

> *A Participant shall at all times act in the best interest of the game and shall not act in any manner which is improper or brings the game into disrepute or use one, or a combination of, violent conduct, serious foul play, threatening, abusive, indecent or insulting words or behaviour.*

As such, it's not just players that feel the wrath of the FA when they say or do something that they shouldn't. Managers' actions on the touchline and at press conferences all have consequences. These can consist of warnings about future behaviour, fines, stadium bans, even touchline bans. Managers can appeal such decisions, but it is relatively uncommon for such decisions to be overturned. Some of the most significant decisions (and sanctions) are set out below.

1. Ex-Newcastle manager Alan Pardew was banned for seven games for headbutting Hull player David Meyler during a game in 2014. He was previously banned for two games in August 2012 for pushing an assistant referee.
2. Ex-Arsenal manager Arsène Wenger received a four-game touchline ban for shoving fourth official Anthony Taylor after Arsenal's 2–1 win against Burnley in January 2017.
3. Sir Alex Ferguson, then Manchester United's manager, served a five-game touchline ban after accusing referee Martin Atkinson of bias and arguing that the game against Chelsea in 2011 needed a 'fair referee'. He already had hanging over him a two-match suspended sentence (which was activated), after accusing referee Alan Wiley of not being fit enough to keep up with players during a game.

4. Paul Ince, while manager of Blackpool, was sanctioned with a five-game touchline ban in 2010 for violently and threateningly shoving the fourth official.

AN UNFORGIVING JOB

Managers live a precarious existence. The pressure is incessant. Like players, managers too will move clubs, countries and continents at the drop of a hat to further their career. Their sacrifices, drive and resilience are rarely acknowledged.

To become an elite manager, it's vital to combine management skills with tactical awareness to bring out the best in the team. Success or failure, depending on how it's measured (by trophies, promotion or avoiding relegation) can mean managers are sacked or appointed, and achievement is incentivised with huge bonuses.

Managers, like players, are paid well at the elite level – but at the lower levels, it can be an unforgiving job. The pressure to succeed can lead to problems with the owners, players, media and the authorities. This pressure-cooker environment is only likely to continue, given the money at stake, and the consequences of success and failure being so high. The sacrifice that managers and their backroom staff have to make shouldn't be underestimated – even if most fans always think they could do a better job.

CHAPTER 7

FOOTBALLERS AND MANAGERS BEHAVING BADLY

Footballers are always going to be in the headlines. Late night drinking, kiss-and-tell stories and mega-transfers create big news. Traditionally, the local and national media has relied on access to players, clubs and managers.

The advent of Twitter and other social media platforms like Instagram and Snapchat has provided novel and more direct channels of communication and interaction. Players can communicate instantaneously with followers. The ease of communication and the instantaneous nature of tweeting players means mistakes and mishaps are inevitable. The more high-profile the individual, the juicier the story.

SOCIAL MEDIA

Social network sites, like Twitter, must be regarded as being in the public domain and all participants need to be aware, in the same way as if making a public statement in other forms of media, that any comments would be transmitted to a wider audience. It is their responsibility to ensure only appropriate comments are used.

This is the advice from the FA to footballers. Below, we'll examine some 'social media gone wrong' moments – to illustrate the ease with which comments in the public domain can lead to serious consequences. Some can be laughed off, others have had more significant consequences. Importantly, the examples given also set out how situations can be best avoided – and contingency plans if the worst does happen.

A RISKY BUSINESS?

Social media is now mainstream. Players need to show common sense on and off the pitch, and clubs need to be prepared for the worst. Damage limitation now extends to the world of social media. The benefit of social media is that the platforms allow players to directly interact with their fans. Never has the impact of being able to communicate so directly and instantly been so exciting for fans and followers alike.

Social media has opened up a Pandora's Box of opinions. The dangers are boundless, and inevitably things will go wrong. With the club unable to ensure prior vetting of communications that are sent out, they are relying on a player to use his better judgement. Mobile phones are being used as multi-platform devices, and texting and instant messaging applications are commonplace. It is easy to see how a tweet could be composed and sent to a wide audience without a thought for the inevitable repercussions. The ability to tweet, snap or insta via a mobile phone means that a simple avenue exists for footballers with time on their hands and something to say. Some have argued that platforms like Twitter have offered the public something they get less and less frequently: outspoken remarks that provoke comment. And it's true: the opportunity for such unfettered communication has only fuelled the popularity of such platforms. Just ask Donald Trump.

Still, dangers lurk. Social media has the capability to get you in trouble instantly. Posts can be removed, but the damage may have already been done: with followers mercilessly retweeting a controversial remark, the process can snowball quickly. A few examples, from a time when social media was less significant than it is today, include:

- Aldershot's Marvin Morgan being suspended, fined two weeks' wages and placed on the transfer list in 2011 for comments on Twitter about Aldershot's fans. After being booed from the pitch, and tweeting that he wished that the club's fans 'would all die', he was unlikely to be able to win them back. Whether the club could have sacked Morgan is another question (possibly for an employment lawyer).
- Former Liverpool FC player Glen Johnson took to Twitter after having his attitude questioned by football pundit Paul Merson. He wrote (in somewhat more blunt terms than described here) that he did not take much notice of those comments given Merson's past drink, drug and gambling problems. No doubt Johnson believed that Twitter was the perfect platform for fighting fire with fire.
- Darren Bent used Twitter to berate Spurs chairman Daniel Levy before his transfer to Sunderland in 2009, urging him in some colourful language to speed up the process. Hours later, an apology was forthcoming, though I think it would be fair to say the pair are no longer Facebook friends.

In more recent years, players, clubs and managers alike have made front- and back-page headlines. None more so than the ex-Everton manager Ronald Koeman, who walked into the middle of a Twitter storm in December 2016 by posting a picture of his Christmas tree covered with red tinsel. That didn't go down well with Everton fans given that arch-rivals Liverpool play in red. It promptly led Koeman to change his colour scheme to a more appropriate blue and white.

The social media world can be an unforgiving place. Nonetheless, it gives players and managers a direct channel to the fans – an avenue that was not possible less than a decade ago. With the benefit of 'speak your mind' comes the responsibility of keeping within the rules. Described below is what happens when players cross the line.

WHEN SOCIAL MEDIA BITES

Issues can arise when players tweet or post particular messages that bring them into trouble with the football authorities. In December 2014, the FA found ex-Liverpool player Mario Balotelli guilty for reposting an Instagram message containing iconic computer game star Super Mario, which said that Mario 'jumps like a black man and grabs coins like a jew'. The message was promptly deleted by Balotelli, who then tweeted: 'My Mom is Jewish so all of u shut up please.' (He was referring to his foster mother, Silvia.) In their charging statement, the FA stated that:

> It is alleged the Liverpool player breached FA Rule E3[1] in that his posting was abusive and/or insulting and/or improper. It is further alleged that this is an 'Aggravated Breach' as defined by FA Rule E3[2] as it included a reference to ethnic origin and/or colour and/or race and/or nationality and/or religion or belief.

Balotelli has previously been subject to racist abuse for being black, and his foster mum is indeed Jewish, but this was no defence to the charge brought by the FA. It was likely that the breach would have been found to be an aggravated breach because he made references in his Instagram post to various nationalities, including Jewish and black stereotypes. Balotelli was sanctioned with a one-game ban and a £25,000 fine.

Below are further examples of players getting into serious trouble for what they said online:

- Ryan Babel, then with Liverpool, became the first player to be sanctioned for misuse of Twitter in January 2011 and was fined £10,000 by the FA. Having been on the receiving end of a number of contentious decisions, he had posted a Photoshopped picture of referee Howard Webb wearing a Manchester United shirt. Babel subsequently removed the tweet, apologised via Twitter and even sent himself to #twitterjail.
- In October 2012, Ashley Cole, then at Chelsea, was fined £90,000 after he called the FA a 'bunch of t**ts' on Twitter; the post was retweeted more than 19,000 times. Cole's outburst came after a commission investigating John Terry for racial abuse was less than complimentary about the evidence Cole had given.
- In August 2012, Rio Ferdinand was fined £45,000 after agreeing with a follower on Twitter that Ashley Cole was a choc ice (black

on the outside, white on the inside). This was the first of two sanctions against Ferdinand: in October 2014 he became the first Premier League player to be banned from playing as a result of a social media message. He replied to a Twitter follower by calling their mother a 'sket', or promiscuous woman. He was banned for three matches and fined £25,000.

- In May 2013, Marseille loanee Joey Barton was banned for two games for calling PSG defender Thiago Silva an 'overweight ladyboy'. Initially, the French Football Association had refused to sanction the player, claiming that they had no power to do so since his words were in English.

- In September 2016, former Burnley striker Andre Gray was banned by the FA for four matches for tweets he had posted in 2012. The tweets, which contained offensive terms, were posted when Gray was playing for non-league Hinckley United. Specifically, he stated in one deleted tweet: 'Is it me or are there gays everywhere? #Burn #Die #MakesMeSick.' The posts were found, presumably by an investigative journalist, after Gray scored his first Premier League goal against Liverpool in 2016. The FA, who had not been previously aware of the tweets, took action.

- Coventry City's defender Chris Stokes was banned for one game and fined £1,000 by the FA for tweeting during Chelsea's 2–2 draw with Tottenham in May 2016: 'This games embarrassing to watch! Bunch of faggots.'

- Fulham player Ryan Tunnicliffe was banned for two matches and fined £5,000 after tweeting in June 2015: 'Happy that Middlesbrough didn't go up, just for the main fact that @Patrick_Bamford is a sausage boy.' This was a reference to on-loan striker Patrick Bamford, and Middlesbrough's play-off final loss to Norwich City in 2015.

The above examples range from silly to idiotic and beyond, and all players were charged with 'aggravated misconduct', but unfortunately such actions are becoming commonplace in sports generally. And as more players embrace social media there are bound to be more incidents. To keep sponsors, managers and teammates onside, football players will need to be thinking long and hard about the consequences of each and every post they make. There are no hard and fast rules.

The usual rule of thumb is not to say anything negative, full stop. That's easier said than done, but there are some other general rules players should follow:

1. **Do not reveal tactical information.** Do not give away any technical or tactical information that could aid the opposing team. When playing at Liverpool in January 2010, Ryan Babel announced 'I've been dropped and not playing tomorrow' before the squad had been announced against Stoke.
2. **Cool off.** Don't tweet until a few hours after games. Otherwise it's more likely that honest but not necessarily appropriate remarks will be made about controversial moments in the game or about fellow teammates, opposing players, the fans or even the manager.
3. **Keep quiet about any naughty business.** Don't broadcast to the world that you've been up all night drinking, gambling and/ or clubbing, etc. Posting pictures of any such 'activities' is also a definite no-no. Everyone has access to a camera on their phone, so players need to be on their best behaviour when out socialising, or there is unlimited scope to get into trouble. Aston Villa player Jack Grealish was photographed drunk on the floor in June 2015 in Tenerife. This was after the season had finished, but clubs usually take a dim view of such behaviour and may at the very least heavily fine the player.
4. **Don't give out personal information.** Don't tell people where you live. And posting bank details on Twitter, even if you have money to burn, is not a good idea.
5. **Avoid arguments with followers.** Justifying your recent 10k-a-week pay rise is unlikely to go down well with fans.

DAMAGE LIMITATION

Most players are on some form of social media. I haven't yet heard of a club insisting on a total ban for their players. If clubs and agents have the resources, all players should be monitored. In any event, anything controversial will spread like wildfire, and it will not be long before both club and player see smoke on the horizon.

The next stage is damage limitation. This may consist of:

- Assessing whether the tweet has recently been posted and whether it is worthwhile to remove it.
- Removing the tweet and apologising via Twitter and other media platforms.

POSTING MESSAGES

It is now common for players to have commercial teams looking after their social media accounts. This has sometimes led to rather awkward outcomes:

1. On leaving Liverpool, Christian Benteke announced on Twitter that he was joining Burnley – only later to make clear that it was actually Crystal Palace. He clarified that one of his backroom team had mistakenly posted the wrong club: 'Oops my bad lol Yes I signed for cpfc and not burnley. Sorry for the little mistake the person that manages my Twitter got a little confused.'

2. Victor Anichebe cut and pasted the whole message from his social media team: 'you can tweet something like "Unbelievable support yesterday and great effort by the lads."'

3. İlkay Gündoğan had to tweet to reassure fans that he had not died. This followed a tribute from the players of Manchester City, who offered Gündoğan their support by wearing shirts emblazoned with his name after he suffered a knee injury in City's 2–0 victory against Watford in December 2016.

4. After playing for bottom-of-the-table Aston Villa in a 6–0 thrashing by Liverpool at Villa Park, Joleon Lescott tweeted a picture of a top-end Mercedes, riling disgruntled fans. Lescott claimed the post was accidental.

Although these examples demonstrate only the superficial perils of social media, there have been two more examples in Spain of players being sacked for their social media posts. In July 2015, Deportivo de La Coruña terminated the signing of Julio Rey after they saw some of the posts he had written on Twitter, including one from three years earlier, when he was just 17, directing offensive remarks at Depor. Similarly, in December 2015, just a short time after Barcelona announced the signing of Sergi Guardiola, they terminated his contract after seeing posts written two years previously insulting Catalonia.

Today, clubs and owners will use the investigation stage of larger transfers to look through a player's social media accounts in order to ensure there are no skeletons in their closet. Using particular keywords, they will undertake forensic searches to ensure there are no previous postings that could cause issues for the club down the line. That is why it is so important for a player to understand the perils of social media as well as the virtues.

Social media is also sometimes considered a distraction for players in the build-up of games. At the end of the 2016/17 season, it was reported that Manchester United had begun to more strictly control its players' use of social media. New guidelines set out where, what and when they can post messages on Twitter, Facebook, Snapchat and Instagram. Specifically, the club did not want its players to post training pictures within 48 hours of a game or on the team bus on the way to games.

'A number of players from across the top leagues and top youth academies contract external marketing agencies to manage their social media profiles. The objective for each agency is simple. Raise and protect the player's profile.

In the cases mentioned above, a number of these players have not employed marketing agencies to work with them on a player's social media profiles. The agencies act as a filter and an insurance system, to ensure the player is not posting anything that could lead to fines, bans through misbehaviour or miscommunication across different territories.'

Ehsen Shah, B-Engaged

WHO DECIDES WHAT FOOTBALLERS CAN AND CAN'T DO?

The short answer is that it depends . . . Football rules are a complex web of interlinking and sometimes overlapping regulations. There are a variety of rules that can apply, depending on whether it's a league, cup or international game.

In addition, players can get into trouble for lots of different things. Players will be disciplined for physically assaulting each other (on or off the pitch), swearing, drug use (or missing a drugs test), or saying things that bring the game into disrepute, whether in an interview or on social media.

Luis Suárez was found guilty by a FIFA disciplinary committee for biting Giorgio Chiellini during Uruguay's final Group D game against Italy in the 2014 World Cup. For this, he was suspended from international football for nine matches and from all football-related activity for four months, and fined around £65,000. This was the culmination of a number of years of the wrong sort of headlines for Suárez – and makes an interesting case study because a variety of rules were used to charge him, based on playing for Ajax, Liverpool and Uruguay.

He shot to international infamy when he prevented a certain goal with a deliberate handball in the 2010 World Cup quarter-finals in South Africa. Asamoah Gyan missed the subsequent penalty and Uruguay went on to beat Ghana. In November 2010, Suárez accepted a seven-match ban for biting PSV Eindhoven midfielder Otman Bakkal on the shoulder. The ban was handed down by the Royal Dutch Football Association, since he was playing for Ajax at the time. In January 2011, Liverpool bought Suárez for £22.8m from Ajax, and during his spell at the club, FIFA and the FA banned him three times in total.

The different footballing bodies have the power to ban, sanction and fine a player depending on which competition he is playing in. By the time he transferred to Liverpool, the Royal Dutch Football Association had already banned Suárez for seven matches. His first and ultimately most serious ban in the UK related to a match between Liverpool and arch-rivals Manchester United at Anfield in 2011. Patrice Evra claimed – and the FA panel agreed – that Suárez used an offensive word seven times in total. The 115-page decision goes into significant detail about the circumstances and context of the conversation and a decision that ultimately came down to the panel believing one player over the other: no one else overheard what was said. Suárez was given an eight-match ban and a £40,000 fine.

In April 2013, the FA again banned Suárez following a game against Chelsea at Anfield, during which he bit Branislav Ivanović. He was handed a 10-game ban, which meant he missed four of the remaining Liverpool games of that season and six of the following season. After missing the start of the 2013/14 season, he scored 31 goals in 32 games.

His punishment for his third biting offence, at the 2014 World Cup in Brazil, was a nine-match international ban and a four-month total football ban – meaning he was unlikely to play competitive football again before November 2014.

This penalty was imposed by FIFA and, importantly, banned Suárez from playing for his club – at the time Liverpool, though he would soon move to Barcelona for a reported £70m+ transfer. The penalty is believed to be the most severe imposed on a player in World Cup history. Previously the longest ban was the eight games imposed on Italy's Mauro Tassotti for elbowing Luis Enrique of Spain in the 1994 World Cup quarter-final.

Before the sanction was imposed, I tweeted that there was always the possibility of Suárez being banned for all football-related activity because the FIFA Disciplinary Code explicitly gives FIFA such an option.

Daniel Geey
@FootballLaw

Re Suarez bite, if found guilty, usually FIFA suspensions relate to national team but sanctions can be "all football related activity".

24/06/2014 20:01

179 RETWEETS **25** FAVORITES

At the time, many doubted that FIFA would take the 'nuclear' option because it had not been previously used against a player found guilty of unsporting behaviour. Suárez appealed the decision to the Court of Arbitration for Sport (CAS), who softened the ban so that it applied to competitive matches only and not other football-related activities (i.e. training and promotional activities). This meant that Suárez could attend the Camp Nou for his unveiling as a Barcelona player after his transfer and that his first game was El Clásico against Real Madrid.

His example perfectly illustrates the different powers held by footballing governing bodies to sanction and ban a player, depending on which competition they are playing in. Suárez was sanctioned before the Royal Dutch Football Association, the Football Association (twice), FIFA and CAS.

GUILTY OR NOT GUILTY?

Ex-Chelsea captain John Terry faced criminal charges of using insulting, threatening or abusive words/behaviour that was racially aggravated. It was alleged that he shouted racist words in the direction of Anton Ferdinand during a match on 23 October, 2011. The magistrates in the criminal case had to decide whether 'the words were used as an insult, or whether it is possible, as the defence assert, that he was, or believed he was, merely repeating an allegation made to him, and dismissing it'.

Terry was cleared of using racially abusive words and/or behaviour. The magistrates believed it highly unlikely that Ferdinand accused him on the pitch of using abusive language but accepted it was possible for Terry to believe at the time that such an accusation was made. Therefore it was possible that what Terry said to Ferdinand in reply was intended not as an insult but as a challenge. Accordingly, the verdict reached by the court was that Terry was not guilty of racial abuse.

However, on 27 July, 2012, the FA charged Terry with using abusive or insulting words and behaviour towards Ferdinand, behaviour that related to ethnic origin, race or colour. What made this element of the process interesting was that the FA had to wait for the criminal proceedings to finish before starting their own disciplinary process.

Terry was subsequently found guilty by the FA of using abusive language towards Ferdinand. On 27 September, 2012, he was banned for four matches and fined £220,000 even though the criminal court had found him not guilty. Many fans wondered how Terry could be found not guilty by the criminal court but guilty by the FA.

The basic reason is that two different tests were applied. For a criminal test, the court must be satisfied beyond a reasonable doubt. In contrast, the FA used a test based on the balance of probabilities.

The distinction between these two tests – reasonable doubt (i.e. being sure) and the balance of probabilities (i.e. the case being more likely than not) – is important. While a criminal court must ensure that 'a defendant is found guilty only if the court . . . is sure of guilt', the FA has a lower test. Believing on the balance of probabilities that Terry 'used abusive and/or insulting words and/or behaviour towards . . . Ferdinand', the FA found him guilty.

WHAT DID ANELKA MEAN?

On 28 December, 2013, Nicolas Anelka celebrated the first of his goals for West Bromwich Albion in a 3–3 draw against West Ham – not with words, but by touching his right shoulder with his left hand and keeping his right arm pointed downwards – a gesture known as the *quenelle*. At this point, it was almost unheard of in the UK.

Anelka justified the sign as 'just a special dedication to my comedian friend Dieudonné'. The problem for many (including the French government) is that Dieudonné is controversial, some of his shows having been banned because of their anti-Semitic content. Anelka denied any racist intent behind his celebration, but Dieudonné had previously been found guilty of making anti-Semitic speeches in France.

Under the FA rules, Anelka was charged with misconduct, specifically behaving 'in a manner which is improper or brings the game into disrepute or [using] any one, or a combination of, violent conduct, serious foul play, threatening, abusive, indecent or insulting words or behaviour'.

After the Terry and Suárez cases, the FA had changed its rules so that it would impose a minimum suspension of five matches. A second breach would incur a minimum suspension of 10 matches. Anelka received a five-match ban and a fine of £80,000.

Some of the longest bans given out by the Football Association to players

- 13 months – ex-Burnley midfielder Joey Barton for betting and gambling offences.
- 9 months – Manchester United's Eric Cantona for his 'kung-fu'-style kick.
- 9 months – Chelsea keeper Mark Bosnich for testing positive for cocaine.
- 8 months – Rio Ferdinand of Manchester United for missing a drugs test. The ruling forced the defender to miss the second half of Manchester United's season and Euro 2004 with England.
- Seven months – Adnan Mutu for testing positive for cocaine.
- Six months – Kolo Touré after failing a drugs test; he had taken a weight-loss drug.
- 12 games – QPR's Joey Barton for a red card and clashing with Manchester City's Sergio Agüero and Vincent Kompany when playing for QPR.
- 11 games – Sheffield Wednesday's Paolo Di Canio for pushing over referee Paul Alcock.
- 10 games –Southampton's David Prutton for shoving referee Alan Wiley.
- 10 games – Liverpool striker Luis Suárez for biting Chelsea's Branislav Ivanović.
- 9 games – Rochdale's Calvin Andrew for elbowing Oldham defender Peter Clarke; the initial ban was 12 games.
- 8 games – Ben Thatcher, when playing for Manchester City, plus a further 15-match ban suspended, after an incident that left Portsmouth's Pedro Mendes unconscious.

BANS AND MISCONDUCT

The question remains: based on the severity of the offence, are the bans dished out for certain on-field offences fair? In short, does the punishment fit the crime? Some of the most common offences to be charged by the FA under a breach of their misconduct regulations are set out below.

DIVING

From the 2017/18 season in both the Premier League and Football League, cheating by way of diving to gain an advantage for your team can be reviewed retrospectively (i.e. by a panel of experts after the game has finished). Disciplinary action can take the form of a two-game ban for the player in question when that player cheated to win a penalty or get an opposing player sent off. In Scotland, a similar rule has been in place for a number of years and players have been subsequently disciplined when diving. The first player to fall foul of this action in the Premier League was Oumar Niasse after he was found guilty of 'successful deception of a match official' during Everton's game against Crystal Palace at Selhurst Park in November 2017, when he 'won' a penalty.

SPITTING

In 2003, El Hadji Diouf, then playing for Liverpool, was fined and suspended for two games after spitting towards Celtic fans during a UEFA Cup game between the clubs in 2003.

In March 2015, Papiss Cissé was given a seven-game ban while playing for Premier League team Newcastle for spitting at Manchester United player Jonny Evans. Evans was suspended for six games for the same offence. An automatic six-game suspension is set out under FIFA regulations; Cissé received a seventh game ban because it was his second red card of the season.

West Ham's Arthur Masuaku was banned for six games by the FA for spitting at Wigan player Nick Powell during the FA Cup tie in January 2018.

FEIGNING INJURY

The FA in 2015 brought in new rules enabling a panel to ban a player for three games if he deliberately tried to get an opponent sent off by feigning injury.

Ex-Brazilian player Rivaldo was widely criticised during the 2002 World Cup when Turkey's Hakan Ünsal kicked the ball to him near the corner flag. Rivaldo clutched his face when it was clear the ball had hit him near the leg, and was fined £4,500 by FIFA. Ünsal was sent off, having received a yellow card beforehand, and Rivaldo later apologised: 'I said sorry to him, but that's football.'

TACKLES

In March 2010, Stoke player Ryan Shawcross tackled Aaron Ramsey, breaking the Arsenal player's leg. Shawcross received the standard three-game ban for a straight red card. Neil Taylor, while on international duty for Wales in early 2017, tackled Republic of Ireland's Séamus Coleman and broke his leg. He was suspended for two games.

BITES

Luis Suárez was suspended for biting opposition players while playing for Ajax (seven games), Liverpool (ten games) and Uruguay (nine games).

HEADBUTT

Marouane Fellaini was banned for three matches in April 2017 for his headbutt on Manchester City striker Sergio Agüero. This was in addition to a previous three-game ban in December 2012 for headbutting Stoke's Ryan Shawcross.

In the 2006 World Final, Zinedine Zidane was infamously banned for three matches for headbutting Italian defender Marco Materazzi in the chest – although he retired from playing in the aftermath of the World Cup. Bastia striker Brandão was banned for six months by the

French authorities for a headbutt on PSG midfielder Thiago Motta in late 2014.

ELBOW

In March 2017, Zlatan Ibrahimović, playing for Manchester United, was banned for three games after elbowing Bournemouth's Tyrone Mings. The referee had failed to notice Mings alleged stamping on his head while Ibrahimović was on the floor (*see* below). In October 2016, Tottenham's Moussa Sissoko received a three-game ban for an elbow in the face of then Bournemouth player Harry Arter.

STAMP

Tyrone Mings was banned for five games after it was recognised that he had stamped on Ibrahimović's head during the game mentioned above. Aston Villa's Jack Grealish received a three-game ban for a stamp on Wolves player Conor Coady in October 2016.

PUSHING THE REF

Playing for Sheffield Wednesday in 1998, Paolo Di Canio pushed referee Paul Alcock and was subsequently banned for 11 matches and fined £10,000. David Prutton received a 10-match ban for pushing referee Alan Wiley in February 2005 in a match against Arsenal.

To many there is no easy answer to why a six-match ban for spitting is the minimum ban when an elbow (usually causing much greater physical damage) is usually a three-match suspension. As an amateur footballer, this author would rather be spat at than elbowed, even though the punishment is significantly harsher for an offence that does no real physical damage. However, to many fans and players alike, there is a real stigma attached to spitting and as spitting releases bodily fluids which could cause a health risk, the authorities may rightly be concerned to stamp out such behaviour too.

RETROSPECTIVE ACTION

For the past decade, the FA has been able to ban players after the game for certain sending-off incidents that were not seen by the referee and their assistants during a game. Such retrospective action enabled the FA to ban Mings after stamping on Ibrahimović, for example.

In all cases, three people (an ex-match official, ex-manager and ex-player) review the highlights of the particular incident. Each person works in isolation from the other. If all three believe the offence was worthy of a red card, the player is charged accordingly.

In addition, since the start of the 2017/18 season, the FA has been able to take action against a player who deceives a match official. Where there is clear evidence that a player dived, earning a penalty or getting the opposing player sent off, a panel will look at the action, and if all of them believe the referee has been deceived, the FA will charge the player. The player will then be judged to have dived or feigned injury and will receive a two-match ban, as in the case of Niasse (*see* page 168 above).

DRUG TESTING

Drug testing is part and parcel of being a professional footballer, and players can often fall foul of the rules. While a positive drug test result or a number of missed tests might seem a black-and-white indication of guilt, it isn't always so clear cut. Such are the bans handed out, as well as the reputational repercussions, the impact a drug case can have on a player's career can be significant.

Former Chelsea goalkeeper Mark Bosnich and Romanian international Adrian Mutu were both high-profile Chelsea football players who tested positive for cocaine and had to serve playing bans. Chelsea sacked both players for breaches of their employment contracts, which left star striker Mutu to foot a bill of €17.1m (*see* below).

Rio Ferdinand is just one high-profile player to have fallen foul by missing a drugs test; he claimed he forgot to take the test and went shopping instead. He was banned as a result. A brief timeline of events is set out below, describing its impact:

- 23 September, 2003: Asked to take a drugs test at Manchester United's training ground, but leaves without carrying out the test.
- 25 September, 2003: Provides a negative test.
- October 2003: Charged with misconduct by the FA for his failure to take the drugs test.
- 19 December, 2003: Banned for eight months by the FA and fined £50,000.
- 20 January, 2004: Ban starts.
- 18 March, 2004: Appeal rejected.
- June 2004: Unable to play in the Euro 2004 tournament with England.
- 20 September, 2004: Plays his first competitive game since the ban (against Liverpool in a 2–1 win).

The effect of either missing a drugs test (a straight ban) or not being present where you should be when the testers come knocking (the whereabouts rule, also known as the 'three strikes and you're banned' rule) mean that it is a combination of the clubs, players, club doctors and agents who are responsible for passing on details of each player's weekday whereabouts for an hour a day. Recently, Manchester City were found guilty of breaching the terms of the rule and not informing the authorities of the whereabouts of their squad at particular times. This happened three times in the space of five months and they were fined £35,000.

MUTU'S EXPENSIVE NIGHT OUT

In August 2003, Mutu transferred from Italian club Parma to Chelsea for €22.5m. He tested positive for cocaine in October 2004, prompting Chelsea to terminate his contract. He was also banned from football for seven months. He appealed to CAS, which decided that Mutu had committed a breach of his contract without just cause. FIFA ultimately ordered him to pay Chelsea €17.1m. Mutu again appealed to CAS, challenging the FIFA decision. In July 2009, CAS agreed with FIFA. Mutu explained that he could not pay the money and Chelsea changed their approach, suing the clubs he joined after leaving Chelsea on a free transfer: Juventus and Livorno. In April 2013, FIFA agreed with Chelsea that the two Italian clubs should be liable for the payment. In January 2015, however, the decision was overturned. This means that at the time of writing Chelsea have still not recovered the money they believe they are owed by Mutu.

The ruling serves as an warning to players and clubs: a player's actions can have severe financial implications. In the case of Mutu, this meant having to pay back most of his transfer fee. This type of high-stakes dispute illustrates the uneasy relationship between player and club. Footballers earn millions, and are transferred for millions more – which means that the consequences for breaching such lucrative contracts can be astronomical.

THE DIFFICULT CASE OF JAKE LIVERMORE

Sometimes a positive drug test and even an admission of guilt can be overlooked in exceptional circumstances. In April 2015, a routine drugs test following a Hull City game against Crystal Palace led to a positive test for Premier League player Jake Livermore. He was suspended by his club in May 2015 and it was revealed that he admitted taking cocaine. The standard sanction at the time for taking recreational drugs was a two-year ban. It was then reported that Livermore had turned to drugs after the death of his newborn baby.

An FA panel decided that the circumstances were so unique and exceptional that no ban should be imposed. Livermore explained that he had suffered bouts of depression and had taken the drug to relieve the stress and anguish of his situation.

The decision had few precedents because the test for exceptional circumstances is incredibly high. In order for no ban to be imposed, particular exceptional circumstances must apply and there must be clear evidence to explain his behaviour. The FA panel deemed that the test had been met and that no ban should be imposed. Indeed, the details of his baby's death in hospital were redacted (blacked out) due to their harrowing nature. It's fair to say that many felt the panel had taken the right decision. The then Hull City manager, Steve Bruce, commented after the decision: '. . . there are obviously some circumstances that make you see he has been in a dark place for a long, long time. All footballers think they are macho men but they have problems just like everybody else.'

BETTING

In August 2014, the FA brought in new rules for players playing in various leagues, including the Premier League and Football League. Previously, players and managers were not allowed to bet on any match or competition in which they were involved or which they could influence.

Prior to the new rules coming into force, players had been sanctioned. Former Tottenham player Andros Townsend was banned for four months (three of them suspended) and fined £18,000 in June 2013; Cameron Jerome, then at Stoke, was fined £50,000, and Dan Gosling, then at Newcastle, £30,000, though both escaped bans. All three players were believed to have bet on games in which they were involved.

A bet includes betting on results, goal scorers, in-game actions, transfers, manager changes, promotions or relegations. It also involves betting or passing on information they pick up during the course of their job (and of which the public aren't aware), such as a player being injured or being ill, which affects the strength of the team.

Nonetheless, the FA decided to change their rules to prevent players, coaches and others from betting on any football game worldwide. The rationale was to make the ban as simple as possible.

Since clubs and leagues are closely associated with them, gambling companies are extremely visible in football – and many players (perhaps inevitably) have not been as aware as they should have been about the ban. The Football League, for example, is sponsored by Sky Bet, and for the 2017/18 season nearly half of the Premier League clubs had gambling companies as shirt sponsors. Allied to this, the majority of clubs in both the Premier League and Championship have official betting partners. Below is just a selection of players who have breached the new rules:

- Joey Barton, then with Premier League team Burnley, was suspended for 18 months (reduced by five months on appeal) for placing 1,260 bets on football matches over a 10-year period between 26 March, 2006 and 13 May, 2016. It was bookmaker Betfair who alerted the football authorities to his betting habits. He pleaded guilty to the charge but argued that a much lower ban than 18 months was appropriate.

- In May 2016, ex-Manchester City defender Martín Demichelis escaped a ban after accepting a betting-related charge. He placed 29 bets on football matches between 22 January, 2016 and 15 February, 2016, though none related to any matches over which he had an influence. The Argentinian was instead fined the precise amount of £22,058 and warned as to his future conduct.

- Nick Bunyard, then manager of non-league Frome Town, was banned by the FA for three years for betting on his own team to lose a game. He was found to have placed 45 bets against his own teams, although the FA commission accepted he was not involved in match-fixing. The line between profiting from betting against your own team and criminal activities is very thin. In a subsequent interview, Bunyard said that he believed players and managers betting on games continues to be 'part of the culture of football'. His is the most significant ban since the new rules came in.

It has been reported that a variety of ex-professional players have lost large amounts of money through gambling problems. The Sporting Chance Clinic was set up in 2000 to deal with the addictions of many footballers and former players. At that time, drugs and alcohol were the main concern. Today, the Clinic reports that around two-thirds of their clients are treated for gambling addiction.

THE PROBLEM WITH EATING A PIE

The scene was set for a monumental David versus Goliath encounter. The FA Cup draw threw up a fantastic game for the neutral with non-league Sutton United hosting Premier League side Arsenal in February 2017.

With cup giant-killing acts relatively rare, the non-league side gave a stellar account of themselves despite the 2–0 defeat.

In the build-up to the game, a betting company had sponsored Sutton's kit and had paid the club for advertising space around the ground because the match was to be broadcast on primetime UK TV. Its reserve goalkeeper, 45-year-old Wayne Shaw, saw that all three substitutes had been used and decided to eat a meat pie, which alerted the TV cameras.

It turned out that a betting company had offered odds at 8–1 for the goalkeeper to eat a pie during the game. The FA investigated and found that Shaw knew about the promotion. Found guilty of breaching the rules, he was fined £375 and banned for two months. The sad conclusion to this story was that he resigned from the club, is unemployed at the time of writing and is reported to be suffering from depression. He said in an interview for BBC Radio 5 Live: 'I've been through depression. I wasn't sleeping right, I could feel myself getting stressed. And I've still got that knot in my stomach.'

Many have since questioned whether the betting company should have done more to protect Shaw. Indeed, the company was fined £84,000 by the Gambling Commission for its role in the publicity stunt and warned it may lose its licence if found to be behind similar activity in the future.

When does showing your underpants cost you £80k?

During Euro 2012, Denmark star Nicklas Bendtner was banned for one match and fined £80,000 for showing the logo of bookmaker Paddy Power while celebrating a goal against Portugal in the tournament. The logo was featured on the waistband of his underpants, and Bendtner argued that these were his lucky pants. That didn't wash with the authorities: UEFA regulations stop players and teams advertising on their kits during matches.

PLAYING A WEAKENED TEAM

In 2009, Wolves were sanctioned with a suspended fine after making wholesale changes to the club's first 11 against Manchester United. In 2010, Blackpool were also fined £25,000 after their manager made 10 changes to the club's starting line-up against Aston Villa. The fines were the result of a Premier League rule that clubs must field a full-strength team. There are similar rules in the Football League (and their cup competitions), FA Cup, Champions League and Europa League competitions.

Wolves boss Mick McCarthy made the changes to his team playing against Manchester United at Old Trafford. Wolves lost 3–0, and McCarthy then recalled nine players to their following fixture against Burnley and won the game.

After Blackpool had drawn 2–2 at home to Everton, manager Ian Holloway rotated his squad, making 10 changes to his starting team for the match at Aston Villa, only four days later.

The number of changes made meant that the Premier League considered that both clubs were not at full strength. It's fair to say Holloway didn't take the decision too well: 'Who the hell are they to tell me my players are not good enough?' He also threatened to resign if the club were punished.

Both managers were motivated by the heavy, upcoming Premier League fixture list, and rotating players to prioritise certain 'more winnable' fixtures. Perhaps McCarthy was too honest in his explanation that Wolves had a relegation six-pointer against Burnley three days after the United game, which was his priority.

What other reasons are there for picking a weakened team? Usually to focus on particular competitions, like the Premier League or the Champions League, and to give established players a rest while also giving younger squad players a chance and greater experience in the first team.

There are a number of factors that can be used in assessing whether a club is fielding its 'full-strength' team. Some have suggested basing an assessment on the players who have started the most number of Premier League games for the club in that season. However, this alone is probably too crude a measure because it fails to take account of form, tactical formation, unavailability due to injury, or player fatigue and the number of games played to date.

The selection of international players is also questionable. It would be difficult for the Premier League to argue that wholesale changes to the starting line-up weakened a team if the majority of those selected played international football. Equally, teams like Manchester City and Chelsea, with squads packed full of internationals, could all be deemed capable of first team action.

Several clubs – including Liverpool and Manchester United – have rotated their squads at various times but without sanction. Two examples are set out below.

- Manchester United had just won the 2008/09 Premier League title with one game to spare. They played Hull City on 24 May, 2009 ahead of the Champions League Final against Barcelona just three days later. Nine days earlier, United had put out its strongest team against Arsenal because at that stage the race for the title with Liverpool was still up for grabs. Once United had secured the Premier League title, manager Sir Alex Ferguson rotated 10 of the starting 11 players for the trip to Hull.
- In May 2007, Liverpool made nine changes from the team that had beaten Chelsea in the Champions League semi-final four days prior to their Premier League game against Fulham. Even with those changes, the starting 11 facing Fulham contained nine internationals.

Why was Ferguson, who made 10 changes for the Hull game, not sanctioned by the Premier League? (This was the same number of changes made by Wolves against United when it was found to have breached Premier League rules.) The answer is that, even with 9 and 10 changes made, international-class players were still present in United's 'weakened' team. The same was true for Liverpool. What is certain is that any manager's ability to change his starting line-up will depend on the strength of the club's playing squad. Interestingly, the strategy paid off for Manchester United, who beat Hull City 1–0, but not for Liverpool, who lost to Fulham 1–0.

In 2007, when Manchester United avoided sanction, Sheffield United were relegated. By fielding weaker teams against those teams with which Sheffield United were competing to avoid relegation, had Ferguson undermined the integrity of the Premier League? Neil Warnock, the manager of Sheffield United, did not mince his words.

> It's a disgrace the Premier League even thought about charging them [Wolves]. They didn't charge United or Liverpool, which were far more expensive mistakes. Have Liverpool been docked points for the team they put out against Fulham or the one Manchester United did against West Ham? I don't think so somehow.

This led the Premier League to reconsider how the 'full-strength team' rule should be applied. Until this point, there had been no accepted definition of what constituted a 'full-strength team', and it was clearly a difficult call – based on player quality, rotation, resting players and player injuries. Blackpool's Holloway had pointed out that a number of the replacements he selected for the Aston Villa game were international players. As a result, the Premier League agreed that a full-strength squad would be any player listed in the club's 25-man squad list. Since this new interpretation, there have been no further sanctions imposed by the Premier League on its clubs. However, in 2016, the Football League did fine 12 clubs for not fielding their strongest line-ups in the Football League's Checkatrade Trophy. Unlike the original Premier League rules, there had been guidance from the Football League explaining that a full-strength policy was:

1. five of the starting line-up were required to have started the previous or following game; *or*
2. five of the starting line-up who have made the most starting appearances in League and domestic cup competitions fixtures during the current season.

Luton, Portsmouth, Bradford, Blackpool, Bristol Rovers, MK Dons, Millwall, Charlton, Peterborough, Sheffield United, Southend and Fleetwood were all fined. Bristol Rovers manager Darrell Clarke complained bitterly: 'I do not like people telling me what players I can and can't pick.'

PREVENTION AND EDUCATION

There are so many ways players and managers can get in trouble. An Instagram post or a stray tweet can lead to an FA ban and/or fine. Players are banned and sanctioned for a variety of reasons; betting, a poor tackle, a stray elbow or abusive behaviour. The sanctions can be significant and the key to change is educating players and managers to avoid such consequences. Just as a manager will try to make sure a particular player doesn't make a silly two-footed lunge during a game, players need to also be reminded about the perils of ill-thought-out social media posts and public comments that can sometimes get them into serious bother.

CHAPTER 8

THE GLOBAL GAME

Where is the balance of power in the global game? Players are at the centre of industry; but their clubs pay them and provide the showcase for them to flourish in the domestic club setting. There is a delicate balancing act for players wanting to represent their country (and in particular to play in the World Cup, European Championship, Copa América and African Cup of Nations) while also ensuring that they are fit and ready for club competition throughout the season.

Major tournaments need star players to generate the best spectacle possible. In turn, star-studded matches can generate huge television audiences, attracting particular brands that want to enter into lucrative sponsorship arrangements. The 2014 World Cup Final between Germany and Argentina attracted a television audience of more than 1 billion.

Over time, tournament organisers such as FIFA and UEFA have successfully commercialised their finals competitions. Previously, clubs received no compensation for releasing their players, which meant that they were effectively gifting their prized assets in the hope that they came back uninjured and in one piece. A power struggle ensued – a multilateral, high-stakes negotiation between clubs, tournament organisers and national associations in relation to the release of players, compensation for such release, insurance in case of injury and an agreement on the number of friendly and competitive international fixtures throughout the football calendar season.

There are now a variety of agreements and 'memoranda of understanding', which provide a coordinated framework acceptable for all. Previously, many felt that FIFA and UEFA exerted a significant amount of power and control over players. Clubs felt the need to rebalance the international ecosystem.

Ultimately, players want to play international football. An appearance at the World Cup, European Championship, Copa América or African Cup of Nations puts a player on a global stage. What's more, a match-winning performance at a major tournament can potentially define a player's career, leading to a dream transfer, higher transfer fees for a selling club and better wages for the player.

CLUB VERSUS COUNTRY

The 'club versus country' debate is a long-standing bone of contention for many of football's stakeholders. Until relatively recently, clubs received little or no compensation or protection from national federations when their players were released for games involving international qualification and major tournaments. Clubs had to release their players and hope for the best.

For example, in the standard Premier League player employment contract is a clause stating that the club in question is obliged to 'release the Player as required for the purposes of fulfilling the obligations in respect of representative matches to his national association pursuant to the statutes and regulations of FIFA'.

National federations often believe clubs put pressure on players to drop out of particular games or use an injury as an excuse after being called up. These issues continue to cause headaches for major tournament organisers like UEFA or FIFA. To maximise the appeal of their tournaments, they want all the top players playing and clubs releasing them to play for their national team. Clubs are obliged to release their players, but things can get a tad difficult if a player retires from international football and/or refuses a call-up.

In addition, there are strict rules around how a player even qualifies to play for a country. As a rule of thumb, a player doesn't need to have been born in the country they represent at international level. In the early days of the World Cup, there were players who exploited the dual nationality rules. One of the most famous was Luis Monti, who played for Argentina in the 1930 World Cup Final and then switched allegiance for the next World Cup to play in the victorious Italian team. Monti was not the only Argentinian to make the switch to Italy, being in a group of players who were known collectively as the Oriundi. It is not uncommon for a tug-of-war to develop between competing nations who want players that are eligible to play for them. This continues to cause issues for players and countries alike.

PLAYER POLITICS

The issue of nationality can be confusing at the best of times. In a globalised age, to be born in one country, grow up in another and live in a third country is more common than it used to be. Take the example of Adnan Januzaj, who broke into the Manchester United first team in 2013. Given that he was born in Brussels, he was eligible for Belgium, and given that his parents are Kosovan-Albanian he was also eligible for Albania, Serbia or Kosovo (although Kosovo did not have a FIFA- or UEFA-recognised team until 2016).

Such examples cause issues for FIFA, the body that determines eligibility for players in international tournament competitions. It has rules defining who can play for a national team.

The most straightforward position is that a national of the country is qualified to play for that nation. So far, so good. If a player wants to choose a new nation to play for and has not yet played in a competitive senior international match for another country, one or other of the following criterion must be met:

1. the player (or a parent or a grandparent) must have been born in the territory of the new team; *or*
2. the player must have lived in the new country's territory for at least five years after reaching the age of 18 (so he will be a minimum of 23 years of age).

For a player to choose a new country to represent, the player must write to FIFA requesting the change based on fulfilling the above criteria. Once the paperwork is submitted, the FIFA Players Status Committee decides on the request. Until the request is processed the player cannot play for any representative national team.

Some have queried whether the 'granny rule' – as it has affectionately been termed – is too tenuous a link. A fair few international managers have exploited the distant genealogy of players, with Jack Charlton proving particularly adept when he was in charge of the Republic of Ireland during his 10-year reign.

The rules for other sports can be very different. World Rugby voted in 2017 to extend the residency qualification for international players in rugby union from three to five years to ensure those selected players have a 'genuine, close, credible and established link' with the country they represent. In cricket, the England team has been awash with players not born in this country, including Andrew Strauss, Matt Prior and Kevin Pietersen, all born in South Africa. For athletes to participate in the Olympic games, Rule 41 of the Olympic Charter states that each athlete must be a citizen in the country for which they compete.

Some have questioned whether the FIFA eligibility rule could be challenged if a player plays a competitive match and then wishes to switch. A relatively recent example came after Kosovo declared its independence in 2008. In September 2016, it played its first competitive international game against Finland in a 1–1 draw. Participating in that game were players who had previously played competitive matches for other nations, including Albania and Norway. Right up to the last moment, a handful of players were still awaiting clearance from FIFA. Permission was granted only a few hours before kick-off, and appropriately the Kosovan goal was scored by Valon Berisha, who had represented Norway 19 times previously. It appears in this instance that FIFA waived its eligibility rule and granted an exemption because the players could not have chosen to play for Kosovo at the time they made their decision to represent Albania and Norway. This does, however, appear to be the exception to the rule.

In one recent example, Florent Malouda represented French Guiana during a Concacaf Gold Cup match against Honduras. The ex-Chelsea

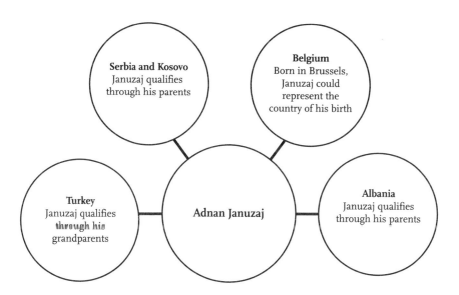

Adnan Januzaj had an incredible number of options when it came to deciding which international team he would represent. In the end, he chose Belgium, the country of his birth.

and France international footballer had 80 caps for France, so FIFA had previously explained to French Guiana that he was ineligible to play. As a result, the team was fined, made to forfeit their match (after originally drawing the game 0–0) and Malouda was suspended for two matches.

Nonetheless, there have been a number of high-profile situations where a player has played international football for one country yet still been able to turn out for another. Instances of players switching are likely to increase as players in a globalised industry live and work in a variety of countries, finding perhaps that they adapt better and/or have the particular attributes that fit the playing style of the new national team.

TO BE OR NOT TO BE – THE NATIONALITY QUESTION

1. Ex-Chelsea striker Diego Costa played twice for Brazil in non-competitive friendly matches, which allowed him to switch allegiances once he received a Spanish passport in 2013.

He represented Spain for the first time a year later. When he played for Spain in the 2014 World Cup, he was roundly booed by the Brazilian crowds for disloyalty.

2. Neven Subotić was born in the former Yugoslavia but represented the United States at under-17 and under-20 level. He elected, however, to play for Serbia after deciding to reject senior call-ups for the United States and Bosnia and Herzegovina.

3. After playing for Brazil in an under-23 tournament for Brazil, Thiago Motta switched to playing for Italy, having qualified to represent the Azzurri via his grandfather. He made his debut in 2011.

4. Premier League star Wilfried Zaha was born in the Ivory Coast, represented England at youth level but elected to play for his country of birth. Zaha also played in two friendly internationals for the English senior side, making his debut against Sweden in November 2012.

BROTHERLY LOVE

You'd have thought it pretty uncommon for brothers to be good enough to play elite international football. However, there are several examples of siblings playing together in World Cup Finals, stretching all the way back to the Evaristo brothers who represented Argentina in 1930. Whether those brothers play for the same team is another question. In fact, there are examples of the nationality rule that may look a bit odd to some.

Take Jonathan de Guzmán. He could have represented Canada, the Philippines or Jamaica but chose Holland after moving to the Netherlands in 1999 from Canada to play for Feyenoord. He played for the Oranje in 2013 for the first time, while his brother Julian elected to represent Canada.

Half-brothers Kevin-Prince and Jérôme Boateng are another case in point. Kevin-Prince was born and brought up in Germany, and represented Germany at under-19 and under-21 level. He was granted a Ghanaian passport in 2010 and began to represent the Black Stars in the World Cup that year, in South Africa. By contrast, his half-brother Jérôme was also brought up in Germany and represented Germany at various youth levels before making his senior debut in 2009. Both brothers, born in the same country, represented different nations and indeed played out a 2–2 draw against each other in the 2014 World Cup in Brazil.

In addition, the Albania v. Switzerland match during Euro 2016 pitted brothers Taulant and Granit Xhaka against each other. It was the first instance of brothers playing against each other in European Championship history.

COMPENSATION

Even while nationality issues were throwing up difficult qualification criteria, clubs and national associations were grappling with another major issue: the obligation on clubs to release players without compensation and with the risk of injury. Matters came to a head at the turn of the millennium.

In September 2000, 14 of Europe's top clubs (Real Madrid, Barcelona, Manchester United, Liverpool, Inter, Juventus, Milan, Marseille, PSG, Bayern Munich, Borussia Dortmund, Ajax, PSV and Porto) organised themselves as the G14. It had no official authority in the footballing world and was initially regarded by UEFA as a maverick pressure group. Yet the G14 was founded as a consequence of the dissatisfaction felt by the clubs with UEFA, and a feeling that clubs should be represented within the formal UEFA decision-making process. The clubs believed they would be more powerful as a formal collective, championing the position of clubs in the wider footballing environment. They were dissatisfied with a number of issues, not just the issues of player compensation and insurance to cover a player's wages when injured on international duty.

The majority of the threats and counter-accusations were played out in front of the world's media. One of these cases involved Abdelmajid Oulmers – a case dubbed as the new Bosman, which commentators predicted would change the game forever.

In November 2004, while playing for Morocco against Burkina Faso, Oulmers was injured and ruled out for eight months. His domestic club, Sporting Charleroi, blamed his loss as the reason for their failure to win the domestic league, eventually finishing fifth. Understanding that the issue was of major importance to all clubs throughout Europe, the G14 supported the Belgium club in its compensation claim against FIFA (as the ultimate global body responsible for setting the rules on player release and compensation) for the injured Oulmers. The G14 further claimed €860m in damages for the costs incurred during the previous 10 years of releasing players for the World Cup without paying for the privilege.

The parties decided to settle this issue, championing negotiation ahead of what might have been years of court cases. The result? Both sides won their respective battles. FIFA secured the dropping of the case while the clubs received compensation for releasing their players.

As a result, and for the first time, clubs releasing their players for UEFA Euro 2008 received up to £3,000 per player per day in compensation. Ex-UEFA president Michel Platini explained: 'Clubs who provide UEFA and FIFA with certain amounts of money through these players should get some compensation and share in these profits.'

It followed that player release compensation was paid both by UEFA and FIFA for their tournaments and was distributed to the clubs depending on how many players played in the tournament (and qualifying rounds). By way of example, the calculation mechanism for Euros tournaments is based on two elements:

1. The number of qualifying matches played by each national team so long as the player is in the 23-man match sheet;
   and
2. The number of players selected for a national team that qualified for the tournament, linked to the number of days each player is present at the tournament.

In the Euro 2012 tournament, €100m was paid out to a total of 575 clubs. Bayern Munich received €3,095,393 – the highest compensation paid.

In Euro 2016, €150m was paid by UEFA to a total of 641 clubs. Premier League clubs received €38,329,085, Liverpool FC receiving €3,394,511 – the highest payment among English clubs. Among the top paid clubs of the tournament were Liverpool, Tottenham, Manchester United, Arsenal and Southampton in the Premier League, along with Juventus, Bayern Munich, Real Madrid, Barcelona and Roma. In Euro 2020, UEFA are reported to be paying €200m.

While such specific detail is not currently available for FIFA tournaments, FIFA provided £1,770 per day to the clubs of footballers who took part in the 2014 Brazil World Cup. It has been reported that clubs will share around £142m per tournament for releasing players for each of the Russia and Qatar World Cups.

INJURY ON INTERNATIONAL DUTY

Relations remain a tad frosty between clubs and international associations, especially when it comes to the thorny issue of international call-ups and players being injured prior to the call-up or as a result of playing for their national team.

There are countless examples of club managers being far from happy about releasing a healthy player, only for him to return injured and not able to play while the club continues to pay his wages. One such example was Arjen Robben. Bayern Munich believed that the medical staff of the Royal Dutch Football Association had 'patched him up' so that he could continue playing in the South Africa World Cup in 2010, regardless of the longer-term impact on his health and the wishes of his club. He was unable to play for the first two months of the subsequent season as a result of a hamstring injury – allegedly suffered in the warm-up games prior to the tournament.

Bayern's chief executive at the time, Karl-Heinz Rummenigge, stated: 'When you hire a car, you have to bring it back in a decent state. Robben was taken from us, then put back in the garage as a wreck. Once again we must pay the bill as a club after a player is seriously injured playing for a national team.'

After various similar conflicts with high-profile clubs and the threat of legal action, FIFA were spurred into action. The solution was a programme called FIFA Club Protection, which began in 2012. Prior to this insurance plan, there was no compensation for clubs whose players were called up and injured on international duty.

When Jack Butland broke his ankle playing for England against Germany in March 2016, his Premier League club Stoke City were able to claim an insurance payout to cover his wages and medical care. There are, however, a few conditions to the insurance, including:

- an initial 28-day 'excess' period, meaning that the club doesn't receive any compensation for the first month;
- the maximum wage insurance pay-out is capped at €143k a week, which should cover most players; *and*
- cover is limited to one year and a maximum pay-out of €7.5m per player.

One other main practical difficulty is that the annual fund is capped at €100m per year. So if there are a number of large claims in the same year, the fund might have already run out of money by the time a player is injured. As Butland was out of action for 13 months, Stoke would have claimed the maximum available. The unlucky Butland also broke his finger again on England duty in November 2017, but because he was out of action for less than a month it would have been unlikely that compensation for this absence would be available.

An example is Everton right-back Séamus Coleman, who was injured playing for the Republic of Ireland v. Wales in March 2017. Under the FIFA programme, Everton were entitled to claim back his reported £50,000-per-week salary for the first year of his lay-off. Coleman returned to the Everton first team in January 2018, thus qualifying for compensation of around £2m, or the equivalent of around 10 months' worth of wages (minus the excess).

A number of clubs and players may also take out separate insurance policies to guard against the financial impact of serious injury or illness. If more than one policy has been taken out, the club or player usually cannot claim twice for the same injury suffered.

PLAYER CALL-UPS

Under the FIFA international call-up rules, clubs are required to release their players for international duty.

The FIFA Player Status and Transfer Regulations Annex 1 'Release of Players to Association' terms state that:

> Clubs are obliged to release their registered players to the representative teams of the country for which the player is eligible to play on the basis of his nationality if they are called up by the association concerned.

This has led to some interesting disputes about the meaning of a 'call-up', the tournament in question and whether a player is entitled to play for their domestic club after an international team has been eliminated from a tournament.

Calling it a day and/or being obliged to release a player for international competition can be controversial. These issues came to a head for Lionel Messi when playing for Argentina in the 2008 Olympics in China, and for Joel Matip and Allan Nyom, of Premier League teams Liverpool and West Brom respectively, when both selected by Cameroon to play in the 2017 African Cup of Nations.

In 2008, the Olympics fell towards the beginning of the footballing season rather than taking place in the traditional closed season across Europe. Clubs were understandably wary of losing their star players for the start of their domestic and Champions League qualifying games. At the heart of the dispute were Barcelona's superstar Lionel Messi, Schalke's Brazilian defender Rafinha and the Brazilian playmaker Diego Ribas from Werder Bremen.

The matter involved a long-standing custom to release under-23 players for the Olympics. This is despite the fact that, under the FIFA rules, the Olympics were not classed as an international FIFA tournament, meaning that the clubs could refuse to release their players.

On 30 July, 2008, FIFA decided that clubs must release their players for the Olympics. Unsurprisingly, the clubs took the matter to the Court of Arbitration for Sport (CAS), although by this stage the Olympics were only a matter of days away.

On 6 August, 2008, CAS disagreed with FIFA, stating that the players didn't need to be released. While FIFA was 'surprised and disappointed' by the decision, Schalke and Werder Bremen both consented to their Brazilian players Rafinha and Diego remaining in China with the rest of their squad. Similarly, Barcelona also reluctantly accepted Lionel Messi's desire to play for his country; he would eventually guide his team to gold. As part of the deal struck with Barcelona, he was apparently excused from specific friendly matches.

Under the FIFA rules, clubs have to release a player if the player is called up for an international game as defined in the FIFA rules. Both Joel Matip and Allan Nyom were selected for Cameroon's provisional 35-man squad for the 2017 African Cup of Nations.

Matip had not played for Cameroon since 2015. Unfortunately for him, he had not officially written to Cameroon announcing his retirement before his call-up to the national team. In the event that he was selected, Liverpool were concerned that they could be sanctioned by FIFA for playing a player who should be on international duty. Liverpool manager Jürgen Klopp was advised by the club's lawyers not to select the player against Manchester United and Plymouth Argyle – something which didn't go down well with the Liverpool manager.

In this moment, we are sure we did nothing wrong. We are sure Joel Matip did nothing wrong. He didn't play for Cameroon since 2015. Since he has been here he has not been a Cameroon national player. In this moment he is not in the squad of Cameroon, so he cannot play for them, but in this moment we have not a 100 per cent guarantee he could play for us. That is the situation.

FIFA's guidance turned on whether the player had to inform Cameroon before being called up of his intention not to be selected. Had Matip provided written confirmation that he didn't want to be selected before being included in the provisional Cameroon squad?

As for Nyom, he travelled to the Cameroon pre-camp but was not selected for the final squad. It was reported that the Cameroon FA still refused to provide their consent for him to play for his club.

Both matters were ultimately resolved after the Cameroon FA relented and provided their consent for both players to play for their respective Premier League teams. Nonetheless both players missed Liverpool and West Brom games, much to the frustration of their clubs.

These situations raise the following questions. Is a player even able to formally retire? What happens if the player's country refuses to accept the player's wishes? In 2016, after French playmaker Franck Ribéry announced his retirement from international football, UEFA president Michel Platini said: 'Franck cannot decide himself whether he plays for France. If [coach] Didier Deschamps picks him, he must come. That's the FIFA rule. If he doesn't come, he will be suspended for three Bayern Munich games.'

Similarly, Claude Makélélé came out of retirement to play in the 2006 World Cup for France, and then promptly re-retired after the tournament. The then French coach Raymond Domenech did not accept the player's request at the time. Chelsea manager José Mourinho accused Domenech of treating the player 'like a slave'.

THE 39TH GAME

In February 2008, the Premier League announced that it was considering the introduction of an 'international round' to its football season, extending the current 38-game season to 39 matches.

Under the proposal, each club would play a 39th game abroad during a weekend in January, starting in 2011. Cities all over the world would bid to become hosts for the matches. Five cities would each host two games. These additional games would most likely be determined by a draw, with the top five teams seeded to avoid playing each other.

With an international round further raising the profile of the already popular league, the amount of money the Premier League could receive from the sale of overseas rights might have again risen substantially – there were estimates of an additional £5 million for each club.

Its advocates, including Richard Scudamore, then the Premier League chief executive, explained that more money could be reinvested in the game, meaning better players, grounds and facilities. The former prime minister Gordon Brown even suggested that some of the money could be used to lower ticket prices.

Such a scheme could also be good for the host cities. NFL games at Wembley, for example, are reported to generate £20m+ for London as visitors from the United States flock to the capital for the game. Diehard football fans could even use the game as an excuse for the annual family holiday. Indeed, Arsène Wenger, ex-manager of Arsenal, and Kevin Keegan, former Newcastle manager, both thought the idea of providing live stadium access to fans who could otherwise watch Premier League games only on television was a noble gesture. Keegan said, 'It will give everybody in the world a chance to see it in areas where they don't get a chance to see football like that.'

Despite the obvious financial incentives for staging the international round, the proposals were met with much hostility. 'GAM£ 39', as it was dubbed, was roundly criticised. The plans would alienate domestic fans, unhappy about their league being taken on tour, while seriously affecting the integrity and, more importantly, the structure of the football season.

The draw method to determine the game 39 set of fixtures was also questioned. Specifically, it could have been especially unfair on the teams battling relegation, if they had to play a third match against, say, the champions elect. Or imagine two teams were battling against relegation, and one of those teams was drawn against Liverpool, while the other was drawn against a relegation rival.

The then Sunderland manager Roy Keane, who was broadly in favour of the extra game, tellingly explained, 'Change is good but that depends who you are playing in that extra game. If it's one of the top four, I might argue.' Ex-Manchester United manager Sir Alex Ferguson was also unhappy, saying that consultations with managers and players should have taken place on a substantive level before the idea was announced to the world.

Commentators also raised concerns about player burnout, saying that some clubs already played too many games. An interesting point was also raised by ex-Fulham manager Lawrie Sanchez, who argued that foreign national associations could well view the Premier League 'coming to a country near you soon' as a threat to their own leagues' viability and popularity: 'other national associations won't be happy about the Premier

League coming into their game, taking sponsors, taking advertising, taking revenue from their game'.

Within a week of the press release, various national and international football associations publicly rejected the idea. Michel Platini, the then UEFA president, described the idea as 'comical' and 'a nonsense idea'. Sepp Blatter, ex-FIFA president, labelled it an 'abuse of association football', while the Asian Football Confederation was one of many to refuse the Premier League to play competitive games in their grounds. The Korean FA expressed 'strong reservations' and the Japan Football Association called the project 'problematic'. Conversely, the United Arab Emirates Football Association and the Hong Kong Football Association backed Premier League plans.

The Football Supporters' Federation launched its 'No to game 39' poll to fight the plans. Game 39 has not since reared its head, and it would clearly be controversial to bring the topic back to the table for further debate.

PLAYERS UNDER PRESSURE

Club versus country battles are nothing new in football. Players are in a continual tug of war between their domestic clubs and international teams. Conflict continues to occur over releasing players for international duty, what happens when players are injured while playing for their country and how much compensation should be paid to clubs for releasing their star assets. While these matters can sometimes bubble over, the wider debate rages about the number of games players should be playing for them to perform at their optimal level. That debate is not going to end any time soon, especially as players are so valuable to club and international teams alike.

CHAPTER 9

FOOTBALL BROADCASTING

The money flow into football has become a torrent in recent times, predominately because of pay TV. For TV executives, football is a must-see driver enabling them to sell wider subscription services and lucrative premium packages. Leagues like the Premier League and competitions like the Champions League provide exclusive must-have premium content for broadcasters to convert millions of fans into long-term pay TV subscribers.

In turn, the monies paid by broadcasters have flowed to leagues and clubs. In recent years, companies have proved willing to pay billions of pounds per season for premium, exclusive content. The result is that clubs (and their players) are the beneficiaries of huge money flows into the game. In the Premier League, clubs receive a minimum of almost £100m for each season they play in the top division. This in turn allows them to spend millions of pounds on player transfers, wages and world-class stadia.

In the 2016/17 season, it was reported that the Premier League was available to watch in more than one billion homes across 188 countries. The global reach and appeal of the Premier League, and football in general, should not be underestimated. Such a cross-continental fan base leads to demand for the live product – which is met by broadcasters receiving lucrative subscriptions and advertising revenues, and clubs selling merchandise and match-day experiences to engaged fans.

In 1992 the latest football revolution in the UK began when Sky bought the exclusive rights to the Premier League. In more recent times, similar models have been adopted by almost all major European football leagues. This symbiotic relationship between live content and football looks set to continue.

PREMIER LEAGUE BROADCASTING RIGHTS EXPLAINED

The current three-year 2016/17–2018/19 global broadcasting deal for the Premier League netted its 20 clubs more than £8bn. Of that, £5.14bn came from two companies: Sky and British Telecom (BT).

Sky is the largest pay TV operator in the UK, and BT the largest provider of UK broadband. The astronomical sums paid by both broadcasters for a variety of live packages of rights are an acknowledgement of their need to retain Premier League matches as a key component of their respective business models.

Both broadcasters see the Premier League as a means of driving subscribers to their platforms as well as being a source of advertising revenue. For some time, consumers have complained that the two companies having exclusive rights means that two expensive subscriptions are needed to watch a complete season. The question for broadcasters is how many 'packages' of live rights and games are needed to retain and attract subscribers to their premium channels and wider broadband and mobile-phone 'quad-play' offerings.

Before we get into the story of the fierce competition between these two consumer-facing entertainment companies, it is important to go back to the early 1990s and the origins of the Premier League and its initial, ground-breaking deal with Sky.

HOW BROADCASTING RIGHTS USED TO BE SOLD

Before the Premier League was formed in May 1992, the Football League sold its top-flight broadcasting rights to various TV companies, including terrestrial broadcasters BBC and ITV. For example, for two seasons starting in 1983, terrestrial broadcaster ITV paid £5.2 million for 10 live matches per season. During the 1985/86 season, such was the serious breakdown in the relationship between the Football League and the television companies that there was no football broadcast at all for the first half of the season. The head of BBC Sport at the time, Jonathan Martin, said during this impasse that 'soccer is no longer at the heart of television schedules and it's not likely to be again'. (How wrong he was!)

After the dust had settled and football returned to the nation's screens, ITV paid £11m per season to show a reported 18 live matches from 1988 until 1992. Until the forming of the Premier League, the Football League distributed this money more evenly across the four divisions. This changed when the Premier League signed a record-breaking, five-year deal with Sky.

On April 1991, it was announced that around 16 clubs, including the top five clubs at the time – Arsenal, Spurs, Liverpool, Everton and Manchester United – were proposing to break away from the Football League and form a new super-league. The breakaway was intended to provide the clubs with a greater share of revenue from the TV and commercial deals. They argued that they deserved a greater share because they were the main attraction and should have the power to invest a greater share of their income in improved stadia and superstar players.

The Football League and its teams were concerned that the trickle-down flow of investment through the football pyramid would evaporate. In the 1992/93 season, against a backdrop of hostility between the Football Association, the Football League and the newly formed Premier League and its member teams, the breakaway teams competed in the Premier League for the first time. The revenue received was split between the original teams – 22 by the time the League was established – and was shared as set out below according to where the team finished and the number of times it was on TV.

As the holder of the exclusive broadcasting rights, the Premier League had auctioned those rights to the highest bidder. In May 1992, Sky, which had begun its satellite broadcasting service in the UK in 1989, paid a stellar £191m for an exclusive five-year live broadcasting deal. BBC won the highlights, to show on the iconic *Match of the Day* show, but ITV – previously, the alternative live terrestrial broadcaster – was left with nothing. For the first time, the top division was broadcast live exclusively on pay TV.

HOW RIGHTS ARE SOLD

The Premier League negotiates broadcasting deals, usually on a country-by-country basis. Companies who wish to bid for the rights receive an invitation to tender (ITT), which provides the conditions for bidding, the broadcasting packages on offer, the technological processes and know-how required, and any financial guarantees required depending on the size of the bidding company. Usually, for each rights cycle, the Premier League will identify the largest countries and sometimes prioritise deals in order of approximate value or geopolitical significance (think the United States and China).

The types of rights available include live, near-live, delayed, longer highlights, internet rights and mobile rights, depending on the particular territory's appetite for a variety of programming requirements.

Ultimately, the response to the ITT will involve bidding significant amounts of money to win the exclusive rights in a particular country. Competition can be fierce, and large fee increases require broadcasters to bid significant sums to attract subscribers and viewers to their stations.

During the 2016–17–2018/19 rights cycle, the Premier League received £3.2bn from foreign non-UK broadcasters. The League has even sold some of the next rights cycle (2019–20/2021/22), to a number of broadcasters. For example, it was reported that SuperSport, the sub-Saharan Africa broadcaster, agreed to pay £168m a year for the rights – more than double the previous deal. Similarly, NBC in the US are paying £128m per season until 2022.

COLLECTIVE AND EXCLUSIVE SELLING

From the Premier League's inception in 1992, its broadcasting rights have been sold collectively. This means that the member clubs act together to form a league, play in competitions and negotiate commercial deals. For some time now, the question has been whether this collective approach is legal. To date, the court and regulators have accepted that the collective selling of broadcasting rights brings important benefits.

Collective selling continues to be an issue because many believe that the clubs joining together to market the live matches limits the number of live games that can be televised (as clubs choose the number of games that they want to sell). The counter-argument is that the Premier League's commercial agreements need to be organised collectively to manage the interests of its 20 clubs and to help fairly distribute revenues received. Suppose Manchester United decided to individually sell their rights to the highest bidder, as Barcelona and Real Madrid did for many years. United would receive huge sums, and obviously these would not be distributed among the other clubs. This in turn would lead to less equal distribution of broadcasting monies, as well as the potential for reduced competitive balance within the League because the club would have considerably more money to spend on transfers and wages.

For similar reasons, the Premier League historically sold its rights on an exclusive basis. This previously meant that only one broadcaster per country could show live Premier League matches. That changed in the UK in 2007, when a broadcaster called Setanta bought some of the live rights and aimed to compete with Sky. Up until that point, from 1992 to 2007, Sky had been the only broadcaster in the UK to televise live football through its Sky Sports subscription channels. This change was prompted by the European Commission, which investigated the lack of competition in the market for UK football rights, and put in place a framework that prohibited Sky from winning all the broadcasting rights packages. It meant that at least one other broadcaster had to win a live Premier League package.

This competitive landscape evolved once more when BT bid for and won live matches from 2013 onwards. At this stage, the Premier League was keen to maximise competition between two companies with deep pockets, and the fierce auction process in turn ramped up the prices paid.

THE MONEY GENERATED

The amount that broadcasters have been willing to pay to screen live games has grown exponentially. In securing Premier League rights, Sky established itself as the leading sports and entertainment platform in the UK. Live football was the undoubted driver to attract and retain subscribers. Without Premier League football, both Sky and BT run the risk of fewer subscribers, reduced advertising revenues and a resulting drop in profits. Over the last two rights cycles, the amounts that Sky and BT have paid to the Premier League have sky-rocketed:

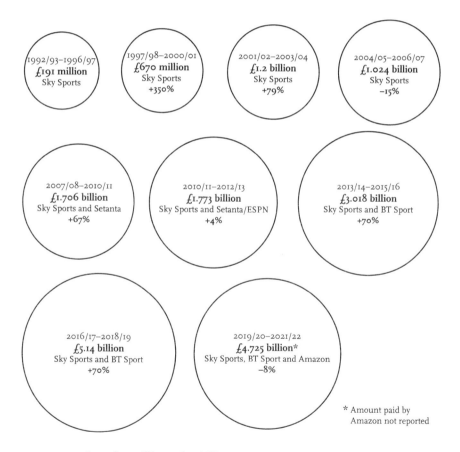

From £191 million to £4.7 billion in just over 20 years, the amounts paid to broadcast Premier League matches have grown exponentially. Competing broadcasters and the astute division of the rights into exclusive packages have helped drive revenues.

Historical Premier League UK live rights table

	1992–97	1997–2001	2001–04	2004–07	2007–10	2010–13	2013–16	2016–19
Amount (£)	191m	670m	1.2bn	1.024bn	1.706bn	1.773bn	3.018bn	5.14bn
Total cost per match (£)*	0.6m	2.8m	3.8m	2.5m	4.1m	4.3m	6.5m	10.2m
Number of games	60	60	106	138	138	138	154	168
Broadcaster(s)	Sky	Sky	Sky	Sky	Sky/ Setanta	Sky/ ESPN	Sky/ BT	Sky/ BT

* Note: numbers rounded up

Summary Premier League UK live rights table for the current 2016/17–2018/19 deal

Broadcaster	Total 2016/17–2018/19 amount paid (£)	Total amount per season (£)	Total per game (£)	Number of matches	Percentage increase on the previous deal	Number of packages won	Previous amount paid (£)
Sky	4.176bn	1.392bn	11m	126	83%	5	2.28bn
BT	960m	320m	7.6m	42	18%	2	738m

For the 2016/17–2018/19 live rights, Sky and BT were awarded the domestic UK rights to show live Premier League matches for three years. The companies paid £5.14bn in total, which equated to a huge 70% increase in rights fees.

The explanation for the 2016/17–2019/20 increase in total cost per match is the competition between Sky and BT, each competing for rights to protect particular broadcasting and broadband markets. With Sky entering the mobile phone market in the UK and BT buying mobile phone operator EE, live premium sports rights are seen as one of the core drivers for 'quad-play' consumer offerings – a bundled phone line, broadband, subscription channels and mobile phone product. Having must-watch live content is seen as the driver for consumers to buy the rest of their technology and communication services through either Sky or BT.

BT also has exclusive rights to Champions League/Europa League matches. It paid more than £1.1bn for these rights for a three-year period ending in 2021.

For the 2016/17–2018/19 rights, Sky paid £4.176bn for 126 games – an increase from the £2.28bn it paid previously for 116 matches. BT had four more games (42 matches per season) than it had in its previous deal and paid £960m per season over the three years of its deal. It had previously paid £738m for 38 matches per season.

In addition, the Premier League announced that the BBC had been successful in bidding for the highlights, to show on its iconic Saturday night *Match of the Day*, having paid £204m.

In the previous 2013/14–2015/16 deal, the total global domestic and overseas figure was reported to be around £5.5bn. As you can see from the above, the money paid by Sky and BT for the domestic market 2016/17–2018/19 rights alone was £5bn+. Even as the domestic deal gets close to topping £5bn, the global appeal of the Premier League continues to grow, with strong competition in a number of key markets, including Asia and the United States. As a result, the latest 2019/20–2021/22 global deal price may end up being north of £8bn.

This is because in February 2018, it was announced that Sky and BT had retained their strong positions in the live Premier League market. Both companies paid a combined reported £4.464bn for the live rights to five of the seven main packages of matches to cover the 2019/20–2021/22 period. The remaining two packages were sold during the summer of 2018 to BT and new entrant Amazon.

BT's additional 20 matches cost £90m, taking their overall spend to £975m, which represented a slight increase on the previous £960m, when there were 10 fewer matches. BT's average cost per match dropped from £7.62m to £6.25m. Amazon bought a package of 20 matches, which consists of two rounds of games shown simultaneously via Amazon Prime per season. Sky paid £3.57bn for its packages of 128 games per season, at a 14% discount on its present deal.

In June 2018 the BBC successfully renewed the rights for its highlights package until at least the 2021/22 season for £211.5m. The package includes the Saturday night *Match of the Day* programme as well as *Match of the Day 2*, *Football Focus* and *The Premier League Show*.

NEW PLAYERS IN FOOTBALL BROADCASTING

For the first time in Premier League history, for the 2019/20 season there will be three companies showing live Premier League matches in the UK. Amazon will be the first to stream its matches exclusively online. The games in the UK will be live-streamed via Amazon Prime (Amazon Prime also has the exclusive UK rights to US Open and ATP World Tour tennis, and non-exclusive rights to NFL games). The price of the deal has yet to be made public.

Amazon Prime is a subscription service, costing £79 per year in the UK, that combines free, unlimited and next-day physical delivery of Amazon products with an online streaming service. The streaming platform provides films, boxsets and now a growing choice of live premium sports content.

Interestingly, Amazon have bought live-streaming rights to only 20 games per season, along with highlights packages. One set of 10 matches is a Boxing Day (26 December) offering, the other is a set of 10 matches during a mid-week set of fixtures in early December. In addition, it has been reported that four of the live games on Boxing Day will be shown back-to-back – a first in Premier League history. While Sky and BT have games throughout the season, Amazon's package is an extremely slim offering of a small number of games within two narrow timeframes. The question is: why has Amazon decided to make the investment at all?

At a basic level, many believe that one of the main objectives is to acquire more Amazon Prime subscribers. The lure of free and quick delivery of physical goods at the speed of a few clicks means people will be more likely to spend on the Amazon website. Evidence from reports at the end of 2017 suggests that US Amazon Prime subscribers spend on average $1,300 per year via Amazon, versus $700 per year spent by non-Prime members. With 100m+ US subscribers in 2018 (as reported by *Variety Magazine*), there appears a clear logic in making the Amazon Prime offering even more attractive to the UK market.

The other driver is likely to be data. Understanding subscribers' physical shopping and online viewing habits gives companies like Amazon the ability to offer the products and services that its customers may wish to buy. Just as Netflix recommends particular programmes through a complex algorithm based on previous viewing habits, Amazon's aim may be to gain greater traction in the UK by analysing people's online and off-line behaviours, in order to attune their product offerings further.

THE LIVE BROADCASTING PACKAGE

UK broadcasters bid for a number of standalone live packages. Historically, the Premier League divided up the matches into a number of packages. For the latest 2019/20–2021/22 auction, there were seven live packages for sale.

These packages varied in size and quality of game. Particular packages give the winning broadcaster 'first picks'. These are first-choice picks of the best game in each game week. Each package has a set day and time. For example, under the latest 2019/20–2021/22 auction process, Sky won the rights to show 128 matches and, most importantly, bought every weekend 'first pick' of matches. They will show matches in the UK at 5.30 p.m. on Saturdays, Sundays at 2 p.m. and 4.30 p.m., and, for the first time in Premier League history, eight games on Saturdays at 7.45 p.m.

HOW THE MONEY IS DISTRIBUTED

The broadcasting and central sponsorship revenue generated from commercial deals is distributed based on a set formula set out in the Premier League regulations (*see* pages 207–209). Revenues are split 50% for a team being in the League in the first place, 25% for where a team finishes in the League, and 25% for how many times a team is selected for a live game in the UK. An amount is also distributed on an equal basis as a result of foreign broadcasting monies received. The monies are distributed to the member clubs, used to cover the running costs of the League, provided to Football League teams by way of solidarity payments or provided to particular charitable, grass-roots or community causes. For example, the Football Foundation, which is part-funded by the Premier League, the FA and the government, provides around £30m each season to grass-roots sport in the UK.

In late 2017, it was reported that some of the top Premier League clubs were lobbying for a change in the way that the broadcasting monies are distributed. From 1992 onwards, the overseas broadcasting monies were split equally between each of the relevant clubs. Based on the 2017/18 season standings, each club would receive an equal payment of £40.7m from all non-UK foreign broadcasting rights revenues regardless of where the club finished in the League. It was reported that teams like Manchester United, Manchester City, Arsenal, Chelsea, Tottenham and Liverpool were keen that the overseas monies should be distributed according to performance rather than just split equally. Those clubs suggested that foreign fans generally want to watch the bigger teams play. The small teams countered this by arguing that the League is only as strong as it is because of its excellent competitive balance. The uncertainty of any team beating another team provides the basis for an exciting and unpredictable League. As such, smaller clubs argued that anything that reduces unpredictability should be avoided.

The result of those 2017 discussions was that for the time being, no changes would be made. In any event, to change the revenue distributions, under the Premier League rules, 14 out of the 20 clubs would need to vote in favour. At that time, there were not enough clubs that thought it was in their interest to change the way the overseas money was distributed.

Fast forward to the summer of 2018, and a compromise was found. The solution was that the revenue up to the amount currently received by non-UK broadcasters (approximately £3.2bn) would still be shared out equally but that any increase in the overseas broadcasting deal (i.e. over and above £3.2bn) would then be distributed according to where each club finishes in the Premier League. This has not previously occurred for the overseas rights element of the Premier League broadcasting deal.

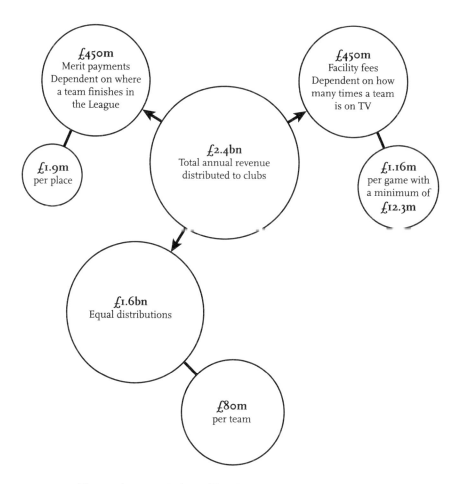

The Premier League is the world's richest league, and all 20 clubs get a share of £2.4 billion per season. Each team is guaranteed over £90 million for the season they are in the Premier League, which includes revenue based on their final league position and the number of televised games in which they appear.

The table on the following pages shows payments made by the Premier League to clubs for the 2017/18 season.

A COMPARISON WITH FOREIGN LEAGUES

While the Premier League still leads the way in relation to broadcasting revenues generated, a number of other leagues receive multi-billion-euro payments for their prized rights. Indeed, over the last decade there

2017/18 Premier League payments to clubs

Club	UK Live	Equal Share	Facility Fees	Merit Payment	International TV	Central Commercial	Total Payment
Manchester City	26	34,812,558	30,390,736	38,625,360	40,771,108	4,838,892	149,438,654
Manchester United	28	34,812,558	32,650,495	36,694,092	40,771,108	4,838,892	149,767,145
Tottenham Hotspur	25	34,812,558	29,260,856	34,762,824	40,771,108	4,838,892	144,446,238
Liverpool	28	34,812,558	32,650,495	32,831,556	40,771,108	4,838,892	145,904,609
Chelsea	26	34,812,558	30,390,736	30,900,288	40,771,108	4,838,892	141,713,582
Arsenal	28	34,812,558	32,650,495	28,969,020	40,771,108	4,838,892	142,042,073
Burnley	10	34,812,558	12,312,666	27,037,752	40,771,108	4,838,892	119,772,976
Everton	19	34,812,558	22,481,580	25,106,484	40,771,108	4,838,892	128,010,622
Leicester City	12	34,812,558	14,572,424	23,175,216	40,771,108	4,838,892	118,170,198
Newcastle United	18	34,812,558	21,351,701	21,243,948	40,771,108	4,838,892	123,018,207
Crystal Palace	12	34,812,558	14,572,424	19,312,680	40,771,108	4,838,892	114,307,662
AFC Bournemouth	11	34,812,558	13,442,545	17,381,412	40,771,108	4,838,892	111,246,515

West Ham United	17	34,812,558	20,221,821	15,450,144	40,771,108	4,838,892	116,094,523
Watford	10	34,812,558	12,312,666	13,518,876	40,771,108	4,838,892	106,254,100
Brighton and Hove Albion	13	34,812,558	15,702,304	11,587,608	40,771,108	4,838,892	107,712,470
Huddersfield Town	10	34,812,558	12,312,666	9,656,340	40,771,108	4,838,892	102,391,564
Southampton	16	34,812,558	19,091,942	7,725,072	40,771,108	4,838,892	107,239,572
Swansea City	10	34,812,558	12,312,666	5,793,804	40,771,108	4,838,892	98,529,028
Stoke City	12	34,812,558	14,572,424	3,862,536	40,771,108	4,838,892	98,857,518
West Bromwich Albion	10	34,812,558	12,312,666	1,931,268	40,771,108	4,838,892	94,666,492
£		696,251,160	405,566,308	405,566,280	815,422,160	96,777,840	2,419,583,748

Source: Premier League

has been a move away from clubs selling their individual rights and towards the English model, by which the League collectively sells the rights of each club to the highest-paying broadcaster. This has been introduced in recent times in Italy and Spain. The recognised benefit of collective selling is that all teams receive a fairer share of the TV rights revenues, which improves the overall quality of the League and leads to more competitive football, which in turn raises the attractiveness of the overall product. 'Competitive balance' is key to a healthy and successful league.

Previously, Real Madrid and Barcelona received over €140m for the sale of their broadcasting rights in 2014/15, while smaller teams like Almeria received €18m. With such huge disparities in income, it effectively became impossible for smaller clubs to compete. Their duopoly was effectively ended in April 2015, when La Liga announced that a collective agreement would start in the 2016/17 season.

The table below sets out the total global rights revenue figures received from broadcasters across a number of the top leagues.

The 2016/17 season

Country	League	Global Broadcasting Revenue per season
Spain	La Liga	€1.484bn
Italy	Serie A	€1.244bn
Germany	Bundesliga	€960m
France	Ligue 1	€819m

Source: Deloitte Annual Review of Football Finance

TELEVISION REVENUE AND THE CHAMPIONS LEAGUE

Domestic leagues are the mainstay for club competitions over a nine-month period. Then, depending on where particular clubs finish, they may qualify for European cup competitions for the following season. In England, the top four teams qualify to play in the Champions League, while the fifth-placed

Premier League team and the FA Cup and League Cup winners qualify for the Europa League.

The Champions League and Europa League are run by UEFA. Prior to 1992, only the champions of each national league were allowed to participate in a knockout competition, the European Cup. This structure changed as a result of negotiations with (and threats from) a number of larger teams. They suggested to UEFA that having more than one team in an enhanced Champions League would be more attractive for fans and broadcasters, with a greater number of top teams playing in a league format before a secondary knockout stage. It was reported that UEFA came to an agreement with the clubs on a new structure, in part to stave off the threat of a breakaway 'Super League'.

Just as domestic leagues sell their lucrative broadcasting rights, so too does UEFA for its prestigious Champions League and Europa League competitions. The result is that a variety of broadcasters across the globe bid to be (usually) the exclusive broadcaster in each country. For example, in the latest Champions League auction, BT paid over £1.1bn for an exclusive three-year deal with UEFA to broadcast both competitions in the UK. This money is distributed by UEFA across the clubs participating in each competition, depending on a number of criteria. These include how they qualified for the competition (i.e. where they finished in their domestic league); how well they performed in the Champions League or Europa League competition; and how much the broadcaster in their country paid for the broadcasting rights.

The Champions League is by far the most lucrative cup competition for Europe's top clubs. More than €1.3bn was shared among the clubs in the 2017/18 UEFA Champions League season. The prize money includes set amounts based on the TV pool (how much a club's national broadcaster has paid for the rights) and also depends on how well the clubs do in each season.

The performance element of the prize money for 2017/18 is set out below (with the 2018/19 figures in brackets):

- Qualification for group stage – €12.7m (€15.25m).
- Group match win – €1.5m (€2.7m).
- Group match draw – €500,000 (€900,000).

- The €500,000 (€900,000) surplus from each drawn match was pooled and redistributed to all clubs taking part in the group stage in accordance with the number of wins they achieved.
- Round of 16 appearance – €6m (€9.5m).
- Quarter-final appearance – €6.5m (€10.5m).
- Semi-finalist appearance – €7.5m (€12m).
- The UEFA Champions League winners can expect to receive €15.5m (€19m) and the runners-up €11m (€15m).

A club in the 2017/18 season could therefore receive more than €57m in prize money as a result of winning all of their group games through to becoming champions.

By way of illustration the 2016/17 champions Real Madrid received:

1. €12.7m for qualifying for the group stage.
2. €6,681,000 in group stage prize money, from three wins and three draws (€1.5m × 3 and €500k × 3 = €6m) + €681k as the additional payment distributed to all clubs from the surplus.
3. €35.5m from the sum of €6m (the last 16) + €6.5 (quarter finals) + €7.5m (semi-finals) + €15.5m (winning the final).
4. €26.1m from the market pool distribution, based on each country's value of the national TV deal.

Madrid's total revenue from UEFA for winning the tournament was therefore approximately €81m.

The top 10 highest-earning Champions League clubs in the 16/17 season are set out below:

1. Juventus €110.4m (finalist).
2. Leicester City €81.6m (quarter-finalist).
3. Real Madrid €81m (winner).
4. Napoli €66m (last 16).
5. Monaco €64.6m (semi-finalist).
6. Arsenal €64.5m (last 16).
7. Atlético Madrid €60.6m (semi-finalist).
8. Barcelona €59.8 (quarter-finalist).

9. PSG €55.3 (last 16).
10. Bayern Munich €54.7 (quarter finalist).

These are fascinating figures, not least because the losing finalist (Juventus) and a quarter-finalist (Leicester City) received more prize money than the winners (Real Madrid). This is the result of UEFA TV market pool distributions. In the UK, the TV market pool distribution is split between where a club finished in its previous season and how successful it is in the current competition – in other words, how deep into the competition the club progressed; the more games played, the more money received. The Premier League champions receive 40% of the TV revenue pool, the team in second place receives 30%, third place 20% and fourth place 10%. Therefore, where a UK team finishes in its domestic league can be very important for its UEFA revenues.

In June 2018, UEFA announced a number of sweeping changes to the way that €2.5bn worth of monies would be distributed for the Champions League and Europa League competitions, in each season from 2018/19 onwards. Of the €1.95bn for Champions League clubs per season, UEFA explained that:

- '25% will be allocated to the starting fees (€488m).
- 30% will be allocated to the performance-related fixed amounts (€585m).
- 30% will be distributed on the basis of 10-year performance-based coefficient rankings (€585m).
- 15% will be allocated to the variable amounts (market pool) (€292m).'

The 10-year performance rankings relate to performance and success in UEFA competitions over the last decade, while the market pool (explained above) will be distributed according to the value of the TV broadcasting deal in the particular country that the club plays its domestic football.

Once the end of the 2018/19 Champions League season has occurred, UEFA will provide breakdown of how the final amounts paid to the clubs were calculated, similar to the Real Madrid example above.

THE DAWN OF THE EUROPEAN SUPER LEAGUE

News reports broke in June 2016 that Manchester United, Manchester City, Liverpool, Arsenal and Chelsea had all met at the Dorchester Hotel in London to discuss the matter of a breakaway Super League involving the elite teams across Europe. The 'Big Five' were represented by Ed Woodward, Ferran Soriano, Ian Ayre, Ivan Gazidis and Bruce Buck. Also at the meeting according to reports was American billionaire Stephen Ross, the owner of the NFL's Miami Dolphins, who runs pre-season and post-season tours and competitions with a number of teams throughout the world.

West Ham co-chairman David Gold believed that the plan 'would destroy football as we know it.' Reports were that the Super League would involve the top clubs breaking away from their domestic league and playing in matches with their elite European competitors on a weekly basis. The competition wouldn't necessarily be based on promotion or relegation but would be by invite-only (i.e. only the biggest clubs would be invited and entry wouldn't necessarily be determined by qualifying in each club's domestic leagues).

The billion-pound question is this: would teams selected for the new European Super League still play in their respective leagues or drop out of domestic competition completely?

This is not, however, a new question, but rather a recurring one. In 1998, it was reported that a company called Media Partners, the Milan-based sports rights agency, was interested in setting up a Super League with a number of top European clubs. Only after reports that UEFA promised an expanded Champions League with 32 clubs (an increase of 16 teams) and the promise of additional club revenue was the idea rejected. Similarly, a competition called the European Golden Cup was mooted as an alternative to the Champions League in 2003.

To say any potential breakaway would be complex and complicated is an understatement. Would FIFA allow players of teams competing in a breakaway league to play in the World Cup, European Championships, Copa América or the African Nations Cup? There would be major fan controversy if local, domestic derbies and rivalries ended. There would also be more unequal distribution of broadcasting rights monies across Europe, the top teams potentially taking more money because of their larger fanbase and media exposure. The remaining national leagues might not be as attractive, having lost the larger teams, and this could reduce broadcasting and commercial revenues. Fans would have the cost of travelling across Europe on a regular basis. Controversy would also revolve around a 'closed league' with no relegation and promotion but an invitation-only basis, which would undermine the pyramid structure of European sporting competition.

More recently, UEFA agreed to change the structure of the qualification criteria for the Champions League. The change from the 2018/19 season onwards now guarantees that the top four clubs in the best-performing European countries (currently, Spain, England, Germany and Italy) will all have places in the Champions League group stages. Previously, the last qualifying place in those leagues had to go through one knockout game.

Some believe that the advent of a breakaway Super League involving Europe's top clubs is an inevitability. Just as occurred with the Premier League in 1992, when the top clubs wanted a larger share of the revenues, top domestic European clubs are looking to UEFA to provide ever-increasing prize money. At some point, the question will return to the surface. And then the real issues to settle will be what form it will take (i.e. will it replace or supplement existing domestic leagues?) and whether entry into the league will be closed (i.e. on an invitation-only basis, guaranteeing the top clubs' participation every year). Many argue that an absolutely closed league, which removes the ability of teams to qualify on sporting merit, is the start of a slippery slope to the model of no promotion or relegation, as used in various US sports.

Ultimately, fans still demand local rivalries. As high-profile as the Champions League is at present, there does not appear to be the demand for clubs to leave their domestic leagues and compete in a European-wide league with Europe's elite teams. AC Milan fans want derbies against Inter, Everton fans want to play Liverpool regularly. One possibility is for the number of games in the Champions League to grow, leading to more guaranteed games over the season. This will mean more games for broadcasters to televise and more revenues for the clubs in addition to their domestic league prize money.

Arguably, there is effectively a European Super League already in place. It's called the Champions League. It's open to many more teams than just the champions of each league, it is no longer a pure knockout competition – giving clubs leeway to lose matches yet still qualify for the later stages of the competition – and it has been expanded to cover more matches across an extended period of time. The revenue generated is now matching that of many domestic leagues (*see* pages 211–213). It would therefore take a brave set of teams to break away from a very lucrative competition.

THE CHANGING WAY WE WATCH SPORT

The Premier League is the most viewed football league on the planet. In the build-up to various broadcast tender processes, it is usually reported that a new broadcaster is vying to enter the bidding, especially for live television rights. beIN Sports, Discovery and YouTube were all mentioned during the build-up to the 2013–16 rights cycle. Amazon became the first company to break the duopoly of Sky and BT when it secured the seventh package for the 2019/20–2021/22 cycle – after Google, Apple, Facebook and Netflix had been the latest in a long line of potential stalking horses. The product is in demand so why wouldn't these global media giants with super-deep pockets be interested?

It could also be argued that they are better placed to maximise the potential of broadcasting rights due to the newer ways football is consumed online. Fans are now viewing matches and highlights through combinations of satellite and internet-enabled TVs, websites, on demand platforms, tablets, apps and smartphones. As a result, there is now less of a distinction between broadcasters like Sky and social media platforms like YouTube and Facebook – both types of companies are content businesses.

This merging of markets is already having profound effects on consumer habits and in some cases is even driving consumer behaviours. Netflix, revolutionising the market for on-demand streaming of films and box sets, delivered via an internet connection, has forever changed the habits of newer and older generations alike. 'Cord cutters' (the name for consumers who are not willing to pay for more traditional and sometimes expensive subscription packages of premium content) are now picking and choosing their subscriptions through more flexible (and usually cheaper) internet offerings rather than the traditional cable and satellite broadcasters. There are, of course, those who do not subscribe at all and who are instead finding a cheaper or even free (and often illegal) service online (more on that later).

If the way that people are watching premium content (including live football) is changing, there is little surprise that new types of technology companies are becoming interested in the type of content that will drive viewers to their particular platforms.

Tech and social media companies, like YouTube, Twitter, Facebook, Snapchat and Amazon, have in recent times made moves into sport. Before their debut into the Premier League, Amazon Prime had already entered the British sports broadcasting market by winning Sky's ATP World Final tennis rights. This followed an agreement in the US with the NFL to stream 10 Thursday-night games (taking over the deal from Twitter, who had previously streamed the matches). In 2017, Facebook streamed live US Major League soccer matches, and secured 25 Major League Baseball games from 2018 onwards. In 2015, YouTube struck an agreement with BT in the UK to show the Champions League final.

For many, this is just the beginning. It shows that technology companies see the value in providing sports content and are here to stay, either in competition with, or complementary to, the main content providers.

The growing truth for many traditional broadcasters is that football fans no longer rely on a TV to watch content. There is growing flexibility (in part due to superfast broadband) to watch live football while second-screening (following comments on Twitter or looking at updated pictures on Instagram).

There are competing pieces of content vying for a fan's attention at any one time. A multitude of fans using multiple screens to share and comment is the new norm. There are a growing number of fans wanting to share particular experiences (in the stadium or watching live) while also hearing opinion and devouring content from pundits and influential opinion makers.

Without even thinking about it, tech-savvy fans are watching live football on a TV, mobile, tablet or in the stadium, and simultaneously seeing what is being said on Twitter about a particular refereeing decision or goal while watching a replay on their subscription app and taking part in a WhatsApp conversation about the controversial decision. This is a trend that will only continue and evolve further.

THE DECLINING LIVE-MATCH AUDIENCE

Reports over the 2016/17 season suggested that English Premier League live viewing figures had fallen to a seven-year low. In June 2017, the *Financial Times* reported that 'average viewing figures on Sky's TV channels fell 14% over the past season according to the Broadcasting Audience Research Board'. The NFL has also witnessed falling viewing figures, with a 10% decline in ratings in 2017, following an 8% decrease in 2016. Regardless of the merits of how the figures are calculated and measured (some take sample sizes while others don't include official online figures), many believe that more thought is needed to understand and service new viewing habits. The large broadcasters in the UK must continue to find innovative ways to reach the diverse sets of fans wanting different things from their football viewing experience – and no doubt have the infrastructure to do so. That is, so long as they continue to bid successfully for those rights in an age when tech companies want a slice of the premium action.

Nonetheless, if more fans find unauthorised, pirated live feeds and do not pay for access to premium football content, broadcasters may start to think twice about paying billions of pounds for those rights.

In addition, the rising cost of monthly subscriptions in the UK has left many supporters increasingly unable to afford the price of two channels (Sky and BT) in order to watch Premier League and Champions League football. Broadcasters like Sky and BT will pay the lucrative sums only if fans keep on subscribing.

Setanta and OnDigital had previously encountered this problem. Both broadcasters had tried to compete with Sky in the live football market but ultimately failed to get a critical mass of subscribers to make a profit. Setanta, a Dublin-based company, went into administration in 2009, three years after winning the Premier League rights and seven years after OnDigital (later, ITV Digital) collapsed. It is not inconceivable that a tipping point may occur when 'must-have' premium football content is no longer the driver for fans and families alike to subscribe to pay TV. If the money dries up or rights values drop significantly, this will impact on the ability of clubs to pay the sky-high transfer fees and wages to attract the best footballers from around the globe.

THE PREMIER LEAGUE SCREENING PACKAGES

The array of Premier League football packages provided to the broadcasting market is diverse. There are potentially five or six live matches per game week stretching from Friday to Monday, alongside staggered mobile, internet and terrestrial highlights packages across subscription, free-to-air, mobile and internet platforms. In the 2016/17 18/19 auction for the Premier League:

- A new regular set of live Friday night matches were screened for the first time.
- Saturday 12.30 p.m. matches have become a regular occurrence.
- There can be no live televised 3 p.m. games in the UK, to protect attendances at matches across the country kicking off at the same traditional time on a Saturday afternoon.
- From 5.15 p.m. in the UK, subscribers to a mobile app can watch three-minute highlights of the 12.30 p.m. and 3 p.m. matches.
- There is usually a live Saturday 5.30 p.m. match.
- Sky Sports has extended highlights of the best game of the day (usually one that has not been televised live).
- The iconic *Match of the Day* highlights programme is screened around 10.30 p.m. on Saturday night (and repeated early on Sunday morning for the youngsters who can't stay up so late!).
- Depending on the broadcaster's pick of matches, games on Sunday can start at 2.15 p.m. and 4 p.m.
- Weekend highlights can be distributed on separate club channels in the days following the match.
- There is a relatively regular Monday night screening of a live Premier League game at 8 p.m.
- There are a number of mid-week fixtures, as well as games around festive holidays, including Easter and Christmas.

WHY CAN'T LIVE FOOTBALL BE SCREENED AT 3 P.M. IN THE UK?

In the UK, live football cannot be broadcast on TV between 2.45 p.m. and 5.15 p.m. on Saturday during the football season. This is based on a UEFA rule that gives a national association the power to prevent broadcasts of its domestic league for around two hours each weekend. The main reason for this is to protect lower league attendances. It has also meant in recent years that El Clásico, the Barcelona v. Real Madrid game, has not been able to be televised in the UK until 5.15 p.m., some 15 minutes into the 5 p.m. game!

The rationale behind the decision is that people may decide to watch a game in the comfort of their own home (or pub) instead. The larger clubs whose matches are televised would deny the lower clubs the prospect of higher attendances.

BROADCASTING PIRACY

Since fans are increasingly internet savvy, many have migrated online in search of matches to watch without paying subscriptions. This means that rights holders like the Premier League must deal with new issues. If consumers can access premium content and circumvent broadcasters that have paid billions of pounds for the privilege to screen the matches, broadcasters will want rights holders to clamp down hard on those accessing the content for free. According to a survey conducted by BBC Radio 5 in July 2017, 'more than a third of Premier League football fans say they regularly watch matches live online via unofficial streams'.

This has become a specific problem in the UK because every other country can show live those Premier League and Football League matches that kick off on Saturday at 3 p.m. Given the ease with which fans can access internet streams and satellite feeds, pubs in the UK have been screening matches on Saturday afternoons for years. This became a concern when some pubs began subscribing to foreign satellite channels or streaming through internet sites to broadcast the matches to their pubs. This meant that they were subscribing to broadcasters other than Sky and BT, who were obviously unhappy, having paid several billion pounds to be the exclusive broadcasters in the UK.

Over the last decade, the Premier League and Sky have brought court actions against many pub owners who subscribed to foreign channels using various feeds from around the world, including North Africa and Greece. Similarly, with the advent of high-speed broadband, many consumers and pubs alike are finding websites that stream live matches for a fraction of the cost (usually because they do not have the rights).

UK broadcasters provide official packages for pubs. These subscriptions can be several thousands of pounds per month. In 2006, Karen Murphy, the owner of the Red, White and Blue pub in Portsmouth, was sued after buying a Greek decoder and decoder card in order to broadcast live Premier League matches in her pub. She argued that as a citizen of a European Union member state, she should be able to source from across the EU the cheapest legitimate subscription to broadcast Premier League matches in her pub. The Premier League alleged that Murphy's actions, among other things, breached its intellectual property rights.

When the European courts finally ruled on the case in October 2011, many believed that Mrs Murphy had won an historic and monumental victory. The court ruled that the way in which the Premier League tendered its rights, by stopping viewers from watching the satellite broadcasts with a decoder card from another European country, was against European law.

However, the court also concluded that the Premier League owned 'copyrighted works' such as the anthem and specifically the logo used in the broadcast. As a result, Mrs Murphy required permission from the Premier League to show those copyrighted works to broadcast the live pictures. As the Premier League would not provide their consent, she remained prohibited from broadcasting the channel.

PIRACY 2.0

Websites streaming live Premier League match pictures without the consent or agreement of the Premier League (or the national broadcasters to whom they sell their rights) appear to be a clear-cut example of a new generation of illegal internet piracy.

The Premier League and others are keen to stress that anyone not buying the legitimate subscriptions to gain access to a live internet stream is indirectly reducing the product's value. This loss in subscription revenue will eventually be reflected in lower broadcaster bids to obtain rights to show live football. And lower bids means less money distributed across the game.

The Premier League continues to devote significant time and effort to monitor particular websites. In July 2017, it won a court battle to block more than 5,000 server IP addresses that were being used to host and stream illegal content.

More recently, Kodi boxes have risen to prominence in the UK. These boxes are legal but can be used to provide easy access to such illegal streams. The Premier League has been keen to stress that such pre-loaded boxes could get users into serious trouble too. In April 2017, it secured a court order to block the rights-infringing video streams of football matches via Kodi set-top boxes. Additionally, there have been several successful prosecutions of individuals selling Kodi boxes.

FOOTBALL AND SOCIAL MEDIA

This hard-line approach to dealing with copyright issues has its detractors, especially in relation to user-generated clips of premium content being shared online.

The Premier League had previously announced that it was clamping down on social media companies for hosting footage and on users for posting the recordings on social media channels such as Twitter and YouTube. It argues that fans using social media are infringing the Premier League's copyright.

As well as selling live rights in the UK to Sky and BT, the Premier League sells a number of near-live mobile and internet rights. In the UK, Sky is one of the current rights holders. Consumers subscribe through access to apps and websites to view the premium, near-live content. If consumers through social media are able to access the very goals and talking points shown, directly competing with the products for which the Premier League has sold the rights, this undermines the value of the product.

The counter-argument from some quarters is that the posting of short fan clips actually enhances the reach of the goals, controversial incidents and important moments of a game. By trying to regulate an ocean of consumer-generated content and ask for each and every posting to be removed, the administrative burden for the Premier League to undertake and for the social media companies to police is significant. Nonetheless, this is very much what it is willing to do to safeguard the huge sums that Sky and BT domestically are willing to pay to ensure fans can only watch the games on their platform. A spokesman for the Premier League has previously explained:

> You can understand that fans see something, they can capture it, they can share it, but ultimately it is against the law. It's a breach of copyright and we would discourage fans from doing it. We're developing technologies like gif crawlers, Vine crawlers, working with Twitter to look to curtail this kind of activity. I know it sounds as if we're killjoys but we have to protect our intellectual property.

So, the Premier League and many other rights holders do liaise with social media companies like Twitter and platform hosts like YouTube to ensure that any copyrighted materials are removed quickly.

DIRECT-TO-FAN SUBSCRIPTIONS

One possible avenue for leagues to consider is, why use a broadcaster at all? Major League Baseball has a direct-to-fan website subscription service, available to purchase for around $80 per season. Indeed, in time for the 2017/18 season, the Football League launched its iFollow platform, giving Football League fans outside the UK and Republic of Ireland the chance to subscribe with a £110 season ticket to watch all live matches via the subscriber's desktop, mobile and/or tablet. (It should be noted that around a dozen clubs, including Aston Villa, Derby and Fulham, refused to sign up to the iFollow platform.)

Some have questioned whether the Premier League will ever go down a path of setting up a website and selling straight to consumers, by-passing the broadcasters entirely. Given the broadcasting money on offer (£5bn+ domestically), this appears relatively unlikely, because the Premier League would face some very large risks, none more so than starting with zero subscribers and no revenue. Another large burden would be the infrastructure and start-up costs, and though this could be outsourced to established industry companies, it's a huge undertaking for the Premier League to take on, especially while companies like Sky and BT are willing to pay large fees to guarantee live football rights on their channels.

'CROWN JEWEL' BROADCAST FOOTBALL EVENTS

While most of this chapter has discussed pay TV's relationship with football and the money that has flowed to the leagues, clubs and players, there are laws in place to prohibit certain sports events from being exclusively on pay TV.

There are a number of events that the UK government believes should be available to be screened on terrestrial television. Wimbledon, the Olympics and the Grand National are three examples. From a football perspective, the World Cup finals tournament, the European Championship finals tournament and the FA Cup final must not be made available exclusively to pay TV broadcasters.

This is the consequence of the EU's Audio-Visual Media Services Directive, which gives the governments of member states the ability to list particular cultural events that are of major importance to its citizens so that they are not shown live on pay TV behind a paywall. As part of the UK's list, it reserves every World Cup and European Championship finals tournament match. UEFA and FIFA challenged the UK government's right to list both tournaments a number of years ago. The wording of the law was important in the overall decision:

> Each Member State may take measures to ensure that broadcasters under its jurisdiction do not broadcast on an exclusive basis events which are regarded by that Member State as being of major importance for society in such a way as to deprive a substantial proportion of the

public in that Member State of the possibility of following such events via live coverage or deferred coverage on free television. If it does so, the Member State concerned shall draw up a list of designated events, national or non-national, which it considers to be of major importance for society.

UEFA challenged the Commission's decision to approve the UK's listing of the entire Euro tournament, arguing that it protected terrestrial broadcasters like BBC and ITV from the competition of pay TV broadcasters. Without operators such as Sky and BT bidding for the rights, UEFA and FIFA argued that they could not receive the actual market value for their tournaments, meaning they had less revenue to pass back to national associations and grass-roots football.

Ultimately, the European court rejected the arguments. Mainly, the court was of the view that the EU directive's aim was to give citizens the benefit of being able to watch for free events that are of significance to the country. Once the UK leaves the EU, the government will have a decision to make in setting out whether they should still maintain a protected list; the current set of lists only applies to EU member states.

A DIFFERENT REALITY: THE FUTURE, NOW

Picture this: the game is about to start, and you put on your augmented reality (AR) headset. You are transported to Anfield, where the crowd has just started singing 'You'll Never Walk Alone', and you look on from the main stand and turn your head to see the Kop in full voice. You're not watching the game in two dimensions from your TV or tablet but are in an actual seat, able to turn your head to see who is in front of you and behind you and to scan 360 degrees around the ground as the match begins. You're in the stadium, on match day – and that's just for starters. What if you want to highlight particular stats about a player, see particular player movements or see where he is on the pitch? A digital information 'overlay' on the screen comes as standard.

This 'basic' view could be combined with videos of goals in other games as they go in, and a social media feed running down the side of your view, enabling you to send messages to your friends or see what the commentator has tweeted. The sounds of the stadium become louder and change depending on the angle at which you turn your head as you become immersed in the AR world.

Clubs may soon be in a position to sell an AR season ticket. Mainstream broadcasting companies like Sky and BT are all heavily investing in such technology to make this very much the reality. It's the future – and probably less than five years away from being a potential mainstream offering. For teams and leagues with armies of foreign fans who can't get to games and who wish to experience a more authentic match-day experience, AR and its equivalent technologies have the potential to change the way fans experience live sport.

This product is just one way the traditional sports world is embracing AR. While the fan match-day experience has game-changing potential, the idea of virtual sponsorship for companies wishing to advertise to sports fans is becoming of real interest to leagues, clubs, players and digital agencies too. At present, physical advertising boards at stadia (be they digital or otherwise) can carry only a limited number of adverts. What if broadcasters, depending on the audience, could substitute real advertising boards at stadiums for virtual advertising boards on the screen while watching the same match? It means that broadcasters can overlay physical adverts and customise them according to which country the fan is in watching the game and the individual preferences (and internet search history) of that fan (e.g. have they been looking online for a new Gap jumper or mobile phone contract?). Five fans in five different countries may view five entirely different sets of advert boards over the whole game. This will become the norm.

NEW CHALLENGES AND NEW OPPORTUNITIES

Broadcasting money is the lifeblood of the football industry. The leagues and clubs have grown increasingly dependent on selling their rights for ever more lucrative amounts. Such are the numbers on offer that one season in the Premier League is worth almost £100m to a club.

Leagues and clubs will go to great lengths to ensure broadcasters receive value for money, meaning a wide variety of kick-off times throughout the weekend as well as clamping down hard on online piracy. Nonetheless, as fans migrate online, the availability of easily accessible content means leagues like the Premier League are facing new challenges to combat online piracy.

The future will see increasingly innovative ways of consuming the match content. Immersive AR experiences are not far off, and in 20 years time, it may seem somewhat basic that we were once watching live football on a screen.

EXTRA TIME

The world of football continues to evolve at a rapid pace. Transfer fees and player wages spiral ever higher, and the financial risks and rewards of promotion and relegation are even more stark. New figures released in 2018 by Deloitte set out that the European football market is now worth £21.9bn. The value of commercial deals and broadcasting rights to a club that wins the play-off final to reach the Premier League will no doubt soon break the £200m mark.

Ultimately, this book was written to help demystify particular elements of the football industry, and help fans to understand the role of players, agents, managers, owners, broadcasters, brands, national associations and international federations. Each participant is heavily reliant on the other to coexist and thrive.

The football money merry-go-round has gone into overdrive. Take the Premier League: over the last three broadcasting deals, pay TV subscriptions have funded huge revenue uplifts for clubs. Though it's true the latest Premier League domestic deal produced relatively flat growth, the figure of more than £4.5bn in domestic revenues is still extraordinary. It was unlikely that domestic growth could be maintained.

It seems that the way younger generations are viewing entertainment content, including live sport, is fundamentally changing. Fans are consuming content on a variety of devices – sometimes at the same time – and TV companies are having to recalibrate their product offerings accordingly, to keep subscription numbers high enough to pay for the lucrative rights. Some have suggested that a saturation point has been reached. Fans, they argue, are overloaded with football and are no longer watching entire games on a regular basis. Instead, they are switching off and cancelling subscriptions. It's far too soon, though, to write off the pay TV subscription model as outdated. Premium live sports will continue to command huge rights fees, including domestic league rights deals for the Premier League, Serie A and La Liga among others, and for international club and country tournaments such as the Champions League, Euro Championships and World Cup.

As club revenues grow, transfer fees and wages will continue on their upward trajectory. As long as eye-watering amounts of revenues continue to be generated through broadcasting deals, match-day monies and brand partnerships, teams can spend what they earn on record-breaking deals. Manchester United and Real Madrid, for example, in 2016/17 generated £581m and £579m respectively. The transfer benchmark has now been been set by Neymar, moving to PSG for a €222m. Though it is likely to be some time before this record transfer fee is broken, global superstars will continue to be sold for astronomical figures. Competition for the top players remains fierce as elite teams compete for a small number of uber-talented players.

Ultimately, transfer spending is demanded by fans, who expect owners to show ambition. Failure to invest adequately in the playing squad can lead to underperformance: not challenging for the league title or promotion; failing to qualify for the Champions League; or worse, relegation. It's Catch-22: spend too little, and never challenge for glory; spend too much, and possible financial ruin awaits. The real challenge is to spend wisely within the rules. This is easier said than done and will continue to be challenging, especially for newcomer owners.

It's impossible to talk about money without mentioning agents (now called intermediaries). While some fans will never believe that they do a good job for players and clubs alike, good agents do in fact bring real value to the table by getting a deal across the line. Nor are they just a necessary evil; most clubs see them as essential. Large deals and the high commissions that agents receive will always grab the headlines, but the vast majority of deals take a huge amount of planning, negotiation and diligent execution. There is real skill in being an agent and many do a fantastic job.

Since the rules were relaxed and more agents have come into the global game, the risk is that many lack the relevant experience, skill sets, networks and expertise to get the best deal for their clients. It's likely, however, that change is on the horizon. Expect to see in the coming years the establishment of a more tightly regulated registration and education system, requiring agents to demonstrate they understand both the industry and its rules. Many will continue to believe that the commissions agents receive should be capped or limited. Others, this author included, take a contrary view: regulating the commission for agents in the football business but not for the agents of actors or musicians seems artificial and unrealistic. Ultimately, it is up to those who pay the agents (the club and/or the player) to decide if they are getting value for money.

With the vast sums of money involved, UEFA's Financial Fair Play regulations and the Premier League and Football League's similar break-even rules have come into their own. The rules have done a great deal of good in reducing club losses caused by unsustainable spending, though there remain plenty of detractors who believe the rules are a way to protect the established clubs from the ambitious clubs wanting to challenge the status quo. It's true that the rules are not perfect, but it would be a mistake to scrap them. Changes will continue to be made, thus giving more leeway to clubs as their long-term financial health improves.

As a consequence of more and more clubs making profits (or reducing their losses), teams are becoming more attractive and valuable to potential investors. Greater cost control plus growing revenues equals an appealing proposition. Football takeovers will continue so long as investors are confident that they can bring new business practices (and forms of income generation) to the table and that core revenues like broadcasting rights will increase in value.

The money on offer for Europe's elite teams continues to grow exponentially. Real Madrid and Bayern Munich in 2016/17 received £200m and £126m respectively from broadcasting rights in figures released in 2018; the Premier League Champions earn almost £150m in prize money before match-day and sponsorship revenues are taken into account; and qualifying for the Champions League group phase from the 2018/19 season will be worth €15.25m and each group stage win a staggering €2.7m.

Such huge revenue streams, especially in the Champions League, mean that a European breakaway league is still a possibility. UEFA have done a good job in pacifying a number of the elite clubs by promising extra money and guaranteed Champions League group stage participation. The more difficult long-term question is whether an actual European league competition could ever replace domestic leagues like the Premier League, La Liga or Bundesliga. That seems unlikely at present, especially if it means an end to domestic competitions and historic rivalries. Fans would rightly go crackers if matches like Liverpool v Everton or Milan v Inter were wiped off the fixture list.

As the game continues to evolve, so too will football rules and regulations – either as a reaction to a crisis or when new issues arise. For example, third-party investment was banned by FIFA only after various integrity controversies occurred throughout Europe and especially South America. The Premier League brought in its own cost control provisions in part because Portsmouth, then a Premier League club, had serious financial difficulties. When new controversies arise, national and international football associations will need to be both nimble and pragmatic – amending rules or creating new frameworks. With its Financial Fair Play rules UEFA demonstrated that it understood concerns about the reality in which a number of clubs were running up losses on a regular basis.

Of course, it's not just clubs that get into trouble. So too do players. There will always be negative headlines and consequences as a result of disciplinary matters, whether on or off the field. Social media has, for better or worse, brought fans within touching distance of the players, many of whom have encountered problems after tweeting without thinking. Players are as flawed and fallible as you or I. The bottom line is that mistakes happen every day – but some take place in front of 60,000+ supporters or 5m Twitter followers, making them more newsworthy.

Nonetheless football has the power to do real good. Jermain Defoe, for example, had a positive impact on the six-year-old Bradley Lowery before his tragic passing from cancer, and there are many more similarly kind, selfless gestures that go unreported.

It may be a little thing like signing an autograph, or it may be a larger gesture, such as Gerard Deulofeu seeking out cerebral-palsy sufferer George Shaw, whose football video wearing a Deulofeu shirt went viral. Then there's Hector Bellerin, who provides boxes full of Puma boots for local London hospices. These are the things I see every day and it's inspiring. Footballers don't live in isolation. Look at Juan Mata donating part of his salary to charity or Andy Robertson volunteering and donating food and his time at a local foodbank. We are all human and most feel the need to make a difference to others less fortunate.

Money may make this the industry go round, but its participants – the players, the managers, the owners and, yes, the agents – do huge amounts of good for the local and wider communities. That shouldn't be forgotten.

ABOUT THE AUTHOR

I've been privileged to have been a lawyer in the sports and football industry for over 13 years. During that time, I have worked on high-profile Premier League and Football League club takeovers, multi-million-pound international transfers and player contract negotiations, player image rights, boot and commercial deals, helping players and agents with a variety of disputes and disciplinary matters, advising clients on broadcasting agreements, and providing legal support on all sorts of regulations including the Financial Fair Play rules, third-party investment, the international FIFA transfer rules and the intermediaries regulations. The work has been so wonderfully varied that one day in the office is rarely the same as the next.

I've blogged on the football industry at www.danielgeey.com for over 10 years as well as writing for various sports, media and entertainment legal journals. I also provide comment and analysis for media outlets including Sky Sports, Sky News, the BBC, ITV, CNN, Bloomberg, the *Daily Telegraph*, *The Times*, the *Independent*, the *Financial Times*, CityAm and TalkSport.

I co-authored the EU law chapter of the seminal legal textbook *Football and the Law*, published by Bloomsbury.

I continue to speak at various global sports conferences on the business of football.

website: www.DanielGeey.com
Email: Info@DanielGeey.com
Twitter: www.twitter.com/footballlaw
Instagram: www.Instagram.com/footballlaw
YouTube: Search Daniel Geey channel

ACKNOWLEDGEMENTS

This whole book adventure would have never begun without my wife Hollie. She prods, cajoles, challenges me and reins me in. She has planned, brainstormed, proof-read, amended and lived and breathed this book with me. It got in the way of holidays, weekends, family time and date nights. This book is as much hers as it is mine.

To my parents, David and Lillian, I'm the midway point of you both. Mum the international tennis player and Dad the criminal lawyer. The Courts are the focal point for you both. It's little surprise I'm a sports lawyer. Sport and hard work were the glue of our family. Thank you both for your unwavering love and confidence in me. Your positivity knows no bounds.

To my brother Matthew, thank you for your spreadsheets, and Hilla for your incredible design input.

To the Phillips and Geey families, this book is really a homage to every lunch, dinner, kick-about and trip to Anfield. The constant debate and laughter about football laid the foundations for me to write this book.

To the Springers, my incredible extended family, thank you for looking after Hollie, particularly on the holidays that I was half-buried in my laptop.

A huge thanks to Neil Swimer, Anne Geey, Robin Phillips, Rabbi Liss, Mike O'Brien, Jake Cohen, John Sinnott, Trevor Rack, Adam Lovatt and Ehsen Shah for reading the book at different stages and offering their constructive thoughts. To Tony Evans for his guidance throughout. To Jake Cooper for endless fascinating chats on the future of broadcasting, how content is being consumed by millennials and the exponential rise of social media.

To my A-level economics tutor Ratesh Dhir, who didn't immediately laugh at my idea to write a book on football after discussing the unusual supply and demand curves for player transfers. To my Master's tutor, Mark James, who in 2003 encouraged me to write my first two journal articles on multiple club ownership and Premier League broadcasting rights. Those articles became the foundation for my future blogs. To my literary agent David Luxton, your powers of publisher persuasion know no bounds and I will always be grateful for your determination and energy to get this project off the ground. As importantly, Matt Lowing and Zoë Blanc at Bloomsbury Sport. Your incredible input from start to finish has improved the book immeasurably.

To Charles, John, Nick and Kerry for putting up with my illusions of actually wanting to become a sports lawyer one day. To the incredible Sports team at Sheridans: Andrew, Chris, Jonny, Katherine, Nic, Sarah and Reyna, I'm grateful to be working with such talented teammates and friends.

INDEX

INDEX

INDEX

'If you want to know and understand how football really works, this is the book for you.'

Guillem Balagué, *Sky Sports*

'It's a pleasure to work with Daniel and he has a great understanding of the football industry. His book should be a must read for football fans.'

Freddie Ljungberg

'Fascinating, brilliant and mind-boggling at times, this book takes you behind the scenes of football. What happens on the pitch is only part of the story. Done Deal is essential reading if you want to get close to the full picture.'

Tony Evans, Evening Standard *and ESPN*

'A myth-busting and hugely entertaining look at the ever more complex machinations of the beautiful game. Essential.'

Raphael Honigstein, ESPN

'Undoubtedly the leader in his field, with Done Deal Daniel has produced a fascinating and comprehensive insight into the global business of football and the ever-changing landscape of the world's beautiful game.'

David Dale, CEO, Football Aid and Field of Dreams

'[Done Deal] is a testament not only to Daniel's vast knowledge on his subject, but also to his ability to present even the most complex ideas in a clear and vivid way.'

Gianluca Vialli

'There are very few people who are as up to speed on the most pressing legal topics within the football industry as Daniel Geey.'

Chris Pearlman, COO Swansea City FC

'A must read for anyone looking to work in football.'

Ehsen Shah, Managing Director, B-Engaged Ltd

'A uniquely insightful and accurate reflection of modern football and its exciting evolution.'

Fausto Zanetton, Founder and CEO, Tifosy Ltd